JN057118

発刊の想い。

これからの世代のみんなが、
日本中と交流をするためには、
「デザインの目線」がとても
重要になっていくと考えます。
それは、長く続いていくであろう
本質を持ったものを見極め、
わかりやすく、楽しく工夫を感じる創意です。
人口の多い都市が発信する
流行も含めたものではなく、
土着的でも、その中に秘められた「個性」——
それらを手がかりとして、
具体的にその土地へ行くための
「デザインの目線」を持った観光ガイドが今、
必要と考え、47都道府県を一冊一冊、
同等に同じ項目で取材・編集し、
各号同程度のページ数で発刊していきます。

d design travel
発行人　ナガオカケンメイ

problems, we will point out the problems while recommending it.
- The businesses we recommend will not have editorial influence.
  Their only role in the publications will be fact checking.
- We will only pick up things deemed enduring from the "long
  life design" perspective.
- We will not enhance photographs by using special lenses. We
  will capture things as they are.
- We will maintain a relationship with the places and people we
  pick up after the publication of the guidebook in which they
  are featured.

Our selection criteria:
- The business or product is uniquely local.
- The business or product communicates an important local
  message.
- The business or product is operated or produced by local people.
- The product or services are reasonably priced.
- The business or product is innovatively designed.

Kenmei Nagaoka
Founder, d design travel

編集の考え方。

・必ず自費でまず利用すること。実際に泊まり、食事し、買って、確かめること。

・感動しないものは取り上げないこと。本音で、自分の言葉で書くこと。

・問題があっても、素晴らしければ、問題を指摘しながら薦めること。

・取材相手の原稿チェックは、事実確認だけにとどめること。

・ロングライフデザインの視点で、長く続くものだけを取り上げること。

・写真撮影は特殊レンズを使って誇張しない。ありのままを撮ること。

・取り上げた場所や人とは、発刊後も継続的に交流を持つこと。

取材対象選定の考え方。

・その土地らしいこと。

・その土地の大切なメッセージを伝えていること。

・その土地の人がやっていること。

・価格が手頃であること。

・デザインの工夫があること。

SIGHTS
その土地を知る
To know the region

CAFES
その土地でお茶をする
お酒を飲む
To have tea
To have a drink

RESTAURANTS
その土地で食事する
To eat

HOTELS
その土地に泊まる
To stay

SHOPS
その土地らしい買物
To buy regional goods

PEOPLE
その土地のキーマン
To meet key persons

A Few Thoughts Regarding the Publication of This Series
I believe that a "design perspective" will become extremely important for future generations, and indeed people of all generations, to interact with all areas of Japan. By "design perspective," I mean an imagination, which discerns what has substance and will endure, and allows users to easily understand and enjoy innovations. I feel that now, more than ever, a new kind of guidebook with a "design perspective" is needed. Therefore, we will publish a guide to each of Japan's 47 prefectures. The guidebooks will be composed, researched, and edited identically and be similar in volume.

Our editorial concept:
- Any business or product we recommend will first have been purchased or used at the researchers' own expense. That is to say, the writers have all actually spent the night in at the inns, eaten at the restaurants, and purchased the products they recommend.
- We will not recommend something unless it moves us. The recommendations will be written sincerely and in our own words.
- If something or some service is wonderful, but not without

京都のふつう

d design travel 編集部が見つけた、
京都府の当たり前。
絵・辻井希文

京都の街と人を守る、赤いバケツ　京都府は、「国指定重要文化財」の建造物の数が、日本一だ。そんな、街その物が宝物である京都府にとって、最も恐るべきは火事である。京都府内を歩いていると、「文化財を火災から守りましょう」のポスターをよく見かけたが、それ以上に目にしたのが、街の至る所の建物の前に置かれた、赤いバケツだ。赤地に白で、「防火用」「消火用」などと書かれており、常に水が溜められている。イザという時には、火の気づいた人が、ザバッと消し止める。ある地域では、バケツは町内会費で一軒に二個支給され、水道代もかからないそうだ。また、水を何日も換えていないと、「お隣はん、どないかしはったんやろか？」と、安否の確認もできるそうだ。

通りの名前を歌って覚える　京都市の市街地中心は、東西を「丸太町通り」から「十条通り」まで、南北を「寺町通り」から「千本通り」まで、合計五〇本以上の通りがあり、北に行く事を「上ル」、南には「下ル」、東には「東入ル」、西には「西入ル」と言う。タクシーなどで行き先を伝える時も、正式な住所よりちょっと下った所」などと通りの名前を伝えた方が、断然、話が早い。通りの名前の覚え歌もあって、南北が「寺御幸」、東西が「丸竹夷二押」だ。「丸竹夷二押御池、姉三六角蛸錦、四綾仏高松五条、雪駄ちゃらちゃら魚の棚、六条三哲通りすぎ、七条越えれば八九条、十条東寺でとどめさす」——すべての通りの頭文字等（現在は名前が違う通りもある）が、見事なリズムで歌詞に組み込まれており、これを歌えれば、もう京都で迷わない！

compared to others. It's normal around here." It is normal in Kyoto to keep doing it for longer than a century.

Singing the names of streets　There are nearly 50 streets in Kyoto, starting from Marutamachi Street and Jujo Street which go east and west, and Teramachi Street and Senbon Street that go north and south. It's a lot easier to say the street names than giving the address when you are in the taxi. There are two songs that would help you memorize the street names: for the streets that go north and south, "Tera Goko", and for streets that go east and west, it's "Maru Take Ebisu". The first characters of each street are presented to be sang with hypnotic melody. If you can remember this, you will never get lost in Kyoto!

Red buckets that protect the city and the people　If you walk around the city, you would come across posters reminding people to be careful with fire to protect historical buildings. But more than these posters, you would see red buckets placed in front of buildings all over the city. With "Beware of Fire" written with white letters, the bucket can be used by anyone who sees fire.

市で買い物、探し物　京都観光の思い出に、「偶然、お寺で市をやってて、半日過ごしてしまった」という人も多いのではないか。京都の市の代表といえば、毎月二一日の東寺の「弘法市（弘法さん）」と、毎月二五日の北野天満宮の「北野天満宮御縁日（天神さん）」だが、他にも、数多くある府内の神社・仏閣では、毎週のように「手づくり市」「がらくた市」「古本市」などの「市」が開かれていて、遭遇率が、かなり高い。どの市に出かけても、境内をぎっしりと埋め尽くすほどの集客で、地元の人にも、観光客にも、老若男女問わず、大人気。欲しい物、探し物が、あってもなくても、不思議と、延々と歩き回ってしまう。そうして見つけて、買えた一品は、がらくたでも骨董品でも、京都の旅の宝物だ。

超・専門店街　京都には、個人経営の小さな専門店が、たくさん、市街地中心部に残っている。髪を切りたければ理髪店、珈琲が飲みたければ喫茶店、豆腐が食べたければ豆腐店。数珠が欲しければ数珠店、杖が欲しければ杖店、箒が欲しければ箒店、靴を修理したければ靴修理店、ジャケットにネームを入れたければネーム店——とにかく何でも、欲しい物の専門店がある。全国的知名度の百貨店「大丸」や「髙島屋」の創業地の百貨店でもある京都は、街全体が一つの大百貨店のような。その道の専門家、職人、凄腕のバイヤーらが、街じゅうに溢れている、"本物の専門店街の都市"だ。しかも、それら専門店街の多くは、創業一〇〇年超えが当たり前で、感心して「老舗ですね」と言うと、必ず「全然、まだまだ。ふつうですし」と謙虚な答え。長く続ける事は、「京都のふつう」なのだ。

Ordinary objects founds in Kyoto by the d design travel editorial department

Illustration: Kifumi Tsujii

Shopping in the city　In temples and shrines all over Kyoto, they sponsor so many different kinds of market every week: "handcraft market", "used books market", "junk market" and others. It's not just popular among the locals but also tourists come, packing up the market. Even if there's nothing I am looking for, I can't help but to browse around to find something unexpected.

Ultra specialized shops　In Kyoto, you can still find very specialized independent shops all over the city. It is as if the entire city is like one big department shop. This is the city that takes pride in craftsmanship, and these shops have been supporting artisans. Most of these shops opened their doors more than hundred years ago. When I make a comment about how long they have been around, most of them reply humbly, "We're still quite young

京好み
あぶらとり紙
よーじや製

京都府の一二か月

KYOTOGRAPHIE 京都国際写真祭（京都市）2015年のテーマは「TRIBE（部族）——あなたは、どこにいるのか？」。フエゴ諸島諸先住民を撮影したマルティン・グシンデの作品など、14組の作品を紹介。通常非公開の「建仁寺内 両足院」等が会場。

Photo: Takuya Oshima

祇園の「節分おばけ」（京都市）厄除けの風習「節分おばけ」。芸妓一行が「お染め・久松」などに扮してお茶屋を巡る姿は、ハロウィンようで面白い。節分の夜、花見小路などで、出会える可能性大！

やすらい祭（京都市）
P.090に掲載

6 5 4 3 2 1

JUNE   MAY   APRIL   MARCH   FEBRUARY   JANUARY

初寅大祭（京都市）1月最初の寅の日に鞍馬寺の毘沙門天で、無量の大福を授かれる。大祭3日間は「魔除けの福笹」授与があり、1月だけ、「あうんの虎」の魔除けを購入可。

新茶見学会（宇治市）「丸久小山園」で年に1度、5日間ほど開催される茶摘み体験と工場見学。取材中、編集部も参加し、見学後、振る舞われた抹茶（新茶）に感激でした（要予約。工場見学のみ、通年実施）。

京都タワー階段のぼり（京都市）一切骨組みがない筒状の京都タワービル。通常非公開の内部を眺めて上がれば、285段の螺旋階段も、あっという間に上がる事ができ、認定証が貰える。例年は年2回開催で、もう1回は10月。

5〜9月 **鴨川納涼床**（京都市）二条大橋から五条大橋まで約100の店が、鴨川に張り出し式などの座敷（納涼床）を設ける。川を渡る風に涼みながら、「モリタ屋」で食べた、すき焼きの味は忘れられない。

京都美山サイクルグリーンツアー（南丹市）美山町で2日間開催の、自然体験とサイクリングの複合型イベント。総走行距離125キロの「ロングライド」の名物は、鹿肉カレー、鮎にぎり、黄金芋のスイーツ。「かやぶきの里」を堪能できる。

伊根のうみゃーもん祭（与謝郡）伊根町 役場正面広場で開催。「伊根まぐろ」はもちろん、珍味「鯖へしこ（糠漬け）」や「鷹池大納言ぜんざい」なども美味なので、ぜひ。

由岐神社例祭 鞍馬の火祭（京都市）由岐神社の奇祭。若衆が大松明を担ぎ「サイレイ、サイリョウ」と囃し、火の粉を撒き散らして街道を練り歩く。神輿の担い棒にぶら下がり、逆さ大の字に足を広げる「チョッペンの儀」は必見。

京都五山送り火（京都市）お盆に迎えた先祖の霊を、再び冥府に送る行事。夜7時頃から、東山如意ヶ岳の「大文字」から順に、山に送り火が点火される。豪快に燃える松明の音に耳を傾けて、心を鎮めて見送るのがいい。

12 11 10 9 8 7

DECEMBER　NOVEMBER　OCTOBER　SEPTEMBER　AUGUST　JULY

京都音楽博覧会（京都市）梅小路公園で開催の京都出身バンド「くるり」主演の野外フェス。2014年は英楽団「ペンギン・カフェ」等が参加。その日限りの演奏に、観客は残暑より熱く盛り上がる。

京都ま冬のブックハンティング（京都市）左京区にある、「恵文社」「善行堂」「萩書房」「ホホホ座」「迷子」の5店舗が開催する古本フェア。「10円本の市」「写真集特集」などの催し多数。貴重なバックナンバーにも出会える。

「ときのあとさき」の演奏会（京都市）アコーディオン奏者の生駒祐子と、コントラバス奏者の清水恒輔の音楽ユニット「mama！milk」が、法然院で演奏。方丈庭園の木々のざわめきや、鹿威し等の自然音と融け合う音色が美しい。

祇園祭（京都市）ひと月にわたって続く祭りのメインイベントは、17日と24日の「辻回し」。山鉾33基が、四条河原町で、一気に方向転換。倒れそうで倒れない、山鉾のしなりに、観客は息を呑む。

Photo: Ryo Mitaura

Furoshiki
specialty shop
Musubi

Yamada Sen-I Co., Ltd.

＊1 d design travel 調べ（2015年4月時点）　＊2 国土地理院ホームページより
＊3 総務省統計局ホームページより（2015年4月時点）
＊4 社団法人 日本観光協会（編）「数字でみる観光」より（2014年度版）　※（ ）内の数字は全国平均値
＊1 Figures compiled by d design travel. Date as of April 2015.　＊2 Extracts from the website of Geographical
Survey Institute, Ministry of Land, Infrastructure,Transport and Tourism.　＊3 According to the website of the
Statistics Bureau, Ministry of Internal Affairs and Communications. Date as of April 2015.
＊4 From Suuji de miru kanko, by Japan Travel and Tourism Association（2014 Edition）
※ The value between the parentheses is the national average.

京都の数字
Numbers of KYOTO

美術館などの数 ＊1（122）
Number of institutions registered under the Kyoto Prefecture Association of Museums
Museums

137

スターバックスコーヒーの数 ＊1（22）
Starbucks Coffee Stores

25

歴代 Gマーク受賞数 ＊1（826）
Winners of the Good Design Award

830

経済産業大臣指定伝統的工芸品 ＊1（4）
Traditional crafts designated by the Minister of Economy, Trade and Industry

西陣織・京鹿の子絞・京くみひも・京指物・京黒紋付染、他
Nishijin-ori (Woven textiles), Kyo-kanoko-shibori (Dyed textiles), Kyo-kumihimo (Braided cord), Kyo-sashimono (Wood crafts), Kyo-kuromontsuki-zome (Black dyeing)

17

JAPANブランド育成支援事業に採択されたプロジェクト ＊1（7）
Projects selected under the JAPAN BRAND program

12

日本建築家協会 京都府の登録会員数 ＊1（88）
Registered members of the Japan Institute of Architects

88

日本グラフィックデザイナー協会京都府登録会員数 ＊1（64）
Registered members of the Japan Graphic Designers Association Inc.

62

府庁所在地
Capital

京都市
Kyoto City

市町村の数 ＊1（36）
Municipalities

26

人口 ＊3（2,724,624）
Population

人

2,636,092

面積 ＊2（8,041）
Area

㎢

4,612

1年間観光者数 ＊4（59,640,000）
Annual number of tourists

人

76,740,000

郷土料理
Local specialties

西京焼
賀茂茄子田楽
ゆば
しば漬け
ちりめん山椒

Saikyo-yaki (Broiled miso-marinated fish)
Kamo-nasu-dengaku (Broiled eggplant with miso glaze)
Yuba (Tofu skin)
Shibazuke (Salt-pickled eggplant and cucumber with red perilla)
Chirimen Zansho (Dried whitebait with sansho pepper)

国指定重要文化財の建造物数 ＊1（51）
Nationally Designated Important Cultural Property (Buildings)

軒

293

主な出身著名人（現市名、故人も含む）
Famous people from Kyoto

北大路魯山人（芸術家・京都市）、阿部牧郎（作家・京都市）、井上梅次（映画監督、脚本家・京都市）、岸田繁（「くるり」、ミュージシャン・京都市）、小林薫（俳優・京都市）、佐渡裕（指揮者・京都市）、野村克也（プロ野球選手・京丹後市）、みうらじゅん（イラストレーター・京都市）、綿矢りさ（小説家・京都市）、他

Kitaoji Rosanjin (Artist, Kyoto), **Makio Abe** (Writer, Kyoto), **Umetsugu Inoue** (Film director, screenplay writer, Kyoto), **Shigeru Kishida** ("Quruli," Musician, Kyoto), **Kaoru Kobayashi** (Actor, Kyoto), **Yutaka Sado** (Orchestra director, Kyoto), **Katsuya Nomura** (Baseball player, Kyotango), **Jun Miura** (Illustrator, Kyoto), **Risa Wataya** (Novelist, Kyoto)

京都号
目次

CONTENTS

昇苑くみひも

I

WIND WOVEN TOWELS

IKEUCHI ORGANIC

EHIME-IMABARI / TOKYO / KYOTO / FUKUOKA / NEW YORK

www.ikeuchi.org

SAMBOA BAR Established 1918
NIKKA WHISKY

白水

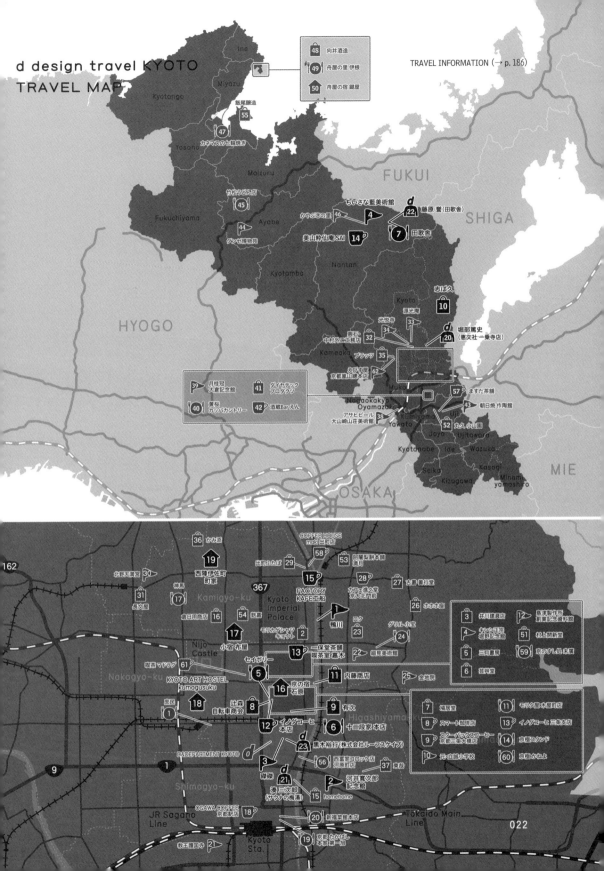

d design travel KYOTO
TRAVEL MAP

TRAVEL INFORMATION (→ p. 186)

48 向井酒造
49 舟屋の里 伊根
50 舟屋の宿 鍵屋

55 飯尾醸造
47
カネマスの七輪焼き

45 竹松うどん店

44 グンゼ博物苑

46 かやぶきの里
ちいさな藍美術館
4
14 美山粋仙庵 SAI
7 田歌舎
22 藤原 誉(田歌舎)

10 志ば久

33
34
32 懐石・中村外二工務店
d 堀部篤史(恵文社一乗寺店)
20
35 えびす屋京都嵐山総本店
62

39 月桂冠大倉記念館
40 黄桜カッパカントリー
41 ダイヤテックプロダクツ
42 酒蔵Bar えん

57 ますだ茶舗
43 朝日焼 作陶館
52 丸久小山園
38 アサヒビール大山崎山荘美術館

下部都市図

36 かみ添
19 西陣伊佐町町家
58
53 阿闍梨餅本舗満月
29 出町ふたば
15 FACTORY KAFE工船
28
27 古書善行堂
26 ホホホ座

30 北野天満宮
31 神馬 長五郎
17
16 倉日用商店
54 鼓月
2 モリカゲシャツキョウト
ロク 23
24 グリル小宝
22 細見美術館

17 小宿 布屋
13 一保堂茶舗 喫茶室嘉木
11 内藤商店
25 金地院

61 喫茶マドラグ
5 セイボリー
16 京の宿 石原
9 有次
8 辻森自転車商会

18
12 イノダコーヒ本店
6 十二段家本店
23 黒木裕行(株式会社ルーフスケイプ)

1 d D&DEPARTMENT KYOTO
3
21
56 志津屋本家コロッケ河原町店
37 東華
15 homehome
2 河井寛次郎記念館
湊三次郎(サウナの梅湯)

18 OGAWA COFFEE 京都駅前店
20 新福菜館本店
19 京都たかばし本家第一旭

21 教王護国寺
JR Sagano Line
Kyoto Sta.
Tōkaidō Main Line

3 井川建具店
4 キンシ正宗堀野記念館
5 三月書房
6 誠孝堂
12 島津製作所創業記念資料館
51 村上開新堂
59 京のすし処末廣

7 鳩居堂
8 スマート珈琲店
9 スターバックスコーヒー京都三条大橋店
10 元立誠小学校
11 モリタ屋木屋町店
13 イノダコーヒ三条支店
14 京都スタンド
60 京極かねよ

162
367
9
022

d MARK REVIEW
KYOTO

1. 京都市の市民が、みんな憩い安らげる、とても長い公園。

流域（距離）は 31 キロ（一級河川としては 23 キロ）。

オオサンショウウオも、カワセミも、カジカ（小魚）も棲む、本当に美しい川。

2. 余計な施設やゴミがない。

美しい景観と環境を保つ、河川整備のお手本。

毎日のように業者による歩道周辺とゴミ箱の清掃があり、

さらに、学生などボランティアによる掃除が日々、行われている。

3. 源流まで、京都の人々に愛され、守られている。

1935 年の大水害を切っ掛けに、10 年以上もかけられた大工事で、

川底を掘り下げ、現在と近い姿に。

鴨川ほど愛される川は、他にない 京都市の中心市街地を真っ直ぐ流れていて、繁華街の人混みからも、直ぐに河川敷に出られて、どこまでも広がる大空の下で、寝転ぶ事も、歌う事も、ビールや珈琲を飲む事もできる。一部の河原には芝生が植えられていて、日光浴や月見を楽しむ人もいる。中洲の繁みから、小鹿が顔を出す事もある。地元の人々は、より長閑な雰囲気の、荒神橋から北が、特に好きなのだそうだ。元々、現在の美しい植栽はなく殺風景だったが、少しずつ桜の木が植えられ、冬にはユリカモメが飛んでくるようになり、凸凹だった道が整備され、自転車でも難なく走れるようになった。そして、現在も、快適に変化し続けている。急勾配の暴れ川であり、七条大橋だけが築一〇〇年を超えたが、三条大橋も五条大橋も、激流に破壊されて流される。鴨川の源流は、北大路から北へ車で約三〇分の、雲ケ畑という美しい名前の山間にある。その山主の久保常次さんは七七歳で、子供の頃、川の中で用を足そうとすると、父親にコテンパンに怒られたと苦笑し、今でも、生活排水などを、そのまま川に流す事は絶対にないと言う。『若木が根を張らなければ、大雨が、そのまま市街地に流れ込んでしまう。きちんと間伐する事が大切です」と、久保さんは話し、川を守る事の大切さ、山仕事の仕方を、大学生や子供達に伝授し続けている。京都の人々が愛しているから、鴨川は美しい。そして、鴨川が美しいから、京都は美しい。（空閑 理）

Kamo River

1. A very long park where Kyoto citizens relax

2. A park without excess facilities or wastes, Kamo River preserves the landscape and environment.

3. A river loved all the way to its source

Kamo River runs through the center of Kyoto. You can always escape the crowds of the business district and go to the riverbed to sing, drink coffee or beer, or take a nap under the expansive blue sky. Part of the riverbed is covered with grass, and many go there to tan and watch the moon. In the past, there were no plants along the river and it was a bit dreary, but cherry trees were gradually planted and the previously bumpy road was fixed. It's now easy to bike on. The origin of Kamo River is located in Kumogahata, an approximately 30-minutes drive north from Kitaoji. Tsuneji Kubo, the owner of the mountain from which the Kamo River flows, explains, "If the young trees don't take root, the rain will flow directly into the city. It's important to thin the trees as need." He teaches university students and children about the importance of protecting the river and how to perform mountain work. The Kamo River is beautiful because Kyoto citizens love it. (Osamu Kuga)

河井寛次郎記念館

京都府京都市 東山区五条坂鐘鋳町569
Tel: 075-561-3585
www.kanjiro.jp
10時〜17時（入館は16時30分まで）
月曜休（祝日の場合は翌日）　夏期・冬期休館あり
清水五条駅から徒歩約10分

1. 京都で作陶し続けた陶芸家の
故・河井寛次郎の元・住居兼仕事場。
1937年、河井寛次郎が自らデザインした建物。
陶芸、木彫、金工、書などの作品を100点以上展示し、
彼の書斎の実物の椅子に実際に座れる。

2.「清水寺」「三十三間堂」などの
神社・仏閣が多い地区にある。
東山の麓、「豊国神社」「智積院」の近くに、ひっそりと佇む。

3.「寛次郎の器でお茶を楽しむ会」など、
家族経営だからできる、民藝本来のよさを伝えている。
1963年開館以来、子供から孫へと遺族で経営を続ける。

デザインが生きる京都生活の遺産　「河井寛次郎記念館」は、河井寛次郎が生前、家族と共に暮らしていた家だ。まず、玄関を入って直ぐ、人さし指が、ビシッと天をさした手の木彫に、僕の寛次郎に対する魅力は一層掻き立てられた。最初の広間は、吹き抜けになっていて、二階へは、故・濱田庄司が寄贈した箱階段を上がる。吹き抜け部分を挟んだ部屋が書斎で、大きな臼のテーブルや、オブジェとしての自在鉤（囲炉裏などで使う木製フック）などが部屋に調和し、重厚で心が落ち着く空間だ。中庭を挟んだ廊下には、台湾の竹職人と造った竹の棚や、金工職人と造った真鍮のキセルなどが展示されてあり、素焼窯の手前の茶室から見える庭には、同級生に貰ったという島根県の大根島の丸い石がある。そして、陶房の先に共同の登り窯がある。大工の家に生まれた寛次郎は、緻密に設計された通路や部屋、襖の把っ手など細部に至るまで、自らデザインし、実兄を棟梁とした郷里の安来の職人達と造った。窯には地元の陶工が集まり、自宅にも千客万来だった、と寛次郎の孫の学芸員・鷺珠江さんは言う。故・柳宗悦は、京都を訪れる際には寛次郎の世話になればいい、と知人に紹介していた。民藝運動の起ち上げメンバーの寛次郎。僕はここに来て、彼の皆に愛される人柄や勤勉さと、彼の生み出した様々なデザインに深く感動した。「河井寛次郎記念館」は年に二回、家族揃って大掃除をするそうだ。誰からも永く愛され続ける素敵な記念館だ。（神藤秀人）

KAWAI KANJIRO'S HOUSE

1. Home and studio of the late Kyoto-based potter Kanjiro Kawai

2. Located in an area with many popular Kyoto destinations

3. With events such as "tea ceremonies using Kanjiro's pottery," it carries on the values of the *mingei* folk art movement.

The entrance hall of the house is built in a wellhole style. To reach the second floor, one must climb the stair-shaped storage cabinet gifted by the late Shoji Hamada. Along the corridor, which circumscribes the courtyard, various objects such as bamboo shelves made with bamboo artisans in Taiwan and brass smoking pipes made with a metalsmith are displayed. The tearoom, located in front of the bisque-firing kiln, provides a view of the garden decorated with a round stone from Daikon Island in Shimane Prefecture, which Kawai received from an old schoolmate. Born into a family of carpenters, Kawai meticulously designed the corridors, rooms, and even the handles on the sliding paper doors himself, and constructed them with artisans from his hometown Yasugi, who worked under his brother, a master carpenter. The kiln drew many local potters. KAWAI KANJIRO'S HOUSE is a wonderful museum that's loved by all. (Shindo Hideto)

磔磔 (たくたく)

1. 京都市市街地にある、伝説的ライブハウス。

1974年、当時流行の民藝調の酒場として開店。
日本中の音楽好きが憧れる、数々の名演奏の舞台。
「磔磔」は擬音で、漢字の「磔」の意味はない。

2. 手造りで改築した、築約100年の酒蔵の、素晴らしい音響。

天井裏の楽屋から見える剥き出しの梁には「大正六年」の墨字。
西岡恭蔵（故）、「ボ・ガンボス」（解散）、「くるり」他多数がライブ盤を収録。

3. ビールに焼きそば、名物の日替わりカレーなど、豊富なメニュー。

会場中央の大黒柱付近にテーブルを出す事が多く、
提灯の下、料理を食べながら演奏を聴ける。しかも美味しい。

京都府京都市下京区富小路通 仏光寺下ル筋屋街 136-9
Tel: 075-351-1321
www.geisya.or.jp/~takutaku/
河原町駅から徒歩約5分
営業時間は、イベントの開場・終了の時間に準ずる
（基本はL.O. 22時30分）　不定休

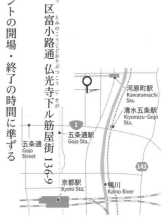

好きなミュージシャンが、ここで演るなら必ず聴くべき四月一六日は、フォークシンガー高田渡の命日で、京都市生まれの息子・高田漣が、その日「磔磔」でトリビュートライブを開いた。一〇〇席ほどの客席も、後方の立ち見席も満員の観客。彼らの背後の壁には、ウィルコ・ジョンソンらの過去公演の巨大な手描き看板がビッシリ。僕の席は壁際のベンチの端で、すぐ前の通路が花道だった。出演メンバーが膝に触れそうな近さで通り過ぎてステージに上がり、『アイスクリーム』『自転車にのって』『銭がなけりゃ』も、『生活の柄』も、そして、「京都で、これをやらないわけには」と『コーヒーブルース』も、次々と演奏して、さっきまでカレーを食べていた隣の叔父さんが、涙を流しながら、微笑みながら、僕らと一緒に歌っていた。高田渡の死去から一〇年、同じ日に、同じ「磔磔」で、息子が歌う親父の歌を、当時の世代の客と息子世代の客が一体となって聴いた。「磔磔」は、開店当時は居酒屋で、「ここで歌いたい」「音楽を聴きたい」という客が次第に、「ライブハウス」という言葉さえもなかった時だが、増え、畳の座敷席がステージになり、障子戸をコンクリート壁にして、京都を代表するライブスポットとなっていった。レコードもCDも売れない現在、音源を購入するよりもライブに行く事の方が自然、という音楽好きが増えている、と僕は思う。だからこそ、この「磔磔」が、京都に必ず在り続けてほしい、と僕は強く願う。（空閑理）

Taku Taku

1. A legendary club located in central Kyoto

2. A 100-years-old sake cellar renovated by hand offers amazing acoustics

3. Plenty of drinks and dishes including beer, fried noodles, and the famous curry of the day

On April 16, the anniversary of folk singer Wataru Takada's death, his son Ren Takada, who was born in Kyoto, performed a tribute show at "Taku Taku." The club was filled to capacity and on the wall behind the audience were giant hand-painted signs for previous shows performed by artists such as Wilco Johnson. The performing members passed at such close proximity that they nearly brushed against my knees, took the stage, and performed a number of Wataru Takada's hits. When

Taku Taku first opened, it was a bar. No one called it a club, but eventually, more and more people started to express interest in performing and listening to music here. The tatami room was turned into a stage and Taku Taku became one of Kyoto's most famous clubs. I think that in this day and age, when neither CDs nor records sell, many music fans are going to see live music instead of buying recorded music. That's why I want Taku Taku to continue its existence. (Osamu Kuga)

ちいさな藍美術館

京都府南丹市美山町北上牧41
Tel: 0771-77-0746
shindo-shindigo.com
11時～17時　木・金曜休（祝日の場合は開館）　冬期休
園部ICから車で約45分

1. 昔話の童話のような景観の、
茅葺き民家の集落「かやぶきの里」にある。
散策したい美山町一の景勝地の北村にある名所。

2. 築200年超えの庄屋を改築した、
藍染め工房兼美術館。
村で最も古くて大きい建物で、小さい美術館。

3. 藍染作家の新道弘之さん自らが館長。
作業工程を目の前で見せてくれ、そのハンカチや、
角袋（反物をバイアス状に縫い上げた袋）などの作品が買える。

京都の小さな、偉大な美術館　京都市市街地から約一時間半車で走った美山町北村「かやぶきの里」は、その入り口から続く坂道の両側に、茅葺き屋根の住宅が建ち並ぶ、美しい山間の集落だ。そこで一番大きな建物の「ちいさな藍美術館」は、丸眼鏡をかけた館長の新道弘之さんが、いつも笑顔で迎えてくれる。「どうぞ、ごゆっくり」と、入館料三〇〇円を払って屋根裏へ案内されると、そこには新道さんが約三〇年間集めてきた、一八世紀の京都琳派模様（装飾芸術）とされるデニムや、大正時代の京都琳派模様（装飾芸術）の型染めなど、僕が初めて見る、国内外の藍染めの衣料品等が約三〇点展示してある。学生時代、有名作家の美術ではなく、庶民の衣服や織物に興味を持ったという新道さん。「こんな素晴らしい物、誰が染めたんや」と、発酵させた植物の葉が、布を鮮やかなブルーに染める藍に魅せられ、卒業後も市内で作家活動を続けてきたが、一九八一年、縁もあり、求めていた静かな活動を北村でスタート。しばらくして、この土地が「かやぶきの里」として「重要伝統的建造物群保存地区」に指定され、多くの観光客が訪れるようになった。それならば、「藍の魅力を多くの人に知ってもらおう」と、二〇〇五年四月、コレクションを展示し、工房を美術館として一般公開。土間で、水道管を利用した道具に、真っ白な生地を丁寧に巻きつけていく新道さん。よい物を、日常で使ってほしいと、考案した藍染めの作業を惜しまず、来館者に見せている。（神藤秀人）

The Little Indigo Museum

1. Situated in Kayabuki no Sato, a fairytale-like hamlet of thatched houses

2. An indigo dye atelier and museum converted from a 200-year-old Shoya house

3. Hiroyuki Shindo, the indigo artist and the museum director

Kayabuki no Sato, a little hamlet in Miyama-cho Kitamura region, is a very picturesque place filled with thatched houses. When you walk into the Little Indigo Museum, the biggest building in the hamlet, you will be greeted by the bespectacled museum director, Hiroyuki Shindo. Up in the attic, which has been converted into an exhibition space, you will see nearly 30 indigo-related artifacts that Shindo has collected over the past 30 years, including a pair of denim jeans from the 18th century. He has been fascinated by indigo—a simple plant, the leaves of which, when fermented, dye textiles bright blue. Originally from Kyoto city, he moved his atelier to Kitamura in 1981. Soon after, this hamlet was designated as a historic site and brought in tourism. He opened the museum in his atelier in April 2005. He wants visitors to see, first hand, his dyeing process and, through that experience, to be inspired to use high-quality indigo-dyed items in their everyday life. (Hideto Shindo)

セイボリー

京都府京都市中京区 東 洞院通
三条下ル三文字町 220 八百一本館
3 F

Tel: 075-223-2320

ランチ 11時30分〜15時 (L.O.)
ディナー17時30分〜20時 (L.O.) 水曜休

www.kyotoyaoichihonkan.com
烏丸御池駅から徒歩約3分

1. 斬新な生鮮食品店「京都 八百一本館」屋上のレストラン。

3 階建てビル屋上の緑が繁る、新 "京の台所"。
生鮮食品や、半調理のお惣菜なども、1 階で販売。

2. 目の前で栽培・収穫される野菜など、新鮮その物の食材。

窓からは、自社の屋上農場「六角農場」が見渡せる。
街中にいる事を忘れさせ、野菜に深く関心を持たせる店。

3. 荘司索シェフによる、創意溢れる料理。

野菜一つ一つの個性を、愛おしそうに楽しそうに、教えてくれる。
シェフと話せるカウンター席が、お薦め。

お腹いっぱい味わう "本当の京都野菜" 六角通りの「辻森自転車商会」隣のスーパー「京都 八百一本館」。三階に上がり、エレベーターの扉が開くと、そこは何と屋外。畑があり、軟らかく肥えた土に、様々な野菜が小さな芽を出していた。作業中の女性に声をかけると、今はスイスチャード（ビートの一系統）を植えていると言われた。よく散歩に来るという地元のお婆さんとベンチで休んでいると、「六角堂」から午後五時を告げる鐘の音が聞こえてきた。一週間後に再訪すると、菜の花が満開。他の野菜も葉の色が濃くなっていて、そろそろ食べ頃という物も多い。この農場に臨むレストランが「セイボリー」だ。

時々、若い料理人が農場に出てきて、ハーブなどをプチプチと摘んでいく。非常に人気で、予約なしでの来店は無謀だが、もしカウンター席が空いていたら、実はそこが特等席。白いワークジャケットをお洒落に着こなした、荘司索シェフが、「お腹、余裕あります？ これも食べてみませんか？」と取って置きの、お薦め料理を出してくれる事も。料理は、目の前の農場や、「八百一」から仕入れた野菜が中心で、食感は新鮮シャキシャキ、盛りつけにも味つけにも創意があって、すべて一級品だとわかるが、「ちょっとした工夫で、もっと美味しくなる」と荘司シェフは、料理のコツを笑顔で教えてくれる。そして、同じ野菜を階下で買って帰る事もできる。"京都の日常" を特別に豊かにしてくれる、新鮮な学びのレストラン。（空閑 理）

Savory

1. A restaurant located on the roof of "Kyoto Yaoichi Honkan," an innovative grocery store

2. The restaurant uses the freshest ingredients grown and harvested on site.

3. Saku Shoji, the restaurant's charismatic chef makes creative dishes.

"Savory" is located on the roof of "Kyoto Yaoichi Honkan," a grocery store adjacent to "Tsujimori Cycles" on Rokkaku Street. Go up to the third floor, and when the elevator doors open, you'll step out onto the building's roof. There's a farm there, and on the rich soft soil, there are many ripe greens and other vegetables that are ready to be eaten. Savory faces this farm. Sometimes, young chefs come to the farm to take some herbs. If a counter seat is open, it's actually your best option. Chef Saku Shoji, dressed in a white work jacket, may ask you, "Do you still have room? Want to try this?" And serve you a special dish. The food is made primarily with ingredients from the farm or Yaoichi. The texture of the ingredients is crisp and all of the dishes are served and seasoned beautifully. All the food there is first class. (Osamu Kuga)

十二段家 本店

1. 柳宗悦、河井寛次郎、棟方志功など、
民藝運動の中心人物が集った食事処。
河井の蓋物、濱田庄司のスリップウエアなど、
家族皆が愛でる作品が飾られた全客間。

2. 正真正銘、しゃぶしゃぶ発祥の店。
先代がデザインした銅製の鍋は、灰汁が出にくく、
茹で汁は、最後にスープとして頂ける。

3. 祇園で一番寛げる、実家のような居心地。
築約150年のお茶屋を改築。
三代目の西垣隆光さん家族が、いつでも笑顔で迎えてくれる。

京都府京都市東山区祇園町 南 側 570-128
Tel: 075-561-0213
ランチ 11時30分〜13時 (L.O.)
ディナー 17時〜20時 (L.O.)
木曜、第2水曜休 (変更あり)
junidanya-kyoto.com
祇園四条駅から徒歩約5分

祇園の"民藝茶屋"「十二段家 本店」の客間には、棟方志功の「釈迦十大弟子」のふすま絵や、河井寛次郎や濱田庄司の皿や花器など、約一〇〇点が、当たり前のように飾られている。全部屋、陶芸家の故・上田恒次が手がけた内装で、和室から洋室に改装した囲炉裏があった部屋も、上田が焼いたタイル敷きのトイレも、まるで「河井寛次郎記念館」のようだ。伊万里焼の大皿に盛られた、海老や賀茂茄子など五種類の前菜。水を張った出西窯の皿を鍋受けに、炭の入った煙突がある鍋で時間。胡麻ダレにさっと浸け、霜降りの近江牛を、あっという間に平らげた。一九二二年、和菓子の店から始まり、花見小路に移転後、お茶漬けの「十二段家」として約四〇年続いたが、戦後、初代は店を閉じた。二代目の西垣光温 (故) は、大阪で書店を営んでいた時、棟方志功の紹介で、河井寛次郎の自宅(現「河井寛次郎記念館」)を訪ねた。そして、そこで見た数々の作品や家具、その生活に感銘を受け、「十二段家」を再スタート。翌年、民藝運動家の故・吉田璋也と試作を重ねてデザインした鍋、河井と吟味してつくった胡麻ダレ。後に、しゃぶしゃぶとして全国へ広まる「牛肉の水炊き」が「十二段家」で生まれたのだ。玄関に飾られている、先代がデザインした大きな鍋は、とても優美な形。これこそ「用の美」だ、と僕は震撼した。(神藤秀人)

一名物しゃぶしゃぶコース」。五秒──それが、僕のお薦めの肉の茹で時間。「名物しゃぶしゃぶ

一九四五年、京都に移り、現在の建物を改築して「十二段家」を再スタート。

034

JUNIDANYA

1. The restaurant that drew the central figures of the *mingei* folk art movement, such as Muneyoshi Yanagi, Kanjiro Kawai, Shoji Hamada, and Shiko Munakata

2. The restaurant, where "shabu-shabu" was invented

3. The most relaxing restaurant in Gion and one that feels like you're at home

In the drawing room of "JUNIDANYA," are approximately 100 works by key figures of the *mingei* folk art movement, including screen paintings by Shiko Munakata, and pottery and vases by Kanjiro Kawai and Shoji Hamada. All the rooms were decorated by the late potter Tsuneji Ueda, and the restaurant feels like "KAWAI KANJIRO'S HOUSE." The five appetizers are served on a large Imari pottery plate and the famed shabu shabu is cooked in a chimneyed pot heated with charcoal sitting on a Shussai pottery plate. In 1921, JUNIDANYA had been open for approximately forty years, but the first owner closed shop after the war. The second owner Mitsuharu Nishigaki reopened the restaurant in 1945, after he moved to Kyoto and renovated the building. In 1946, he designed the special pot with the late Shoya Yoshida, also a member of the *mingei* movement, and created the sesame sauce with Kanjiro Kawai. (Hideto Shindo)

田歌舎（たうたしゃ）

京都府南丹市美山町　田歌上五波 1-1
Tel: 0771-77-0509
カフェレストラン 11時30分～14時30分（完全予約制）
※冬季はカフェも予約制（12月～3月は土・日曜・祝日のみ営業）
月・火曜休（臨時休業あり）
ガイドツアー、体験　火曜休（要予約）
tautasya.jp/about
園部ICから車で約50分

1. 美山町の食材の自給自足のレストラン。

古代米、鹿や猪の肉、鴨の卵、山菜などが食せる、
鹿肉を、ここの名産とも言わしめた、美山町の名店。

2. 狩猟体験やキャンプなどを通じて、美山町の自然の豊かさを広めている。

森に入り、食材を採取し、調理するプログラムがあり、
由良川の河原などで食べる、店特製弁当は絶品。

3. 森を拓き、建物すべてがセルフビルド。

湧き水を引き込む独自の水道システムと、67枚の太陽光発電。
レストランやトイレなどの建材には、伐採した杉材を使用。
ドアノブは、狩った鹿の角を使う。

野生的レストラン　国道三八号線の由良川上流にある、八角形の山小屋風レストラン「田歌舎」は、直ぐ目の前に、田んぼが広がり、ヤマガラなどの多くの野鳥のさえずりや、川のせせらぎが聞こえ、田歌地区の自然を肌で、ありありと感じられる美しい環境。料理は、近隣の森で狩猟する鹿や猪、田畑で作る米や野菜を使い、さらに味噌や酢、山椒などの調味料も、ほとんどが自家栽培。僕達は、鹿肉の「リングソーセージ」と、コシアブラの「山菜ピザ」を注文した。二〇〇三年、現在の調理場で、たった一卓だけのレストランからスタートした「田歌舎」は、二〇〇八年に宿泊棟、二〇一一年に現在のレストランを建てた。建材は杉材を使い、デザインなど、すべてを自分達で行った。動植物や昆虫が多い原生林のツアーガイドや、捕獲した鹿や猪を食べる狩猟体験など、様々な珍しいイベントを企画。現在、ほとんどの部位が食べられる物として需要も拡大しつつある鹿だが、「田歌舎」では、ロースなどの上等な部位以外も「鹿ケバブ（シシケバブの鹿版）」などの創意ある料理に美味しく調理する。代表の藤原誉さんは、多くの人々に、自然の中で暮らす事の大切さと楽しみ、そして、それが誰にでもできるという事を伝え広めたいと努力を重ねる。「鴨の雛、見た？」と、満面の笑顔の誉さん。稲の合鴨農法も、今年で七年目だ。僕は、料理に添えられた自家製のパンに、鴨の卵を使ったタマゴサラダをのせ、実に頬が緩んだ。（神藤秀人）

Tautasha

1. As self-sustaining restaurant in Miyama

2. Promotes the richness of Miyama's natural environment through camping and hunting classes

3. Its owner opened the forest and built the restaurant himself.

There is a farm in front of "Tautasha." You can also hear birds singing and the river flowing there. It's a place where you can really feel nature. The food is made with deer and boar hunted in neighboring forests and produce from the restaurant's own farm. The miso, vinegar, and spices are also almost entirely homegrown. In 2003, "Tautasha" started as a single-building restaurant operating out of the kitchen that's still used today. In 2008, a building for lodging, and in 2011, the current restaurant building was built. The buildings are made of Japanese cedar and were designed and constructed by its owner Homaru Fujiwara. Tautasha also organizes tours of the virgin forest, which offers a rich variety of animals, insects, and plants, and tours in which participants and hunt and cook the game they kill. Fujiwara says he wants to share the importance and joy of living in a natural environment and show that anyone can do the same. (Hideto Shindo)

辻森自転車商会

京都府京都市中京区 東 洞院六角上ル三文字町

Tel: 075-221-5732

9時〜18時　日曜、祝日休

tsujimori.com

烏丸御池駅から徒歩約3分

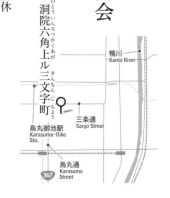

鴨川
Kamo River

烏丸御池駅
Karasuma-Oike Sta.

三条通
Sanjo Street

烏丸通
Karasuma Street

367

1. 京都生活に欠かせない自転車の、風情ある専門店。

新しく、お洒落な店だと入りづらい、年配の地元客も、ここなら、「自転車、調子ええよ」と、気軽に立ち寄れる。

2. 六角通りの名所的存在になっている、築100年以上の建築。

六角通り沿いの壁に取り付けられた、古い自転車が看板代わり。

3. どんな依頼も断らない、自己流で可能な限り対応して整備してくれる店。

先代が体調を崩して閉める事になった自転車店を、専門知識や経験がないながら、独学で引き継いだ現店主。

80年以上も前の自転車を乗れるように修理した事も。

京都暮らしの必需品　京都市には、自転車店が実に多いが、「この店で買いたい」と、僕が強く思ったのは、六角通りと東洞院通りとの人通りの多い交差点にある「辻森自転車商会」だ。瓦葺きの木造建築の外壁には空襲を知らせるベルが残り、看板の「ホンダ」の朱色が映えている。

ショーウインドウには、「ブルーノ」など最新デザインの自転車が並ぶ一方で、東洞院通り沿いは、店と通りを隔てる物は何もなく、開け放たれた作業場がある、今では珍しくなってしまった昔ながらの自転車店だ。行き交う人の多くが足を止め、自転車を停め、「ちょっとサドルが歪んでしもて」「チェーン外れてもうた」「ダイちゃん（店主の愛称）！　パンク、パンク！」などと、店主の宮本大輔さんに話しかけ、数分後、「バッチリや、ありがとう！」と漕ぎ去っていく。

僕が自転車を選んだ約一時間で、声をかけてきた人は五〇人は下らない。修理や部品の取り寄せの相談などはもちろん、道を尋ねる観光客、子供が大きくなったよと顔を見せに来る常連のお客さん、靴の底が取れた、タンスが倒れないようにしたい、恋愛相談……自転車とはまったく関係ない、仕事にならないような相談もあるが、「建物と一緒に、この町で生きているような感じです」と店主は笑う。自転車を買うだけでなく、買った後も、特に整備が必要でない時でも、必ず立ち寄りたくなるのは、京都の人々の勤勉な仕事ぶりと、心の優しさが、この店の人間模様から見えてくるからだ。（空閑 理）

Tsujimori Cycle

1. A bicycle shop with great ambiance; bicycles are essential for Kyoto living

2. Housed in an over-100-years-old building and landmark of Rokkaku Street

3. A bicycle shop that will accept all requests and respond within the repairperson's ability

There are many bicycle stores in Kyoto, but the one that made me want to buy a bike there is "Tsujimori Cycle," located at the busy intersection of Rokkaku and Higashinotoin Streets. In the window are the latest models from "Bruno" and others, but the side of the shop facing Higashinotoin Street is completely open and houses the work area. It's an old school bicycle shop, the likes of which are quickly disappearing. Many people biking by stop and talk to the shop owner Daisuke Miyamoto. In the hour it took me to choose a bicycle, no less than 50 people stopped in to talk to him. People asked about repairs and parts and tourists asked for directions. Some of the questions had nothing to do with bicycles, but Miyamoto laughed and said, "It's all a part of living in this city with this building." Now I've bought the bike, but I still want to visit the shop. (Osamu Kuga)

9

有次（ありつぐ）

京都府京都市中京区錦小路通 御幸町西入ル
Tel: 075-221-1091
www.kyoto-nishiki.or.jp/stores/aritsugu/
10時～16時　水曜休　1月1日～3日休
河原町駅から徒歩約5分

**1. 押しも押されもせぬ、
最高の庖丁と料理道具の店。**

「道具は、使う人が自分で手入れする事で、その人の手の一部になる」と、客一人一人に、物を大事する心を伝え続け商いする。

2. 頑固一徹、決してブレない、商いの姿勢。

世界中から観光客が訪れる、信念とスタイルを貫く店。支払いはクレジットカードやトラベラーズチェックは不可、現金のみ。

**3. 数十年前の商品でも修理できる、
万全のアフターケア。**

「刃が錆びたり減ったりしても、修理できる物しか、つくらないのが職人」と、全国の職人や技術者を養成する事も使命とする店。

物の命は大切だ 三〇年以上も前に両親が結婚記念に贈られたという銅製の薬罐を、僕は会社の同僚から預かった。一部が凹み、把っ手の籐は取れて、内側の錫は黒く変色していた。これを修理ができるか訊いてみてほしいというのだった。購入した「有次」は京都市の「錦市場」にあり、客が溢れる店内を通して店員の方は「ほな、見ましょ」と包みを解くなり、「こんな使ってもろうて、よかったなあ。ココとココと……ココや」と、修理箇所を瞬時に判断、料金表と照合して見積もりを出してくれた、かかった時間は、わずか五分。三〇年以上も前の商品なのに、ほぼ同じ形の現商品を持ってきて、修理する薬罐の隣に並べて「こんなふうにキレイに直ってきます」と見せてくれた。その対応に感激していると、ベテランらしい店員の方は「道具とは、そういうもんやから」とクールだが、嬉しそうに微笑んでくれた。同行の編集部の佐々木晃子も感動して、「自分も『有次』の物が欲しい」と、庖丁を買う事になり、時間をかけて一本を選んだ。また、希望すれば、無料で名前を彫ってくれ、研ぎ方を丁寧に教えてくれながら、刃を仕上げてくれる。「よく切れるように」という以上に「長く役に立ってこいよ」「疲れたら、里帰り（修理）に来いよ」と想いを込めるのだそうだ。道具には、大事にすれば、いつまでも生き続ける命がある。それが、掌に握って、ハッキリと感じられる店。（空閑理）

Aritsugu

1. The finest knife and cookware shop in the world

2. A shop that sticks to its beliefs and style and draws customers from around the world

3. The shop offers comprehensive aftercare service. It will repair products sold decades ago.

A colleague gave me a copper kettle, which she said it was given to her parents as a wedding gift over 30 years ago. A part of it was dented, the handle had come off, and the interior had turned black. He wanted me to see if it could be repaired. "Aritsugu," where it was purchased, is located in Kyoto's Nishiki Market. I walked through the crowded shop to the counter at the back and explained the situation. The clerk commented, "So nice that it was used so much. Here, here, and here." Immediately assessing the parts that needed mending, he looked at the price list and gave me an estimate. It took all of five minutes. He brought a new, almost identical product and said, "It'll look like this when we're done." The shop will also engrave your name if you desire. Used with care, good tools will last forever. This is a shop that clearly conveys that fact. (Osamu Kuga)

志ば久（しばきゅう）

京都府京都市左京区大原勝林院町58
Tel: 075-744-4893
9時〜16時　水曜休
www.shibakyu.jp
大原バス停から徒歩約10分

1. 伝統の紫蘇からつくる、名物「志ば漬」。

頑なに種と畑を守り、個性の味を追求し、
自分たちで、徹頭徹尾つくる、大原だけの「志ば漬」。

2. 大原を盛り上げる、リーダー的な父子二代。

父が販売と企画を担当し店頭に立ち、
息子が営業と製造を担当して畑に立つ。
「いいとされる物」ではなく、「いいと思う物」だけを、つくって、売る。

3. 必ず、三千院詣での手土産にしたい、美しい包装紙。

「お好きな色を選んで」と、紙の手提げ袋は5種類で、
全種類、集めたくなるほど素敵。

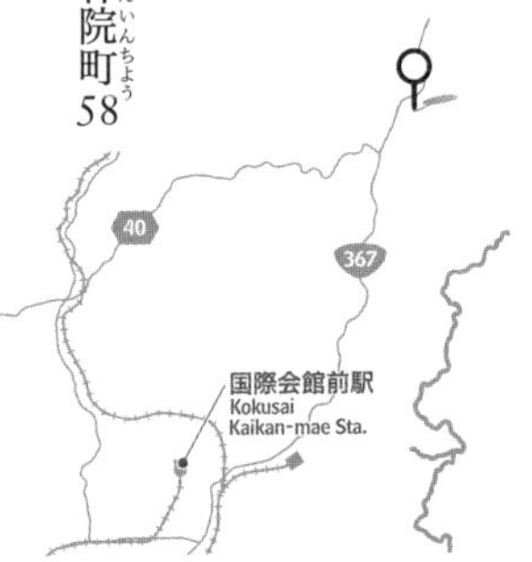

国際会館前駅
Kokusai Kaikan-mae Sta.

大原の男ふたり「京都大原三千院」は、京都駅から車で約一時間。参道の傍らを流れる呂川（りょせん）とも読む）の清流に、楓の木漏れ陽が射して、キラキラと光っている。観光客は多くなく、モリアオガエルも棲むという、清々しく、素敵な道だ。その道沿いに、「志ば久」はある。藍染めの暖簾が爽やかな民藝調の書体で書かれた看板や、藍染めの暖簾が爽やかだ。代表商品はもちろん「志ば漬」で、その主原料の紫蘇の畑は、店のすぐ裏にあり、育てている久保統さんが案内してくれた。「志ば久」の紫蘇は、毎年、自家採種。

大原は、周りを山に囲まれた小さな盆地で、花粉などが外から飛んできにくいため、「志ば久」の紫蘇は、原種に近いと言われている。僕が訪れた時に満開だったのは菜の花で、観光客の目を楽しませ、枯れたら紫蘇の肥料になり、蕾は漬け物になる。約一か月後に再訪すると、小さな葉っぱが二、三枚だけだった紫蘇が立派に育って、ビニールハウスから少し離れた畑に植え替えられていた。

久保さん家族で、一本一本、手植えで作業する。そして、その畑は、大原の里山が眼下に広がる素晴らしい眺望でもあり、その風景を、観光客が畑の中を歩いて見れるように、畝一本分は紫蘇を植えずに残して、道にしてあった。畑の入り口には、久保さんの父が土に立てた、手描きの観光案内板があり、「この先、見渡す限り、大原の里」とある。旅人の心に残るのは、深い歴史でも壮大な物語でもなく、この真心と素直さなのだ、と僕は思う。（空閑 理）

Shibakyu

1. Shibazuke pickles made with heirloom shiso leaves
2. A father and son team that leads the revitalization of Ohara
3. Beautiful wrapping paper, which you must get as a Sanzen-in temple souvenir

"Kyoto Ohara Sanzen-in" is an hour drive from Kyoto station. The sunlight filtered through the maple leaves plays radiantly upon the surface of the Ro River, which runs serenely along the path to the temple. It's a beautiful approach. "Shibakyu" is located along this path. Its folk craft style sign and indigo-dyed shop curtain are brilliant. Its most popular item is the "shibazuke" pickles. The shiso leaves, which it's made of, is grown just behind the shop. Hajime Kubo, who grows them, showed us the farm. He and his family plant and grow all the shiso by hand. The farm is also a beautiful sight and a path just wide enough for tourists to walk through has been left open. A sign placed at the entrance of the farm by Kubo's father reads, "From here on, is Ohara village as far as the eye can see." I thought to myself, "What make the strongest impressions on a travelers' heart are earnestness and sincerity."
（Osamu Kuga）

内藤商店

京都府京都市中京区三条大橋西詰北側

Tel.: 075-221-3018

www.joho-kyoto.or.jp/~sankoba/omiseyasan/naito/naito.html

9時30分〜19時　不定休、1月1日〜3日休

三条駅から徒歩約3分

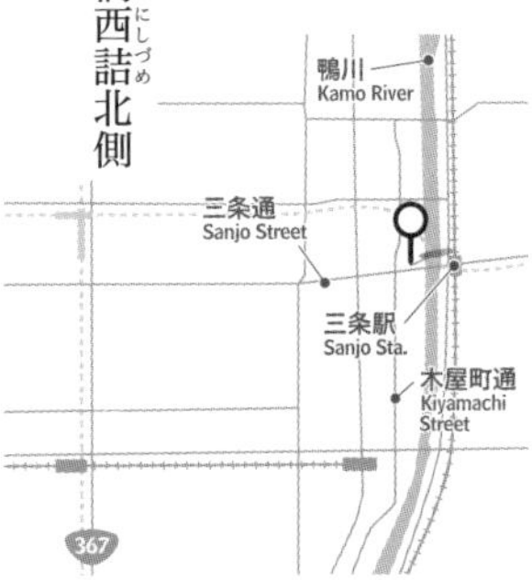

1. ひと目で惚れ込む、棕櫚製品の専門店。

職人の業が生きる箒、束子、バスマット——全商品、逸品。
つくる技術の素晴らしさ、正しい使い方を、自信をもって、
笑顔で伝える店。

2. 少しずつ、確かな物だけを、無理せずに販売。

看板も掲げず、インターネット通販も、取り置きもしない。
ここだけの一級品を買うためには、足で行くのみ。運も必要。

3. 京都の街中で、製品が使われ、その美しい風景を担っている。

京都中の寺や旅館、カフェや書店、セレクトショップなどで、
この店の箒やマットが使われている様子に、京都だけの風情を感じる。

毎日使う、最高級品　鴨川に向かう三条通り、三条大橋の手前に、そこだけ時間が止まっているような、間もなく創業二〇〇年の棕櫚製品の専門店がある。表の棚には整然と束子が並べられ、それらはコロッケみたいで美味しそうで、手に取ると軟らかく、肌触りがいい。そして、鴨居から下げられた箒を指さして、僕は、間抜けな質問をしてしまった——「これは箒ですか?」と。それほど、その箒は美しかったのだ。七代目の内藤幸子さんは「キレイでしょう。これは室内用」と、笑顔で一つを取って、使い方を教えてくれた。体の正面で垂直に近い角度に立てて持ち、毛束の底面で、やさしく撫でるように掃く。絨毯や畳の奥のチリも、きちんと掃き出せる。棕櫚を束ねる細工は濃やかで、ほっそりとした柄は黒色の淡竹で、それを使う人の動きまで美しく見せる。しかし、他の取材予定があって、その時は買えず、翌日再訪すると、その箒は売り切れていた。次の入荷を尋ねると、室内用の箒の職人は一人切りで、長い柄の箒を一二種類、短い柄の箒を五種類、それらを順番につくっていて、同じ箒が入荷する日は、はっきりとは言えないという。だが、その一週間後に店の前を通ると、箒が定位置に下がっていた。その時は違う種類の箒だったが、僕は迷わず買った。「キレイやから、って飾らはる言う人もおるけど、使うたほうが箒もキレイになりますし。いい箒ですし、使うたほうが箒もキレイになってくださいし」。京都がキレイな理由を聞けた。(空閑　理)

Naito Shoten

1. A shop specializing in hemp-palm products, which you'll fall in love with at first sight

2. A shop that humbly sells only a small number of items, and only what it truly believes in

3. Its products are used throughout Kyoto and help maintain its beautiful appearance.

On Sanjo street, towards the Kamo River and just before Sanjo Ohashi bridge is a hemp-palm store that's nearly 200 years old. Walking into it is like traveling back in time. At the front of the store are rows of delicious scrubbing brushes that look like croquettes. I pointed to a broom and foolishly asked, "Is this a broom?" It was so beautiful that I was unsure. The seventh-generation owner Sachiko Naito answered, "It's beautiful, isn't it? This one's for interior use." She smiled and showed me how to use it. It's great for cleaning carpeted floors and dust caught between tatami mats. When I visited again the next day, the broom had been sold. When I asked when she might restock it, she replied that there's only one person that makes the indoor brooms, and that he's making seventeen variations in order, so that it was difficult to say when. A week later, however, the same broom was hanging in the same place. I bought it without hesitation this time. (Osamu Kuga)

イノダコーヒ 本店

京都府京都市中京区堺町通三条下ル道祐町140
Tel: 075-221-0507
www.inoda-coffee.co.jp
7時〜17時30分 (L.O.)　無休
烏丸御池駅から徒歩約5分

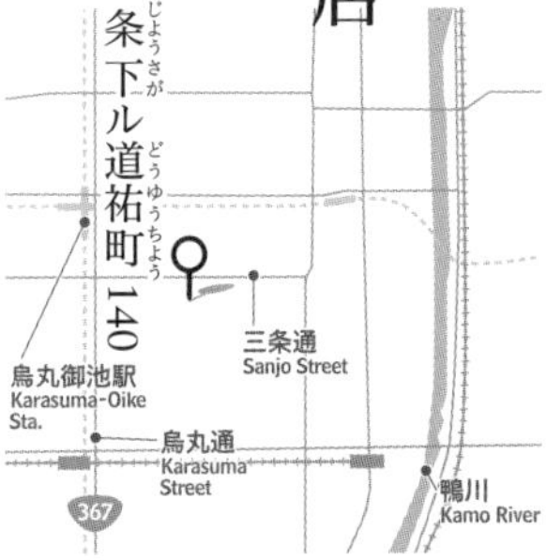

1. 1947年開店の、京都の珈琲文化のシンボル。

素晴らしい格式ある接客と、快適な居心地。
料理は美しく盛りつけられ、赤いポットのロゴマークが
随所に映えている。

2. 1999 年に火災に遭うも、京都の人々に
愛された以前の面影を見事に復元。

防火地区で木造建築の許可が下りず、コンクリート造りだが、
木造かと見間違うほどの外観で、2000 年に再開。

3. 数々の名物メニューと、オリジナルブレンド
「アラビアの真珠」の美味。

定番は、ビーフカツサンド、それとエビフライを挟んだロールパンセット。
月替わりのキャンペーンメニューも、オレンジジュース（フレッシュ）も美味。

イノダに会いに　三条堺町にある、地元客からも観光客からも愛され続けている名店「イノダコーヒ本店」。入り口の焦げ茶色の暖簾を、皆、笑顔で潜って出入りする。瓦葺きで、黒い外壁の、古い蔵のような、格式ある建物だが、実は二〇〇〇年に新築された物と知って、僕は非常に驚いた。前年の火災の被害や、老朽化などを理由に、出来る限り同じ物を新店舗に使用。再建後の変化を心配して、毎日工事現場を見に来ていた常連客もいたそうだ。外観は、解体前と同じように仕上げ、窓のサッシはアルミだが、まるで木製のように塗装され、ステンドグラスや庭の池も、〝イノダそのまま〟に、見事に再現を果たした。入り口の左側の、赤・白・青のトリコロールの外観の「メモリアル・ルーム」は、手作業で大切に解体し、出来る限り同じ物を新店舗に使用。一九四七年当時の姿に戻し、その写真に写っている時計やレジなども再設置。禁煙室を希望すれば照明を低く落としたレトロな雰囲気の旧館に通され、喫煙室を希望すれば、広く、天井が約五メートルの吹き抜けが清々しい、モダンな新館に座れる。椅子とテーブルは原則として以前に使用していた物を手直しして使用している。新しく増設した物も、まったく同じデザインで制作され、どの席に座っても、以前の雰囲気を味わえる。変わらない事、皆が愛する「イノダ」で在り続ける事――素晴らしいサービス、美味しく、色も美しい珈琲や料理と同じく、〝イノダだけの、美味しい〟おもてなし〟を味わえる名店本店。（空閑理）

Inoda Coffee Honten

1. Symbol of Kyoto's coffee culture opened in 1947

2. Damaged by fire in 1999, it retains its original appearance loved by Kyoto locals

3. Offers many famous items including the delicious "Arabian Pearl" blend

The main branch of Inoda Coffee has been loved by locals and tourists alike for years. Everyone enters and exits the shop through its dark brown shop curtain with a smile. With its tiled roof and black exterior wall, it looks like an old cellar building, and I was surprised to learn that it was rebuilt in 2000. The exterior was finished to replicate the original building. The window frames, for example, are aluminum, but have been painted to look like wood. The stained glasswork and pond in the garden have all been restored to retain the original Inoda Coffee's appearance. The "Memorial Room," painted red, white, and blue, and located to the left of the entrance, has been restored to its 1947 form with the original clock and cash register. Ask for the non-smoking section, and you'll be lead to a low-ceilinged, dimly lit retro-feeling room in the old wing. Ask for smoking, and you'll be led to the new wing, which features a modern, refreshing well-type structure with a five-meter high ceiling. (Osamu Kuga)

一保堂茶舗
喫茶室 嘉木

京都府京都市中京区寺町通二条上ル
Tel: 075-211-3421
10時～17時（L.O.16時30分）　第2水曜休
www.ippodo-tea.co.jp
京都市役所前駅から徒歩約5分

1. 本格的な京銘茶を手軽に楽しめる、日本茶専門店の喫茶室。
喫茶メニューは、日本茶のみ。店には"散策のお供"に最適な、急須で淹れるテイクアウトがある。

2. 清水焼の急須など、オリジナルの茶器で教わる体験型喫茶室。
客一人一人に、丁寧に教える1煎目。「お茶の淹れ方教室」などのイベントも定期開催し、出張営業もする。

3. 飲んだ後、気に入った日本茶を購入できる。
商品に合わせたパッケージのデザインが秀逸で、選ぶ楽しさと、贈る喜び、両方が味わえる。

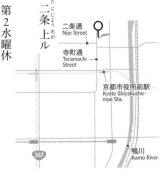

二条通 Nijo Street
寺町通 Teramachi Street
京都市役所前駅 Kyoto Shiyakusho-mae Sta.
367
鴨川 Kamo River

自分で淹れる、最高の京銘茶　洋菓子店「村上開新堂」や「三月書房」などがある、銀杏並木の寺町通り。中でも日本茶の専門店「一保堂茶舗」は、重厚で趣ある店構えだ。店内には、茶壺がずらりと棚に並び、白衣姿の男性と、白い三角巾を被った女性が、カウンター越しに接客していて、皆、明るく活気がある。「嘉木」は、店に併設された喫茶室で、店頭で販売する日本茶の、ほとんどが頂ける。

七人掛けのカウンターと、二人掛けのテーブルが一二席あり、僕はカウンターに座り、玉露を注文した。しばらくして、急須一つと茶碗四つ、そして和菓子が運ばれてきて「ご説明いたしますね！」と、女性店員。「玉露は、まず、お湯を茶碗に入れます。そして、四つの茶碗を使ってお湯を転がし、六〇度位に冷まし、茶葉の入った急須へ。同じように、三煎までお楽しみください」と、一煎目を付きっきりで教えてくれた。一七一七年、茶と雑貨を扱う店として創業した「一保堂茶舗」。本当に美味しい日本茶を届けるために、一九九五年、体験型の喫茶室「嘉木」をオープン。「最後の一滴に、旨みが凝縮しているんです」と教わり、淹れ方も伝えよう。ピタリと手に収まる急須で、自ら注いだ美しい金色の玉露は、とても香ばしく、お出汁のように旨みのある初めての味わいだった。隣では、外国人観光客が、なんと抹茶を点てていた。そして、その笑顔の傍らには、英語も堪能な女性店員。僕は、土産に季節限定の新茶を購入した。（神藤秀人）

Ippodo Tea Main Store in Kyoto Kaboku Tearoom

1. A Japanese tearoom where one can enjoy authentic Kyoto tea casually

2. An experiential tearoom where one can enjoy original tea pottery

3. One can purchase any tea leaves you like

The Ippodo tea main store is beautiful. Inside, tea urns line the shelves, and staff in white cheerfully welcome customers over the counter. Kaboku is adjacent to the tea shop. When I ordered a cup of *gyokuro*, the female staff cheerfully explained it in detail as I sipped it. Ippodo opened its door in 1717, selling tea and other things. In order to teach people how to make tea in a manner appropriate to the leaves they sell, they opened Kaboku in 1995. At the next table, tourists from abroad were making maccha tea, and next to them stood staff who spoke fluent English. As a gift, I bought new tea leaves only sold this season. (Hideto Shindo)

1. 由良川、古民家、水車小屋、桜や銀杏の
木々などの美しい景色が、全席から眺められる。
主役級の借景を見に、必ず窓際席に座りたい。

2. 春はアマゴ、夏は鮎、秋は椎茸、冬は
猪などの、美山町の旬の食材の料理が最高。
カフェ利用だけでは勿体ない、店主・山田剛志さんが調理する、
四季折々を彩る料理。

3. イギリス人杜氏フィリップ・ハーパー氏の
日本酒が買える。
ここでしか買えない、3銘酒「和く輪く京美山」「美山粋仙」
「和く輪く」は、店主の父・文男さんの造った日本酒。

美山粋仙庵 SAI

京都府南丹市美山町 内久保下カルノ541
園部ICから車で約40分

日吉駅
Hiyoshi Sta.

園部IC
Sonobe
Exit

162

美山町の四季に心底惚れた親子の店　僕が美山町を訪れたのは五月で、桜のシーズンは終わっていたが、緑々とした新緑が美しく、気持ちのよい日だった。「かやぶきの里」から由良川を下流に車で約五分、川沿いの岸壁の上に建っている古民家が、「美山粋仙庵 SAI」だ。黄緑色の暖簾を潜って中に入ると、川側の壁がすべて窓になっていて、由良川を見下ろせる絶好のロケーションだ。僕は、靴を脱ぎ、座敷の奥へ進み、窓際に席を取った。店主の山田剛志さんの父・文男さんは、一九九一に美山町の自然に魅せられ、大阪から美山町樫原に移住し、改築した古民家で、一日一組限定の宿「美山粋仙庵」を営んでいた。父の背中を見てきた剛志さんも、父の生活、美山町の自然に魅力を感じ、二〇〇八年、夫婦でこの町に来た。父の宿で二年間修業し、江戸時代の油屋だった建物を買い、家族皆で改築した。窓からの、その美しい景色を一番に重視し、客間を造った。父の友人の「木下酒造」杜氏のフィリップ・ハーパー氏が醸す、茅葺き民家の古茅を肥料に使った「和く輪く京美山」などの日本酒は、蔵を改築した隣の酒店で、主に母の悦子さんが販売している。僕は、アマゴの塩焼きがメインの「春菜御膳」を食べ、食後に美山産の黒豆茶を頂いた。川の流れと水車のゴトゴト回る音が、とても心地いい。帰り際、実家の父への土産にと、日本酒「和く輪く京美山」を購入し、大満足して帰路に就いた。（神藤秀人）

050

Miyamasuisen-an SAI

1. The view of Yura River, old houses, water mill, cherry blossom and ginko trees from every table

2. Serves seasonal local dishes: Amago trout in spring, ayu fish in summer, shiitake mushrooms in autumn, and boar in winter

3. Can purchase Philip Harper's sake

Miyamasuisen-an SAI is an old house built atop the river cliff. Through the yellow-green curtain, you find that the entire wall is a window with a view of the river. I sat at the window seat. Fumio Yamada, the current owner's father, moved to Miyama-cho in 1991 and renovated an old house to open Miyamasuisen-an, an inn. Takeshi Yamada, his son, moved here in 2008 when he fell in love with his father's lifestyle and the beauty of Nature in this town. He apprenticed at his father's inn for two years, bought a building built in the Edo period, and renovated it with his family. Japanese sake distilled by Phillip Harper, his father's friend, is sold next door to the restaurant. I ordered the Spring Special and drank black bean tea made in Miyama. With the sound of the water mill and the river current, it was such a lovely time. (Hideto Shindo)

※現在休業中。

FACTORY KAFE工船

京都府京都市上京区河原町通 今出川下ル梶井町 448
清和テナントハウス 2F G号室
Tel: 075-211-5398
12時〜21時　火曜休（祝日の場合は営業）
出町柳駅から徒歩約5分
ooyacoffeeassocies.com

1. 府内で焙煎する、「オオヤコーヒ焙煎所」の珈琲が飲めて、豆が買える。

珈琲は、一人一人、客の好みを訊き、ガラス作家の辻和美さんの切り子のグラスで頂ける。

湯飲みや、お盆は、店主の父の漆作家・瀬戸國勝さんの制作。

2. 京都生活で必須の自転車も買える、斬新な喫茶店。

鴨川、下鴨神社など、京都の自転車観光の拠点に必ず寄りたい。

3. Tシャツ展や、タイの物産展など、珈琲と必ずセットの独自イベントがある。

様々なイベントを開催し、京都の珈琲を多岐にわたって発信する。

異文化交流的な喫茶店　出町柳の白い雑居ビルの二階の一室に「FACTORY KAFE工船」がある。店は“逆L字形”「Ｌ」になっていて、入って右に焙煎機、左に「TORCH」の珈琲器具などが展示され、正面は六席のカウンターだ。左に行った小さなスペースには、使い古した何工具類や自転車が数台、天井や壁から吊られていて、「KAFE工船」とは別経営の自転車店「バッチグーバイシクル」が併設。珈琲は、数種類の豆に、それぞれ四段階の焙煎度合い、二通りの淹れ方があり、僕は、「グアテマラの、浅ヤキの、こってり」を頼んだ。店主の瀬戸更紗さんは、寺町にあったカフェ「パチャママ」で働いていたが、店主のオオヤミノルさんは焙煎業に専念するため、二〇〇三年に店を閉じた。瀬戸さんは、それでも京都でカフェをやりたいと、二〇〇五年、再びオオヤさんの下で焙煎業を学び、二〇〇七年、「KAFE工船」をオープン。当時は、雑貨店「factory zoomer / wall」も入って、三つの店が同室にあった独自の店舗スタイルだった。

「私は、珈琲は料理だと思うんです。でも、なかなか認めてもらえなくて。だから、私達の珈琲の横に、私達の選んだ、美味しい物、カッコいい物を置いて味わっていただきたい」と、瀬戸さん。今後、洋服の展示会や、花の展覧会も開催するそうだ。丁寧にネルで淹れた珈琲を、僕は、酒を飲むように、ゆっくりと味わった。そして、本気で同店で自転車を買おうと思っている。（神藤秀人）

FACTORY KAFE KOSEN

1. Where one can drink and purchase Ooya coffee baisenjo, made with coffee beans roasted in Kyoto

2. A café where one can also purchase bicycles, a must for living in Kyoto

3. Curates original events that match up coffee with t-shirts or Thai-made products

The L-shaped shop displays a coffee roaster to the right and coffee-related goods to the left; as you walk in, you face a 6-seat counter. In the small corner to the left, they display used tools and bicycles hanging from the ceiling and walls. FACTORY KAFE KOSEN is run by a bicycle shop. Sarasa Seto, the owner, used to work at a café in Teramachi, but the café's owner, Minoru Ooya, wanted to focus on roasting beans, so the café was closed in 2003. Seto's desire to open a

café in Kyoto convinced her to train under Mr. Ooya, and eventually she opened FACTORY KAFE KOSEN in 2007. Back then, there were three shops under one roof. She is planning to have clothing and flower exhibitions in the near future. (Hideto Shindo)

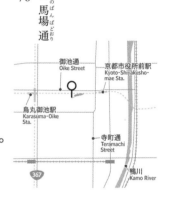

京の宿 石原

京都府京都市中京区　柳馬場通
姉小路上ル柳八幡町76
Tel: 075-221-5612
1泊朝食付き1名 14,040円〜（2名利用時）
烏丸御池駅から徒歩約5分

1. 元は骨董商だった古い町家を、大切に使い続ける旅館。

ビルが建ち並ぶ、京都市市街地中心に風情ある佇まいを遺す、
現在は1泊朝食付きの"片泊まりの宿"。

2. ユーモアとデザインのセンス溢れる、ご主人手造りの備品。

照明器具は、フランク・ロイド・ライトをイメージしたデザイン。
ガレージには、茶目っ気たっぷりにカスタムされた、
日産「ブルーバード510型」1970年式も。

3. 故・黒澤明の晩年の定宿。現在も、同じ部屋に泊まれる。

1980年「影武者」で初逗留。「八月の狂想曲」「雨あがる」の脚本を
ここで書き、書き物机の天板にサインが遺る。

おもてなしとは、当たり前の事　御池通りから姉小路を下った所に、「原石」と書かれた看板があって、最初は何だろうと思ったが、反対から見ると左右が替わり「石原」と読めた。石原元治・弘子さん、ご夫婦の旅館で、建物内部は迷路みたいだが、客室も食堂も風呂も、皆、坪庭に面するように設計されていて、刻一刻と光の射し方が変わり、風がよく通って気持ちがいい。木の柱に土の壁、ほっそりとした格子窓に障子紙——とても落ち着く。黒澤明（一九九八年没）の晩年の常宿で、長い時には一か月以上、ここに泊まって、脚本を書いたり、仲間達と食事したりした。そして現在、その部屋は特別扱いされずに、一見客だった僕達も泊めてもらえた。熱い風呂にフカフカの布団、清潔な洗面所、すべてに不足がなく、手が届き、心がこもっている。「たいした宿や、あらしません。『おもてなし』は『わざとらし』、ヨイショせずに、ありのままでね」と、ご主人は笑う。翌朝、朱塗りの木卓で朝食を食べ終えて、黒澤明も使った灰皿や湯呑みで一服しながら坪庭に目を遣ると、「黒澤さんは、早く仕事を終えると、そこで亀を眺めてらっしゃいました」と料理名人の奥さんが教えてくれた。坪庭には、何と今も亀がいて、愛嬌よく首を、こちらに伸ばしてくれた。今、ここにある目に見える物と、それらが想像させてくれる物、それらに変わりがない事に、自分は、そして、きっと黒澤明監督も、惹かれたのだ、と僕は思った。（空閑理）

Ishihara

1. An inn housed in an old townhouse previously occupied by an antique dealer

2. Handmade fixtures that exude humor and good design sensibility

3. The inn was regularly used by Akira Kurosawa in his later years and you can stay in the room that he stayed in.

"Ishihara" is an inn owned by Hiroko and Motoharu Ishihara. The interior of the building is like a labyrinth, but the guestrooms, dining room, and bath are all designed to face the courtyard and the light changes from moment to moment. The air also circulates nicely and comfortably. The wooden pillars, earthen walls, latticed windows, and paper screen doors are all comforting. Akira Kurosawa was a regular guest in his later years and he stayed sometime for an entire month

working on scripts and dining with friends. After breakfast, I had some tea and a cigarette, using the same ashtray Kurosawa used. As I looked at the courtyard, Hiroko Ishihara, co-owner and master chef told me that when Kurosawa finished work early, he would sit where I was sitting and stare at the turtle in the courtyard. Amazingly, the same turtle still lives in the courtyard. When I peered out to find it, it accommodatingly turned its head towards me. (Osamu Kuga)

※2021年より休業中、再開予定あり。

小宿 布屋（おやど ぬのや）

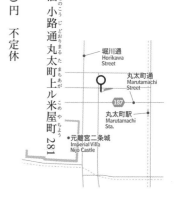

京都府京都市上京区 油小路通丸太町上ル米屋町 281
Tel: 075-211-8109
www.nunoya.net
丸太町駅から徒歩約10分
1泊朝食付き1名 9,000円　不定休

1. 築100年以上の町家建築を、細部にまで拘って再築。

新建材の壁や天井などで、様変わりしてしまっていたが、職人集団「京町家作事組」に依頼して、元の姿に、見事に戻した。

2.「清潔・静寂・安心」がモットーの、ご主人夫婦のホスピタリティ。

宿泊は1日2組まで、門限は22時、入浴は23時まで、テレビなし——それらが実感させる、必ずリピーターになりたい最高の居心地。

3. ご近所の「麩嘉」の生麩や、西陣の老舗豆腐店の豆腐などを使った、とても美味しい朝食。

土鍋で炊く白飯は、ふっくらツヤツヤ。食後の珈琲は談話室に席を移して、本を読みながら、ゆっくりと過ごせる。

小さな宿だからできる事、そのすべてが「布屋」は、明治中期に建てられた、築一〇〇年超えの町家建築。格子戸を開け、奥に細長い土間を通って靴を脱ぎ、談話室でチェックインする。そこに置かれた拭き漆の木卓と長椅子、そして、同じ仕上げの本棚が、とても美しい。本が生き生きと見え、一冊手に取ってみたくなる。以前はホテルマンだったという宿主の布澤利夫さんに訊くと、建物を改築した「京町家作事組」の職人が設えた物だという。建築にピタリと収まっていて、とても自然。正しい寸法があるんだ、本棚も建築なんだ、と僕は刮目した。そして、本棚だけではなく、布澤さんの奥さんが選ぶという、部屋の湯呑みやグラス、茶筒などの細かな備品、檜風呂や、その蓋の設計、バスマット、花容れや、そこに挿してある山野草も、手塩にかけてない、という事が、まったくない。この町家は、布澤さんが生まれ育った実家でもあり、当時は、天井には新建材を張って、窓にはアルミサッシを嵌めて、「普通の家」に改築してしまっていたそうだが、設計に半年、施工に半年かけて、左官さんも庭師も大工さんも、水道工事も電気工事も、拘りと腕がある職人集団が力を込めて、自然に復元した。そして、宿主夫婦と常連客によって、よく使われ続け、大切に手入れされ続け、ますます生き生きと、居心地がよくなっていく。「古民家再生」とは、こういう事か、と僕は実感した。（空閑 理）

Oyado Nunoya

1. A meticulously restored townhouse that's over 100 years old

2. The hospitable husband and wife owners' motto is "cleanliness, quiet, and safety."

3. The delicious breakfast is made with locally sold wheat starch and tofu.

I checked in in the common room. The wipe-lacquered wooden table, long chair, and bookshelf in the same room were beautiful. "Nunoya" owner Toshio Nunozawa, a former hotel-keeper, explains that they were made by the same artisans that restored the building. This old townhouse is the same house that Nunozawa grew up in. When he was raised in the house, it had been reno-vated for comfort, rather than ambiance, with ceilings made of new materials and aluminum window frames. With the help of a plasterer, carpenter, electrician, and plumber, and with half a year spent on design and another half on construction, a group of remarkably skilled artisans restored the townhouse to its natural, beautiful state. Used and kept up carefully by regular guests and the owners, the inn has become more vibrant and comfortable with age. (Osamu Kuga)

1. 自分のペースで美術鑑賞できる "アートホステル"。
グラフィックデザインは「UMA / design farm」、
空間デザインは「dot architects」。

2. 経営者はアーティストで、
「京都造形芸術大学」講師。
アートを教えながら、展覧会やイベントを企画・運営し、
風呂掃除やベッドメイキングも行う、矢津吉隆氏の経営。

3. アートファンにも、そうでない人にも、お薦めの
安心感と清潔感、快適な宿。
バーでは、ハンドドリップで淹れてくれる珈琲が飲める。
事前予約すると、美味しい朝食もつくってくれる (プラス料金)。

KYOTO ART HOSTEL
kumagusuku

京都府京都市中京区壬生馬場町 37-3
Tel: 075-432-8168
kumagusuku.info
大宮駅から徒歩約 5 分

"アートと夜を過ごしたら" 編集部の佐々木晃子は、リュックサックを一つ背負ってドミトリー (相部屋) のゲストハウスを渡り歩く、旅慣れた女性だが、彼女のイチ推しが「クマグスク」だった。「私はアートに詳しくないけど、よかった。アート好きなら尚更だと思う」と。確かに僕はアートが好きで、美術館やギャラリーに、よく行く。しかし、時を忘れて見入ってしまう展覧会は、数年に一度で、たいてい二時間もすると バテてしまう。ギャラリートークは魅力的だが、終了後、家に帰るのが辛い。だが「クマグスク」は、まったく、その心配はない。アーティストの矢津吉隆さんが経営する "アートホステル"、つまり、美術鑑賞しながら泊まれるホテルなのだ。一階にはバスとトイレ、受け付けと小さなバーがある。その先は中庭で、外壁に映像作品がプロジェクターで映し出されていた。チェックイン時に展覧会のパンフレットを貰って、二階の部屋に行ってベッドに寝転び、ビール片手にそれを読む。各部屋や廊下などの共用部分にも、作品が展示されていて、自分のペースで作品を見る事ができる。旅先の夜は長い。シャワーを浴びた後、僕は部屋着でバーに行って、矢津さんに珈琲を淹れてもらって、ここの作品や最近見た展覧会について会話した。同じ日に泊まった副編集長の神藤秀人は、作品の前に置かれたソファーで眠ったり起きたりしながら、夜明け方まで、そこにいた。こういうアートの見方、こういう旅の仕方、こういう時の流れ方があるのだ。(空閑理)

Kyoto Art Hostel
kumagusuku

1. An "Art Hostel," where you can look at art at your own pace

2. The proprietor is an artist and lecturer at Kyoto University of Art and Design

3. A comfortable, clean, and safe inn recommended for art-fans and non-art-fans

I like art and often visit galleries and museums. After two hours of looking at art, however, I'm usually beat. No need to worry about exhaustion at "kumagusuku," an "art hostel" run by artist Yoshitaka Yazu. This is a hotel where you can look at art and spend the night. On the first floor are a bath, toilet, reception desk, and a small bar. Further in, there's a courtyard with a video piece projected on an exterior wall. Upon checking in, you'll be given a brochure explaining the works on display. You can then go up to the second floor to your room, lie down, and read the brochure with a beer in your hand. There are works displayed in the hallways and individual guestrooms and you can view them at your own pace. Associate editor Hideto Shindo, who stayed there with me fell asleep and awoke repeatedly in a sofa placed in front of an artwork until the sun started to rise. (Osamu Kuga)

※2022年春より宿泊施設は閉館。ギャラリー、ショップを備えた複合施設「kumagusuku」として運営。

1. 京町家の一棟貸し切り。

伝統的な町家の特色ある大部分は維持し、トイレ、バス、
床暖房や空調設備などを、大胆に改築・新設して、快適さを追求。

2. 織物工房を併設。職人達の仕事の様子を、
2階から眺められる。

織物工房と居住部の通用口は施錠でき、プライバシーも万全。

3. キッチンに冷蔵庫、食器等完備。

暮らすように、京都に泊まれる。
食事は、精進料理や京料理の仕出しを取るのも、お薦め。

西陣伊佐町 町家

庵 町家ステイ

京都府京都市上京区大宮通上立売上ル西入ル
www.kyoto-machiya.com

京都の「町家に泊まる」と「伝統工芸を観る」の融合宿「庵 町家ステイ」は、空き家になったり、取り壊されそうになっていた、古い町家を京都に遺そうと、それらの居住性を高く改築し、一泊から宿泊できるようにした画期的なスタイルだ。茶室と庭がある数寄屋風町家や、窓から鴨川を眺められる隠れ処風町家など、どれも個性的。宿泊目的の観光客だけでなく、交流会やパーティーの会場として借りる地元の人も増えている。現在、利用できる一棟の中で、最も特色があるのが、「西陣伊佐町 町家」だ。西陣織りの織元が点在する地域にあり、この町家の隣も織物の会社だ。チェックインは現地で行い、スタッフの方が玄関で迎えてくれ、鍵を受け取ったら、その町家はもう "我が家" だ。玄関から続く土間は、「火袋」と呼ばれる吹き抜けで、京都で「おくどさん」と呼ばれる台所の跡と井戸がある。普通の町家であれば、その奥には坪庭があり、それを借景とした寝室や居間等があるのだが、この町家の奥には何と、手織りの帯工房がある。廃墟同然になっていた別の織元の工房跡を、地元の織物会社が買い受け、「庵」に依頼して、手織りの工房を再築し、表の住居部分を宿泊できるように改築した。二階のリビングからは、下の織物工房の全景を見る事ができ、午前八時頃に、職人達が出勤してきて、織機のガシャンガシャンという音が聞こえてきて、何げなく一日の仕事が始まった。"非日常的だが、日常の京都に住める" 稀有な宿屋だ。（空閑 理）

Iori Machiya Stay
Nishijin Isa-cho Machiya

1. Rent an entire townhouse in Kyoto.

2. Adjacent to a textile studio, you can watch the artisans from the second floor.

3. Equipped with a kitchen, refrigerator, and dishes, you can live in Kyoto like a local.

"Iori Machiya Stay" is an innovative project offers lodging starting from a single night in old townhouses that were vacant or slated for demolition, and have been renovated for comfort. Increasingly, it is used not only by tourists, but also by locals who rent it out for parties. Currently, there are 11 houses available. The most striking is the "Nishijin Isa-cho Machiya" townhouse. In the back of it is a functioning textile studio. An abandoned textile studio was purchased by a local textile company, which hired "Iori" to renovate the studio into a lodging space. From the living room on the second floor, you can see the entirety of the textile studio. The artisans arrive at eight and start their workday on their looms, just as they should. (Osamu Kuga)

※2022年より宿泊事業は休業。

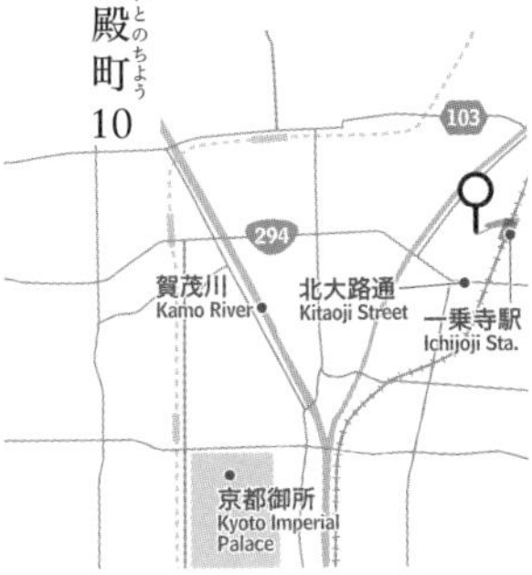

1. 日本中から、海外からも、ファンが訪れる
「恵文社 一乗寺店」店長。

コンセプトや付加価値に頼らず、振り回されもせず、
客が自分で探して、素晴らしい本と出会える店。

2.「イメージの京都」ではない、
ありのまま京都を伝え続ける、文筆家で編集者。

そこで生まれ育ち、一人の地元客としても、京都の事を熱く語る人。
自伝的な京都案内本など、魅力的な著作多数。

3. 長い時間の中で形づくられた、
"数値化できない価値"を大切にする人。

マーケティングや計画性よりも、縁や必然性を重視し、
時代の流れを冷静に柔軟に感じ取り、本当に大切な物を選び取る人。

恵文社 一乗寺店

堀部篤史

京都府京都市左京区一乗寺払殿町 10
Tel:075-711-5919
11時～19時 元日休
www.keibunsha-books.com
一乗寺駅から徒歩約5分

特別ではない特別な店 京都市は、個性的な新刊書店や古書店が幾つもある"本の街"だ。そのイメージを、府外、海外の、特に若い人々にも浸透させたのは「恵文社 一乗寺店」だと僕は思う。この店を目当てに京都を訪れた人々が、出町柳から叡山電車に乗って一乗寺駅で降り、有名な観光地以外にも、魅力的な小さな店や美しい景色が多くある事を知る。そして、それらを巡り歩き、観光地ではない "本当の京都らしさ" に気づく。そして、思う——自分の故郷にも「恵文社 一乗寺店」があったらいいのに、と。「恵文社 一乗寺店」の広々とした店内には、音楽が低く流れているが、とても静かに感じられ、一人で本の世界に没頭できる、素敵な居心地だ。店長の堀部篤史さんは、自身の好みやセンスを、取り扱う本や、それらの売り方等に反映させて「恵文社 一乗寺店」があったらいいのに、と。「恵文社 一乗寺店」はこうだ。堀部の個人店だ」とイメージを持たれる事を、断固、忌避する。

「その本がいいか悪いかは、お客さん一人一人の考え。合理化も均一化もできない」と。現在、欲しい情報は、インターネットで、すぐ検索できるが、書店は、そうではない。無目的でも立ち寄りたい馴染みの喫茶店や居酒屋の定番料理やクセの強い名物のような多くの本があって、それらを自由に選ぶ事ができ、長く過ごしたい居心地と、無口な店主がいる。早くも安くもスマートでもないが、自分が住む街に在り続けて欲しい店——堀部さんがいる「恵文社 一乗寺店」は、そんな店だ、と僕は思う。(空閑理)

Keibunsha Ichijoji
Atsushi Horibe

1. Manager of "Keibunsha Ichijoji,"
   which draws fans from all over Japan
   and abroad

2. A writer and editor that documents
   the true face of Kyoto

3. A man who appreciates
   "unquantifiable values" shaped over
   long periods of time

Kyoto is a book-town. It's home to numerous new and used bookstores. "Keibunsha Ichijoji" has spread this image, particularly to young people living outside of Kyoto. Its spacious interior is perfect for losing yourself in the world of books. Its manager Atsushi Horibe wants to avoid his store being seen as a reflection of his sensibility or tastes, either in terms of book selection or sales style. He explains, "Whether a book is good or bad is a question each customer must answer. It cannot be rationalized or made uniform." Like a favorite café or bar, which you drop into without any purpose, at "Keibunsha Ichijoji," you can freely select from a choice of unique dishes as well as standards. It's a shop comfortable enough to linger in with a quiet manager. (Osamu Kuga)

※2015年に恵文社を退社。掲載情報は2015年7月のものとなります。

d
21

サウナの梅湯

湊 三次郎

京都府京都市下京区木屋町通上ノ口上ル岩滝町175
Tel: 080-2523-0626
14時〜26時（土・日曜 6時〜12時 朝風呂あり） 木曜休
清水五条駅から徒歩約5分

1. 閉業した老舗銭湯を復活させ、
自ら番台に立つ経営者。
施工は僅か2か月。常連客や観光客を問わず、
会話を楽しめる、親しみある接客。

2. ライブ、映画上映会、手づくり市など、様々な
イベントは、脱衣場の男女の仕切り壁を外して開催。
間近のカフェ「efish（エフィッシュ）」などに次いで、
若者が集まる場所を五条につくった。

3. 釜焚きや、番台業務を体験させる、
学生ボランティアを採用。
若い世代にも、銭湯のよさを伝えている。

京都の下町文化を守る青年　僕が初めて「サウナの梅湯」を訪れたのは、二〇一五年五月五日のリニューアルオープンから一週間経つ前で、鴨川納涼床が出始めた、暑い日だった。出町柳から白梅町、そして祇園から五条へ自転車で走ってきた汗を流そうと、愛嬌ある丸メガネの湊三次郎さんに四五〇円（大人）払って男湯の暖簾を潜った。常連のおじさんから「案内しようか！」と、「梅湯」の再開が嬉しくてたまらないらしく、声をかけられた。青や水色のタイルが可愛く、電気風呂や薬風呂などの五つある湯船の、側面の噴水がレトロで珍しい、深い湯船に顎まで浸かった。

静岡県出身の湊さんは、京都外語大学在学中、全国の六〇〇軒以上の銭湯を巡り、故郷の銭湯事情について論文まで書いたほどの大の銭湯好き。卒業後、アパレル会社に就職したが、「銭湯やりませんか」と企画部に提案した事もあった。そして、二〇一四年十二月、学生時代に手伝っていた「梅湯」が閉まってしまう事を知り、湊さんは「京都の必要な銭湯を残していきたい」と、前職を辞し、二四歳という若さで「梅湯」を継いだ。ボイラーの操作法、濾過機の清掃、帳簿の付け方などはアルバイトで学び、大学の後輩などにも修復の手伝いを呼びかけた。今後、釜焚きの熱源を利用した陶磁器作家などの下宿所を二階に造りたい、と湊さん。銭湯に留まらず、銭湯のまま、銭湯だからこそできる事を熱心に考え、実行し続けている。（神藤秀人）

Sauna Umeyu
Sanjiro Minato

1. The owner who revitalized a closed historic public bathhouse

2. Bathhouse converted for live events and movie nights

3. Volunteer system for students to experience heating water with fire

I paid ¥430 to owl-glassed Sanjiro Minato and entered the man's locker area. Choosing from five different kinds of baths—electric bath, medicinal bath, and others, all with blue and white tiles—I submerged into the tub with a retro-looking spout on the side. Mr. Minato, originally from Shizuoka Prefecture, went to nearly 600 bathhouses in Japan while he was a student at Kyoto Foreign Language University and eventually wrote his graduation thesis on the history of bathhouses in Shizuoka. That is how much he loves public baths. When he found out that Umeyu, a bathhouse he worked at while he was a student, had closed down, he quit his job and took over its management at age 24 to preserve the historic Kyoto bathhouse. One of the future plans is to lend out the upstairs rooms to artists, taking advantage of the heat from the fire to heat up water. (Hideto Shindo)

田歌舎

藤原 誉
ほまる

京都府南丹市美山町 田歌上五波 1-1
Tel: 0771-77-0509
園部 IC から車で約50分

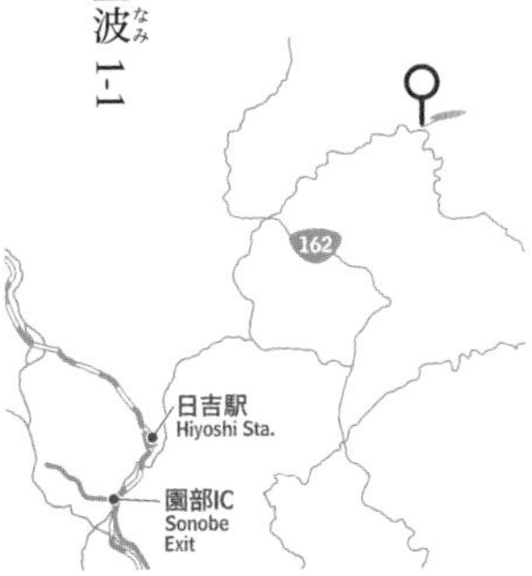

1. 大工、狩猟、農業、遊び、を
自己習得したアウトドアの達人。
アウトドア活動体「田歌舎」を設立し、レストラン、宿泊施設、イベント、
様々に、美山町に人が集まる切っ掛けをつくった。

2. 京都大学の研究林「芦生の森」を守る、陰の立役者。
芦生の原生林のアウトドア体験では、
観光客にマナーを伝え、目一杯楽しませる心優しき野人。

3. 自然を守り活かす「野生復帰計画」の
起ち上げメンバーの一人。
「芦生自然学校」「江和ランド」「田歌舎」の、三つから成る
活動体に参画し、自然と共存する素晴らしさを、人々に伝える強い意志。

美山町の救世主　二度目に僕は、トレッキングの参加で「田歌舎」を訪れた。朝の九時半に集合し、ガイドの吉田佑介さんと共に京都大学の研究林「芦生の森」に入った。

由良川源流へと続く、木材搬出用のトロッコの線路を進み、鹿、猪、ハクビシンなどの生存の形跡、枝木の先に生えるタラの芽などの山菜、足下の水溜まりには、大好物のクレソンを見た。ブナやトチの巨木、鯑（小魚）の群れ。

京都府の自然の奥深さに、正直、僕は驚いた。「田歌舎」に戻ると、代表の藤原誉さんが、「どこ行ったの？　トロッコ路？　よかったやろ」と、何げなく言って颯爽と耕耘機に乗って田んぼへ行ってしまった。彼は、大学時代、豊かな自然の中で自給自足的な暮らしをしたい、と卒業後、軽自動車を買い、テントと釣竿を持って美山町へ来た。そして、大工をしたり、ラフティングや養鶏場を経て、三〇歳前に「田歌舎」を起ち上げた。全国の子供達と、キャンプや農作業、川の清掃などを行う、通年制の自然教室にも関わり、「一度に、一億人を変える事はできないけれど、一〇人の子供から、やがて同じ志を持った人間を増やしていける。そして、数年後、彼らが成長し、自分の暮らす環境を考えてほしい」と誉さん。二〇二〇年、「芦生の森」は、京大の貸借契約が切れ、今以上に観光客の出入りが自由になるかもしれない。しかし、貸借の延長、その規模を含めた交渉は、これからだ。あの美しい森を守っていくのは、この人、そして教え子だと僕は思う。（神藤秀人）

Tautasha
Homaru Fujiwara

1. A self-taught master of the outdoors and an expert in the arts of carpentry, hunting, farming, and play

2. An under-recognized, but leading figure behind, and protector of, Kyoto University's forest research station "Ashiu no Mori"

3. Founding member of "Wild Revitalization Project"

As a university student, Homaru Fujiwara dreamed of living off the land. After graduation, he bought a compact car, and moved to Miyama with a tent and fishing rod. He worked as a carpenter, rafted, and operated a poultry farm before opening "Tautasha" in his twenties. He is also involved in year-long nature classes, which teach children about camping and agriculture and volunteer work, such as cleaning rivers. "You can't change a hundred million people at once," he

explains, "But you can start with ten children and cultivate people with the similar ambitions. Several years later, when those same children grow up, I want them to think about the environment they live in." In 2020, Kyoto University's lease on "Ashiu no Mori" will expire and it may then be opened up to tourists. The negotiations over the extension and scale of the lease, however, have yet to take place. I believe Fujiwara and his students will save this beautiful forest. (Hideto Shindo)

d23

1. 京都の町家に、軽快な発想と、
快適な居心地を与える一級建築士。
町家を「財産」として大切にし過ぎず、
「家」として思い切り使って親しめるように、力を尽くす人。

2. 数十年後の変化まで考える、
長いスパンの視点の持ち主。
「町家も町も、人よりも長生きするから」と、20年後、30年後に、
別の建築士やオーナーが、どう改築したくなるか、まで考えて設計する。

3. 日本各地の伝統的景観を、その地元の人々と共に、
適切に変化させ、そして、守る人。
地元の人々と交流して、双方の理解を深める事に、
時間と労力をかける事を、決して厭わない。

株式会社ルーフスケープ
黒木裕行（くろき ひろゆき）
京都府八幡市美濃山ヒル塚 100-9
Tel: 075-925-8420 （株式会社ルーフスケープ）
www.roofscape.jp

新しく、古い物を遺す建築士　黒木裕行さんに、僕が初めて会ったのは五年前で、黒木さんが設計した「庵町家ステイ」の各物件を案内してもらった。「建物を『箱』ではなく『家』なんです」と言ったりしますが、町家は『箱』ではなく『家』なんです」と、それぞれ、どんな人が、どのように住み、その家を大切にしていたか、自身の思い出のように語ってくれた。これまで黒木さんは、滋賀県の長浜市、奈良県の五條市、島根県の津和野市、長崎県の五島列島の小値賀町などで、様々なプロジェクトを進めているが、今回の「京都府号」取材で訪れた中で、僕が最も美しいと思った伊根町でも進行中のプランがある。伊根町には、鏡のように波が静かな伊根湾に沿って舟屋が建ち並ぶ「舟屋の里」があり、その一部が殺風景な空き地になっている。そこに海上タクシーが着岸できるようにし、地元の海産物の土産店やレストラン等が入る舟屋の町並みをつくり、その間を歩く道の先には、伊根祭の祭礼船を展示するという計画だ。まだ着工前だが、地元の人々と話し合い、食べたり飲んだり泊まったりして理解を深め合い、現在も一年がかりで年間の潮位の変化を調査している。取材当時の黒木さんのオフィスは、ライブハウス「礫礫」から歩いてすぐ、街の中にあった。このオフィスもまた、京都の町家を改築した物だ。新しく場をつくる事で、古くから続く、その町の大切な風景や風情は、地元の人々と共に遺す事ができる——今からでも遅くはないのだ。（空閑 理）

068

Roofscape Architect
Hiroyuki Kuroki

1. A first-class registered architect adding nimble concepts and comfort to Kyoto's traditional townhouses

2. A man with a long-term perspective who takes changes several decades ahead into account

3. A man who works with locals to appropriately transform traditional landscapes allover Japan

Hiroyuki Kuroki, the man behind "Iori" showed me each property in his "Iori Townhouse Stay" lodgings. He told me who had lived in each one and how they had lived in it as if from his own experience and memory. He is currently at work on a project in Ine, which I thought was the most beautiful part of Kyoto. Along Ine Bay, where the water is still as a mirror, there is a village of boathouses and a part of that has become a desolate open lot. The project will repurpose that

lot as a dock for water taxis and create boathouses with local restaurants and stores selling souvenirs of local seafood. Kuroki has discussed the project with locals and gained their understanding. Currently, he is engaged in a yearlong research of the annual tide change. By creating a new place, and with the help of locals, the landscape and ambiance of a town can be saved. (Osamu Kuga)

d MARK REVIEW
TRAVEL INFORMATION

1. Kamo River

2. KAWAI KANJIRO'S HOUSE
- Gojozaka Kanei-cho 569, Higashiyama-ku, Kyoto, Kyoto
- ☎ 075-561-3585
- ℹ Open daily 10:00–17:00 (admission until 16:30), Closed on Monday (If Monday is a national holiday, closed the following day), Closed during summer and winter break
- ⏱ 10 minutes by foot from Kiyomizu-Gojo Station, Keihan Main Line

3. Taku Taku
- Sujiya-cho 136-9, Tominokoji-dori Bukkoji Sagaru, Shimogyo-ku, Kyoto, Kyoto
- ☎ 075-351-1321
- ℹ Closed occasionally
- ⏱ 5 minutes by foot from Kawaramachi Station, Hankyu Kyoto Main Line

4. The Little Indigo Museum
- Kita-kamimaki 41, Miyama-cho, Nantan, Kyoto
- ☎ 0771-77-0746 (Reservation required)
- ℹ Open daily 11:00–17:00, Closed on Thursday and Friday (Open on holidays), Closed occasionally, Closed during winter season
- ⏱ 40 minutes by car from Sonobe Exit, Kyoto-Jukan Expressway

5. Savory
- Yaoichi Honkan 3F, Higashino-toin-dori Sanjo Sagaru Sanmonji-cho, Nakagyo-ku, Kyoto, Kyoto
- ☎ 075-223-2320
- ℹ Lunch: 11:30–15:00 (Last order), Dinner: 17:30–20:00 (Last order), Closed on Wednesday
- ⏱ 3 minutes by foot from Exit 5 of Karasuma-Oike Station, Kyoto Municipal Subway Karasuma Line and Tozai Line

6. JUNIDANYA
- Gion-machi Minamigawa 570-128, Higashiyama-ku, Kyoto, Kyoto
- ☎ 075-561-0213
- ℹ Lunch: 11:30–13:00 (Last order at 13:30), Dinner: 17:00–20:00 (Last order at 20:30), Closed on Thursday and the 2nd Wednesday (Open on holidays)
- ⏱ 5 minutes by foot from Gion-Shijo Station, Keihan Main Line

7. Tautasha
- Tota Kamigonami 1-1, Miyama-cho, Nantan, Kyoto
- ☎ 0771-77-0509
- ℹ Café & Restaurant: 11:30–14:30 (Reservation only) During the winter season, the cafe also requires reservations (From December to March, only open on Saturdays, Sundays and public holidays), Closed on Monday and Tuesday
- ⏱ 50 minutes by car from Sonobe Exit, Kyoto-Jukan Expressway

8. Tsujimori Cycle
- Higashino-toin-dori Rokkaku Agaru Sanmonji-cho, Nakagyo-ku, Kyoto, Kyoto
- ☎ 075-221-5732
- ℹ Open daily 9:00–18:00, Closed on Sunday and holidays
- ⏱ 3 minutes by foot from Exit 5 of Karasuma-Oike Station, Kyoto Municipal Subway Karasuma Line and Tozai Line

9. Aritsugu
- Nishikikoji-dori Gokomachi Nishi-iru, Nakagyo-ku, Kyoto, Kyoto
- ☎ 075-221-1091
- ℹ Open daily 10:00–16:00, Closed on Wednesday, Closed from January 1 to 3
- ⏱ 5 minutes by foot from Kawaramachi Station, Hankyu Kyoto Main Line

10. Shibakyu
- Ohara Shorinin-cho 58, Sakyo-ku, Kyoto, Kyoto
- ☎ 075-744-4893
- ℹ Open daily 9:00–16:00
- ⏱ 10 minutes by foot from Ohara Bus Stop, Kyoto Bus

11. Naito Shoten
- Sanjo-Ohashi Nishizume Kitagawa, Nakagyo-ku, Kyoto, Kyoto
- ☎ 075-221-3018
- ℹ Open daily 9:30–19:00, Closed occasionally, Closed from January 1 to 3
- ⏱ 3 minutes by foot from Sanjo Station, Keihan Main Line

12. Inoda Coffee Honten
- Sakaimachi-dori Sanjo Sagaru Doyu-cho 140, Nakagyo-ku, Kyoto, Kyoto
- ☎ 075-221-0507
- ℹ Open daily 7:00–17:30 (Last order)
- ⏱ 5 minutes by foot from Exit 5 of Karasuma-Oike Station, Kyoto Municipal Subway Karasuma Line and Tozai Line

13. Ippodo Tea Main Store in Kyoto Kaboku Tearoom
- Teramachi-dori Nijo Agaru, Nakagyo-ku, Kyoto, Kyoto
- ☎ 075-211-3421
- ℹ Open daily 10:00–17:00 (Last order at 16:30), Closed on 2nd Wednesday
- ⏱ 5 minutes by foot from Exit 11 of Kyoto-shiyakusho-mae Station, Subway Tozai Line

14. Miyama Suisen-an SAI
- Uchikubo Shimo-karuno 54-1, Miyama-cho, Nantan, Kyoto
- ⏱ 40 minutes by car from Sonobe Exit, Kyoto-Jukan Expressway

15. FACTORY KAFE KOSEN
- Kawaramachi-dori Imadegawa Sagaru Kajii-cho 448 2F Room G, Kamigyo-ku, Kyoto, Kyoto
- ☎ 075-211-5398
- ℹ Open daily 12:00–21:00, Closed on Monday (Open on national holidays)
- ⏱ 5 minutes by foot from Demachiyanagi Station, Keihan Main Line and Eizan Main Line

16. Ishihara
- Yanagino-banba-dori Aneyakoji Agaru Yanagi-hachiman-cho 76, Nakagyo-ku, Kyoto, Kyoto
- ☎ 075-221-5612
- ℹ Prices, one night with breakfast start from ¥14,040 per person (one room with two people)
- ⏱ 5 minutes by foot from Karasuma-Oike Station, Kyoto Municipal Subway Karasuma Line and Tozai Line

17. Oyado Nunoya
- Aburanokoji-dori Marutamachi Agaru Komeya-cho 281, Kamigyo-ku, Kyoto, Kyoto
- ☎ 075-211-8109
- ℹ Prices, one night with breakfast start from ¥9,000 per person (one room with two people), Closed occasionally
- ⏱ 5 minutes by foot from Marutamachi Station, Kyoto Municipal Subway Karasuma Line

18. KYOTO ART HOSTEL kumagusuku
- Mibu-banba-cho 37-3, Nakagyo-ku, Kyoto, Kyoto
- ☎ 075-432-8168
- ⏱ 5 minutes by foot from Omiya Station, Hankyu Kyoto Main Line

19. Nishijin Isa-cho Machiya (Iori Machiya Stay)
- Omiya-dori Kamitachiuri Agaru Nishi-iru, Kamigyo-ku, Kyoto, Kyoto

20. Atsushi Horibe (Keibunsha Ichijoji)
- Ichijoji Haraitono-cho 10, Sakyo-ku, Kyoto, Kyoto
- ☎ 075-711-5919
- ℹ Open daily 11:00–19:00, Closed on New Year's Day
- ⏱ 5 minutes by foot from Ichijoji Station, Eizan Main Line

21. Sanjiro Minato (Sauna Umeyu)
- Kiyamachi-dori Kaminokuchi Agaru Iwataki-cho 175, Shimogyo-ku, Kyoto, Kyoto
- ☎ 080-2523-0626
- ℹ Open daily 14:00–26:00, Closed on Thursday
- ⏱ 5 minutes by foot from Kiyomizu-Gojo Station, Keihan Main Line

22. Homaru Fujiwara (→7. Tautasha)

23. Hiroyuki Kuroki (Roofscape Architect)
- Minoyamahiruzuka 100-9, Yawata-shi, Kyoto
- ☎ 075-925-8420 (Roofscape Architect)

ORIX Rent-A-Car
KYOTO-MIYAMA
DESIGN TRAVEL

美山をドライブしよう！　http://car.orix.co.jp/　オリックス レンタカー

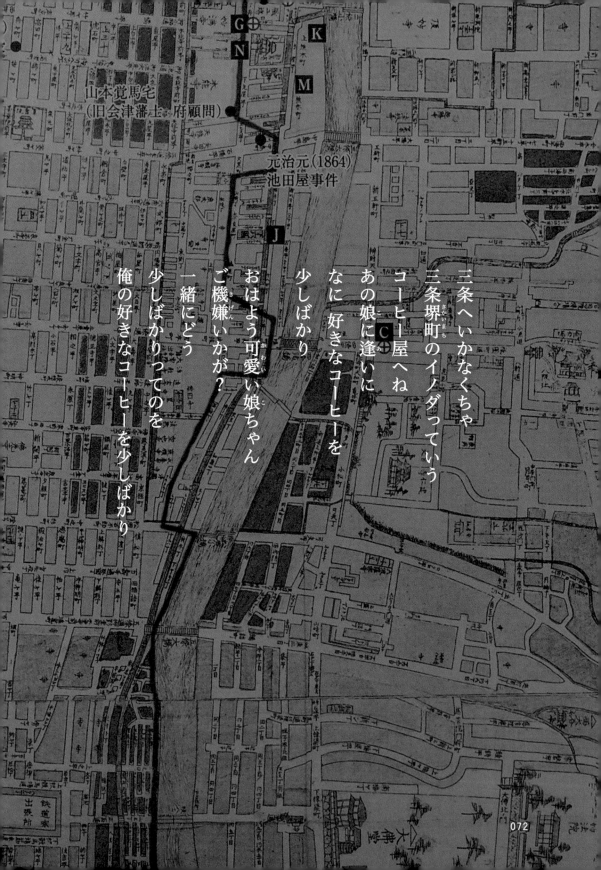

山本覚馬宅
（旧会津藩士　府顧問）

元治元（1864）
池田屋事件

三条へいかなくちゃ
三条堺町のイノダっていう
コーヒー屋へね
あの娘に逢いに
なに　好きなコーヒーを
少しばかり
おはよう可愛い娘ちゃん
ご機嫌いかが？
一緒にどう
少しばかりってのを
俺の好きなコーヒーを少しばかり

いい娘だな

ねえ、熱いのをお願い

そう、熱いのをお願い

そう、最後の一滴が勝負さ

オレの好きなコーヒーを少しばかり

三条へいかなくちゃ

三条堺町のイノダっていう

コーヒー屋へね

あの娘に逢いに

なに好きなコーヒーを

少しばかり

あんたもどう？

少しばかりってのを

「コーヒーブルース」高田渡──
『イキテル・ソング～オールタイム・ベスト～』KING RECORDS（二〇一五年）より
（ルビは、本誌編集部による）

JASRAC 出 1507492-501

天保10（1839）
初代源蔵の生家

B

わが国
初

編集長が、自転車で行く

空閑トラベル I

京都市市街地編。中京区、下京区を中心に

Osamu Kuga
空閑理

Kuga Travel 1: Editor's travel notes

EPARTMENT KYOTO by 京都造形芸術大学

本誌の取材の仕方は、約二か月にわたる現地滞在の間に、四七都道府県、それぞれにある（に違いないと僕達が確信している）「その土地らしさ」とは何か？を見つけ出し、それを軸にして、「d マークレビュー」記事や、その他の取材先を決定していくという事が、基本です。だから今回の「京都府号」では、まず、「京都らしさ」とは何か？を見つけ出さなければいけなかった。「はんなり」「みやび」「あはれ」「一〇〇〇年の都」、そして「いけず」——いろんな情報は聞いていた。たくさん本も読んだ。でも、"そんなイメージの京都"と、"現実の京都"は、かなり違っていたなというのが、取材を終えた僕達の実感です。

「京〇〇」「本家〇〇」「創業〇〇〇年（三桁が珍しくない）」「〇〇御用達」、そんな文字が、京都府内を旅していると幾らでも目につきました。ですが、僕達が、こここそ！と考えて選び、取材させていただいた店や場所の多くには、看板にも暖簾にも、「そんなん、要らん事ですし」と、掲げていなかったのです。屋号さえも、表に出していなかったり、ほんの小さくしか書かない店も多かったのです。

真の京都らしさとは、「京都らしい」かどうか、そんな事より、自分達の範囲で、今ある物を大事にして、一つ一つ、毎日毎日、自信と確信を持って世に出せる、本当にいい物だけをつくる、売る、使う、直す——そういう仕事の中にあるのだ、と僕達は考えました。

今回の京都府取材中、「一面だけを見て、『京都とは、こうだ』と決めつけてほしくない」と、地元の方々から何度も言われました。だから今号「京都府号」では、何か特色的な物事をクローズアップした「特集記事」は設けず、僕達編集部が見てきた、多種多様な京都の姿を、できるだけ多く紹介したいと考え、この「空閑トラベル」では、京都市市街地を中心に、「Ⅰ 生活圏内の自転車編」「Ⅱ 日帰り小旅行のバスと電車編」「Ⅲ 最低一泊のレンタカー編」の三編に分けて、ご紹介する事にしました。

When our editorial department works on a new issue, we stay at the featured prefecture for nearly two months to discover the uniqueness of the area. While there, we write our "d mark review" as well as use that as a starting point to discover other things. Of course, for the Kyoto issue, we had to first discover what makes Kyoto uniquely Kyoto.

Throughout my stay here, I discovered that the philosophy of Kyoto—what makes this city special—is to cherish what you have right now and the work ethic is one of "working one day at a time" to create (and sell, use, and/or fix) only items that you take pride in.

Many times during my two-month stay, I had locals tell me not to categorize and define Kyoto. So, for this issue, I decided not to write my column, "Kuga Travels," in its usual format; instead, I divided it into three different articles: 1. "Kyoto by Bicycle," which focuses in the inner city of Kyoto; 2. A Day Trip by Bus; and 3. An Overnight Trip with a Rental Car.

(→p. 077)

宿はなし

　今回の「京都府号」取材のために、僕が、最初に京都府にやって来たのは三月末で、かなり肌寒かった。四月に入って、鴨川の河川敷のソメイヨシノが咲き始め、やっと満開、と思ったら、見頃を迎えて直ぐ、大雨と大風で、あっという間に散ってしまった。「一年中、観光シーズン」とされる京都だが、桜の時期はピーク中のピークだそうで、「何で、こんな時期に取材なんか」と、出会った誰しもに呆れられた。まったく宿が取れないのだ。宿泊施設は旅館もホテルも、カプセルホテルでさえも、どこも満室。滋賀県の大津市のビジネスホテルでさえも満室だった。桜はない、晴れ間は少ない、店は行列、宿はなし。

　それでも、世界中から訪れる観光客は入れ替わり立ち替わり、「京都駅ビル」の巨大なコンコースから吐出され、「京都タワー」の写真を撮り、無数にある観

in the rest area of the sauna in Shijo-Omiya and ate *gyoza* at the first shop of "Gyoza no Osho" nearby. I met with Ryuki Obara of "D&DEPARTMENT KYOTO" at "Shomin", a standing bar, until the closing time early in the morning. It was fun for a while, but I was feeling exhausted. Finally, Sayaka Nakagawa, the designer at D&DEPARTMENT, let me and our editorial department staff stay at her parents' apartment in the city.

Teramachi Street on a bicycle

The first purchase I made when I settled in Kyoto was a used bicycle. I began to run out of fresh clothes, so I also bought shirts at "MORIKAGE SHIRT KYOTO". The apartment was close to the palace. I often went southward on Marutamachi Street, passing Ebisugawa Street, which was lined with furniture shops on both sides—one of them being "Ikawa Tateguten", a used joinery shop. Kyoto as a city is full of old *machiya*-style houses, inns, shops, and bars, but Ikawa Tateguten deals with (→p. 079)

光スポットへと散らばって、(つまり、僕達の約二か月の京都取材の期間中はずっと)、街から人々が溢れていて、ほとんど宿を予約できなかった。

京都府が抱える大きな課題の一つは、増え続ける観光客に対する宿泊施設の不足だと、よく耳にする。実際、僕達も困った。だが、一方で、京都に住む人々は、宿泊施設はもう要らない、と感じているようにも思えた。

仕方がないから、僕は主に四条大宮にあるサウナの仮眠室で連泊して、近くの「餃子の王将」の日本一号店で餃子を食べ、やはり近くの「庶民」という名前の、いつでも店から客が溢れるほど賑わっている立ち呑み店で、

「D&DEPARTMENT KYOTO」の小原龍樹さん(彼は以前は嵐山で人力車を曳く俥夫だった)や、そこで出会った人々と、閉店まで飲んだりした。すごく楽しかったが、僕は見る見る疲弊していき、その状況を見かねて、

「D&DEPARTMENT PROJECT」のデザイナーの中川清香さんが、京都市市街地からほど近い、ご両親が所有するマンションの空室を、編集部の宿泊室として提供してくださる事になり、有り難く、使わせていただいた。という事で、今回の「京都府号」取材の旅は、宿なしで始まり、予期せず住み処を得て、京都生活をスタートする事になった。

自転車に乗って。 丸太町通りから寺町通りへ

京都生活が始まって、最初に買ったのは中古の自転車。シャツは途中で着替えがなくなり、「モリカゲシャツキョウト」で新調した。そのシャツを着て、自転車に乗って、鴨川を走ったり、コーヒーを飲みに行ったり、必要な本や日用品を買いに行ったりした。マンションは、京都御苑(京都の人は、「御所」と

No vacancy

I came to Kyoto in late March, when it was still cold. People say that Kyoto is a great tourist spot all year around, but the cherry blossom season, unfortunately, is the peak tourist time. Everyone I met laughed at me for coming at this time, and they were right: I couldn't book a hotel room anywhere. Not at *ryokan*, not at business hotels, and not even at capsule hotels. For the next two months, Kyoto was overflowing with people: during my stay, I watched people coming out of "Kyoto Station" in herds, always taking photos of "Kyoto Tower" as they exited the station, and going on their way to see one of the numerous tourist spots scattered throughout the city. And, of course, I couldn't book a hotel for the entire time.

One of the pressing issues Kyoto faces is not enough hotels to accommodate its increasing numbers of tourists, as we experienced firsthand. On the other hand, I got the feeling that the residents felt there were already enough tourists in Kyoto.

Because I didn't have any other choice, I spent several nights

呼ぶ）の近くにあった。丸太町通りから南に下って、家具店が多く連なる夷川通りを走った先のクリーニング店にシャツを出した。その途中にある「井川建具店」が興味深かった。京都には古い町家や旅館、商店、酒場、いろいろと残っているが、この店は、解体になった古い家の建具を、多く扱っている。京都の物ばかりではないそうで、都道府県や地域で、それぞれ寸法が違うらしい。京夷川通りから堺町通りを下ると「キンシ正宗堀野記念館」がある。虫籠窓の町家の見学を兼ねて訪れる人も多い、酒造記念館。名水「桃の井」が敷地内に湧いている。

夷川通りを西へ走り続けると、名店犇めく、寺町通りに突き当たる。まずは、朝九時開店の「一保堂茶舗」。どうやって、この安心感をつくり上げてきたんだろう？と感心してしまうほどの素晴らしいサービス。とはいえ、併設の喫茶室「嘉木」は、恒常的に満席。遠方から、はるばる来て、一服もできずに諦めて帰る観光客も多かった。現在、町歩きのお供に最適な、テイクアウトサービスもある。しかも、きちんと一杯ずつ淹れてくれる。そのラベルデザインは、塩川いづみさん。もちろん美味しい。

一保堂から寺町通りを少し下ると、左手に飾り棚が素敵な洋菓子店「村上開新堂」、右手には、僕の知り合いに非常にファンが多い書店「三月書房」がある。「三月書房」は、一見どこにでもありそうな、小さな書店だが、棚に詰まった一冊一冊の本が、何か「自分の領域」を持ち、それぞれが存在を強く主張していて、不思議な緊張感がある。新刊本ばかりだが、えっ!?と驚くような一冊が見つかったりする。僕には、建築家の故・白井晟一の作品集が光って見えて、何だか緊張してしまい、なぜか（なぜだ!?）買わずに手に取ったのだけれど、何だか緊張してしまい、なぜか（なぜだ!?）出てきてしまった。寺町二条を南に行った所にある「芸艸堂」は、日本唯一の手摺木版・和装本の出版社で、看板には「WOODCUT PRINTS」とあった。葛

of Hokusai Katsushika, Jakuchu Ito, and Sekka Kamisaka, the Meiji-era Japanese painter and designer, and whose work we used as the cover for this Kyoto issue.

Once you cross Oike Street, Teramachi Street turns into a shopping arcade, and you have to get off your bicycle. To the right is "Kyukyodo", an incense and calligraphy shop established in 1663. Because there's a gift-and-letter exchange culture in Kyoto, stationery needed for these frequent forms of communication needs to be simple but beautiful, with high-quality paper that allows, I hope, the words to come smoothly out of my pen.

For breakfast and lunch, go straight down the arcade to "Smart Coffee". They are known for their pancakes, but you should also try their French toast. But be sure to take a friend: the portions are that big, and that good. The simple white tables on the first floor are designed in such a way that although the restaurant is small, it doesn't feel small when you sit down. The second floor opens up at lunch time. (→p. 081)

飾北斎や伊藤若冲、本誌「京都府号」の表紙にも使用させていただいた、明治時代の日本画家・図案家の神坂雪佳の作品集などの版元だ。

御池通りの横断舗道を渡ると、寺町通りはアーケード商店街になり、その先は、自転車は下車がルール。入り口左手に本能寺（今はビル。「ホテル本能寺」まである）がある。右手に、一六六三年創業の、お香と書画用品等の店「鳩居堂」がある。何かを貫ったり贈ったりするコミュニケーションが京都では多く、重視されるというから、それに使う便箋や封筒は、定番的で、極シンプルだが、絶妙なツヤとハリ、きちんと細部までデザインされていて、ペンを走らせると書き味も違う。一枚一枚、大事に使おうと思うと、書く文字が丁寧になり、内容には心がこもる。幾つか選んでレジに持っていくと、それらが、パリッとした包装紙に包まれて、それと同じ鳩柄の紙袋に入れられて、「いい物を買えた」

used joineries for houses taken from dismantled houses. Depending on the area and neighborhoods, joiners come in various sizes.

Further down Ebisugawa Street to Sakaimachi Street, there's "Kinshi Masamune Horino Memorial Museum", a brewery museum.

When you follow Ebisugawa Street westward, you come across Teramachi Street. If it is in the morning, stop by the "Ippodo Tea Main Store in Kyoto", which opens at 9am. They

have started a take-out service, if you want a take-out of green tea to accompany you on your tour. Izumie Shiokawa designed the tea labels. And, of course, the tea is delicious.

If you walk a bit down Teramachi Street from Ippodo, there's "Murakami Kaishindo", a patisserie shop, to the left, and "Sangatsu Shobo", a bookshop with quite a big following, to the right. "Unsodo", in the southern part of Teramachi-Nijo, is the only publisher of woodblock and Japanese bound books. This is the woodblock studio that prints collector-quality works

という気持ちになった。

モーニングでも、ランチでも、そのまま少し下った「スマート珈琲店」へ。

「これぞホットケーキ！」というホットケーキが名物だが、ジューシーなフレンチトーストも捨てがたい。二人で行って、シェアしましょう。一階のシンプルな白い天板のテーブルは、狭い店内でも脚が自由になるように設計されていて、座ってみると、思ったより広々としている。この店のデザインは、確かにスマートだ。ランチタイムは、二階が洋食のレストランになる。

三条へ行くんだよ

さらに寺町通りを下ると三条通りとの交差点に出る。その角に、すき焼きの

At the end of April, the view of the Kamo River from the Sanjo Bridge changes: with the start of wood platforms allowed from May 1, the shops along the river begin building the platforms on the river.

From Sanjo Street, go down Kiyamachi Street along Takase River. You'll come across the "Rissei Elementary School", a closed elementary school that was established in 1927. The building has been converted to a shopping center. At "Rissei Cinema Project" on the third floor, they were playing

Trainspotting, directed by Danny Boyle.

Go up Kiyamachi Street from Sanjo Street and you will come cross "Morita-ya Kiyamachi", an old house converted to a sukiyaki restaurant. The entrance is at the end of a narrow stone-paved path, and the hall faces the Kamo River; when in season, a wooden platform is erected over the river.

Further up the street, near the Nijo Street crossing, is the "Shimadzu Foundation Memorial Hall". "Even failures can help people," says Koichi Tanaka (2002 Nobel Prize winner (→p. 083)

名店「三嶋亭」がある。いかにも格式があり料金も高そうな、でも一度は行ってみたいな、と思わせる重厚な佇まいで、創業時から現在地にあるというガス灯を見上げて、何度前を通り過ぎた事か！ ちなみに、地元の人に訊くと、すき焼きは、「店に行ってまで食べた事はない」「いい肉を買ってきて、家でやる」という人が多かった。

「三嶋亭」から三条通りを東へ行けば河原町通り、さらに進むと鴨川があり、三条大橋の手前に本誌 d マーク記事の「内藤商店」があり、その二軒向こうの鴨川沿いにスターバックスがある。せっかく京都に来たのにスターバックスか！ と思われるかも知れないが、疲れたり、キレイなトイレを探したりする時、スターバックスがあると、やはり助かる。カウンターに座って、ふと隣を見ると海外からのバックパッカーが座っていて、「Kindle」で自分の国の言葉で本を読んでいたりして、その風情に、僕はホッとした。何もわからない、誰も知らない土地で、慣れたカフェに入って読みたい本を読むのも、旅でしかできない事なのだ。しかし、トイレに行くと、一〇分も前の人が出てこなかった。後ろに並んでいた叔母さんに、「たぶん髪でも洗ってるんでしょう」、というジョークを言ってみたが、言葉が通じず、身振り手振り、伝わるまで時間が、かかった（それでも、前の人がトイレから出てくるまでさらに一〇分かかった）。

四月末には、三条大橋から眺める鴨川の風景がガラリと変わる。五月一日の納涼床解禁に合わせて、一斉に、その設営が始まるのだ。河川敷にはクレーン車が入っているけれど、木槌でガンガン叩いたりして、基本的には手作業で建てているようだった。納涼床は、つい最近まで、梅雨明けの七月がスタートだったのに、観光地化が進み、どんどん、その期間が延びているそうで、地元の人は「まだ寒いし、雨も降りますし」という感じ。もっともっと昔、江戸時代は、川の中洲の砂利に、直に席をつくる「床几」というスタイルが定番だったのだそう

Let's go to Sanjo

Go down Teramachi Street and you'll come to the Sanjo Street crossing. There, at the corner, is the famous sukiyaki restaurant, "Mishima-tei". How many times did I pass by that restaurant, look at its expensive-looking façade and the gas lamp which is said to have been from the time the restaurant opened its doors a hundred years ago? On a side note, Kyoto residents almost never eat sukiyaki at restaurants; they all say that they buy good meat at shops and cook it at home.

Past Mishima-tei, go east on Sanjo Street toward Kawaramachi Street. Go straight and you'll get to "Starbucks Coffee Kyoto Sanjo Ohashi" along the Kamo River. When you are tired or looking for a clean bathroom, Starbucks can save your life. I sat at the counter and felt a sense of relief when I saw a backpacker from abroad reading on a Kindle. Of course, when you are in a foreign land where you know no one, a familiar café is comfort. That's one of the beauties of traveling: you can open a book and read, not caring about the time passing.

で、元々は鴨川ではなく、貴船山の貴船川で行われた（現在もある。観光地化している）のだそうだ。ちなみに、このスターバックスにも納涼床席がある。

三条通りから高瀬川沿いに木屋町通りを下ると、一九二七年に建てられた「元・立誠小学校」があり、現在は閉校になっているが、校舎は若者達で溢れ返っていた。「京都ふるどうぐ市」が開催中で、中庭にはコーヒーや菓子店のブースもあった。三階には常設の映画館「立誠シネマ」があり、この日は午後からダニー・ボイル監督の「トレイン・スポッティング」を上映していて、羨ましく思った。

三条通りから木屋町通りを上ると、古い料理旅館を再活用した、すき焼き店「モリタ屋 木屋町店」がある。細い石畳の路地を歩いた奥に店の入り口があり、奥座敷は鴨川に面していて、シーズンには納涼床も出る。二条通りとの交差点近くに「島津製作所 創業記念資料館」がある。「失敗も、人の役に立つ」とビデオで語るのは、田中耕一さん（二〇〇二年ノーベル化学賞受賞。島津製作所の社員）。「島津製作所」は一八七五（明治八）年に創業、理化学機器を製造し、教育分野をはじめ、京都の近代的な科学振興に貢献した企業だ。

その創業に至る歴史的背景を紹介する展示の一部として、京都市市街の〝碁盤の目〟の地図が展示されていた。だが、その見慣れているはずの地図は、かなりな広範囲を、赤い線で囲ってあった。一八六四年の禁門の変（蛤御門の変）で、幕府軍（薩摩・会津・大垣・桑名、そして新撰組）と長州など、つまり京都の人から見たら、他所者と他所者とが、京都中心市街地で大砲でも何でも使って町で戦いを繰り広げ、この赤い線で囲まれた部分が焼けて失われたのだという。約一五〇年前の事である。燃え広がる炎を止める術もなく、町がどんどん焼けていったことから、この事件を「どんどん焼け」と呼んだのだそうだ。

さて、三条通りへと引き返す。何はともあれ、「三条へ行かなくちゃ」。三条堺町に「イノダコーヒ」の「本店」はあるが、そのすぐ近く、三条通り沿いに、

onions and Chinese cabbages? When I imagined what he would paint, even the crowd stopped bothering me.

Go eastward through the marketplace and have a drink at the "Kyogoku Stand", an *izakaya* on Shinkyogoku Street. Open from noon to 9pm and closed on Tuesdays, it's always crowded, no matter the time.

Go through the arcade, and go eastward on Shijo Street. With the night wind comes the sound of the bells. I would look up to find people practicing for festivals on a second floor of a building at the crossing. With the windows open, you can hear the music mixing in with spring night air, traveling far. The Shijo-Karasuma neighborhood is the center of Kyoto; cars and buses drive by nonstop in front of the building. The only people who stop walking to listen to the music are tourists; others go by indifferently. Music mixing with the traffic sounds indicates that the festival is coming closer and closer each day. And perhaps this has been going on for years—the traditional mixing with the new, creating a rhythm of Kyoto.

(→p. 085)

「三条支店」もある。「三条支店」の奥の喫煙席は、コックコートの紳士がキビキビと働く厨房を、ぐるりと囲んだ円形のカウンター。口に布が被せられた大振りの琺瑯ピッチャーに、おたまでお湯が注がれるのだが、これがまさかのネルドリップ！　豪快だ。目の前で、あの濃厚な名物コーヒーは、こうやって淹れているのか！というのを見る事ができ、「本店より好き」というファンも少なくないだろう。でも、僕は本店も好きだ。

四条へ。伊藤若冲の故郷・錦市場

堺町通りを下っていくと、四条通りの手前に、ド派手な極彩色のアーケード街が横切っている。これが錦小路通りで、高倉通りから寺町通りまでの間が「錦

---

in chemistry and an employee of Shimadzu Corporation) in the video.

Go back a bit on Sanjo Street. No matter what, you have to go to Sanjo. There's "Inoda Coffee Honten" at the edge of the Sanjo neighborhood, but there's also "Inoda Coffee Sanjo" along Sanjo Street. There, you will find, near the smoking section, a round counter surrounding the kitchen, and a man wearing a chef's white uniform. You can see the entire process of Nel drip coffee here: a man pouring hot water into a pitcher.

To Shijo, and to Nishiki Marketplace, the home of Jakuchu Ito
When you go down Sakaimachi Street, you'll come across a vividly hued shopping arcade right before Shijo Street. This is the "Nishiki Markpetplace". There are many shops selling vegetables and fish, as well as pickles and *fu*, lining both sides. Tourists and shoppers push each other out of the way to move. The famous painter, Jakuchu Ito, with his unique perspective, was born here in Nishiki. If he were still alive, would he paint people here who come from all over the world? Or would he just paint green

市場」。野菜や魚など生鮮食品や漬け物や麩などの加工食品、お茶や饅頭などの土産店などが犇めき合い、そして初詣でみたいに、観光客が、ギッシリと押し合うように歩いている。江戸時代の絵師で、森羅万象を実に濃やかに、極めて緻密に、ユーモラスに、そして独創的に描いた伊藤若冲は、ここ、錦の生まれだった。僕は学生時代に、相国寺「承天閣美術館」で開催された、若冲画の「動植綵絵」三〇幅と「釈迦三尊像」三幅が一堂に会した画期的な展覧会を見て、猛烈に感動した事を覚えている。今、もし、若冲が生きていたら、錦市場に世界中から集まってくる人間を描いただろうか。それとも、やはり白菜やネギを描いただろうか。そう思うと混雑も愉快だ。

錦市場を東に抜けて、新京極通りの居酒屋「京極スタンド」で一杯飲む。観光客も地元の常連客も、酒飲みも定食利用客も、入れ替わり立ち替わり、自由に楽しむ店。営業時間は正午から夜九時の火曜定休で、毎日大入り、活気が、すごい。「京極スタンド」を出て、アーケード街を抜けて、四条通りに出て西へ進むと、夜風にのって鈴の音が聞こえてきた。四条烏丸の交差点近くのビルの二階で、祭りのお囃子の練習をしているのだ。窓ガラスを開け放っているから、太鼓や笛の音が、遠くまで聞こえてくる。たくさんのバスやタクシーや自転車が、ビルの前を通り過ぎていく。その音色に聴き入るのは観光客くらいで、京都の人々は足を止めないし気にも留めない。エンジン音やクラクション、横断歩道のパッポパッポ音に混ざって、お祭りの音が、そして、お祭りが一晩毎に近づいてくる。こうして、毎年毎年──これが京都のリズムなんだな、と僕は思った。

そのまま変わらずに、面白くなっていく五条

河原町通りを下って五条通りを越えて、高瀬川沿いから少し鴨川側に入った

blossom trees. Umeno, the bookshop owner, thinks that these trees were planted during the trauma of World War II when they were so much food shortage all around the city as well as the country.

The Rhythm of Kyoto

We bought a handmade broom and a tin dustpan from the "Kura Daily Store" to clean the apartment; the store is located in the shopping area near Horikawa Street. If you go eastward and walk northward along Senbon Street, you'll hit "Shinme", one of the best-known *izakaya* in Kyoto. Everything I ate was delicious, but the most delicious was the sake made out of six different sakes. You never got bored, and you never get a hangover. I ordered several glasses every time I went.

On the way back to the apartment, close to the palace at night, I would come across the lush green of the palace trees. Suddenly the temperature would drop and my breath would turned white. From Marutamachi Street on, (→p. 087)

路地にある「五条モール」へ。お茶屋を改築した古い建物で、しばらく空き家だったが、食事処や木工作家のアトリエや書店、貸しギャラリーなどが入って、生まれ変わった。その書店「homehome」の店主うめのたかしさんを訪ねると、白黒の毛色の「オセロ」という名前の猫と遊んでいた。うめのさんは、以前、本誌「福岡県号」の書評を週刊誌に書いてくださった事があり、現在は浄土寺の「ホホホ座」（当時「ガケ書房」）のメンバーでもあり、週末は、ここで自分の店を開いている。週刊誌の記事はとても嬉しくて、編集部で回し読みし、何度も読んだからか、初対面の気がしなかった。話し込んでいると、すぐ裏にある、廃業した銭湯「梅湯」を復活させようとしている湊三次郎さんがフラッとやって来て、立ち話は続いた。楽しかった。京都はよく、「街全体がミュージアム」とか、「アミューズメントパーク」とか、喩えられるそうだけど、大学キャンパスみたいだな、と僕は思った。すぐ近くには、京都のカフェブームを牽引した「エフィッシュ」があり、また、河原町通り沿いにはおしゃれなゲストハウス「レン」が開業したばかり。茶筒の「開化堂」もある。五条、これからも、さらに面白くなりそうです。「梅湯」は目の前に高瀬川が流れ、散りかけの桜の木が立っている。ここから、さらに下ると、桜だけではなく、多種多様な樹木が植えられているが、それは戦時中、食べる物がなくなっても食べられるように、果樹を植えた名残だろうと、うめのさんに教えてもらった。

京都のリズム

賃貸マンションの掃除用に、棕櫚製の箒と束子を買った。「倉日用商店」で買った。「倉日用商店」は、丸太町通りから堀川通りまで出て、少し上った通り沿いの商店街にある。荒物や民藝品などキ製のチリトリは「倉日用商店」で買い、ブリキ製のチリトリは「内藤商店」で買い、ブリ

Gojo, always the same, always changing

Go down Kawaramachi Street, cross Gojo through an alley toward the Kamo River, and you'll come across the Gojo Mall. For some time it was unoccupied, but now the building is occupied by restaurants, ateliers of artists, bookstores, and galleries. When I visited the *homehome* bookshop, the owner, Takashi Umeno, was playing with Othello, his black-and-white cat. He once wrote a review of this magazine for a weekly magazine in Fukuoka; he is a current member of "HOHOHOZA" and runs this bookshop on the weekends. When I was there, Sanjiro Minato—the owner of "Ume-yu", the public bath house—stopped by. Right nearby, there's "Effish", which started the café boom in Kyoto, and "Len", a guesthouse, has just opened its doors. There's also "Kaikado", a teashop. Interesting things are happening in Gojo.

In front of Ume-yu, the Takase River flows slowly, lined by cherry blossom trees. If you go along the river, you'll see that there are many fruit-bearing trees planted amid the cherry

幅広く取り扱っていて、チリトリの他に、宮城県の和紙の名刺入れも気に入って僕は買った。周辺の、お薦めスポットを細かくリサーチを繰り返して、情報が古くならないように書き込んだマップを無料配付している。夜は、さらに西へ移動して、千本通りに出て北上し、名居酒屋「神馬」へ。細長い舟屋造りで、奥まで続く長いカウンター。黄色っぽい照明を低く落とした店内は、入った瞬間勝負あり、もう美味しそうだ。事実、何を注文しても美味かったが、清酒が灘六種のオリジナルブレンド、飲み飽きず、飲み疲れもせず、こればかり、何合も頂いた。

マンションに戻ろうと、御所の近くまで戻ってきて、鬱蒼と繁る御苑の木々が見えてくると、急に寒くなる。吐く息が白くなる。丸太町通りから先は、御苑をすっぽりと靄がかかっていて、闇の中にずっと続く街灯の白い光の点々が、たちまち、ぼやけて見える。翌朝、日が高く昇ってしまってから再び御苑に行くと、カラリと晴れて、空気は澄んで、キレイな青色で、遠くまで見通せた。中は広々としていて、自転車に乗ったまま御苑の中を通り抜けてもいいのだが、敷き詰められた砂利にハンドルを取られて、ペダルも重く、うまく走る事ができない。それで、みんな同じ、一本の轍的な上を走る事になるのが、少し可笑しかった。

現在の長岡京市に長岡京が遷都されたのが七八四年、そして、京都市市街地に平安京が遷都されたのが、七九四年とされ、以降、一八六九年まで、日本の首都であった京都。その間、数多の為政者達が、この都市を支配し、時には侵略し、栄華を極め、巨大な建築物を遺していった。町をつくりかえ、そして争い合い、殺されたり、没落して、歴史に名を刻んだ偉人達は、皆、尽く、京都からいなくなってしまった。どうしてだろう？　複雑怪奇だ。

だが、それでも、京都が京都で在り続けたのは、どんなに荒れ果てても土地を捨てず、誇りを忘れず、商いを守り、頑なに生き続けてきた京都の市民、一般民

people in Kyoto refuse to give up their control to outsiders. Long-time residents in Kyoto never praise rich people who come from outside, who buy up land or take stuff from others; they never acknowledge these outsiders as being from Kyoto. No matter whether these outsiders become the majority or hold power, no matter how much they try to change the city, the Kyoto-ites know that in a decade, in fifty years or in a century, they will eventually leave. That's how it's been throughout history. The essence of a city relies in finding its own rhythm to evolve, to change. The rhythm in Kyoto is like a river or stream: it's long, slow, narrow, sometimes rapid, sometimes too still, but the rhythm is its own, not imposed by anyone else. Kyoto stubbornly holds onto its own rhythm and its way of life. That's what makes Kyoto the city it is.

衆の存在が在ったからだ。「京都らしさ」の根底にあるのは、温故知新の追求ではなく、"盛者必衰のあはれ" なのかも知れない。権威や経済力を振りかざす支配者や他所者などに、京都の人々は京都を譲らない。他所からやって来て、人の物を取ったり奪ったりして富豪になった者など、京都の人々は決して褒めないし、愛さない。相手が多数派になって、権力と実行力などを以て、町を変えようとしても、それらの者は、一〇年、三〇年、五〇年、一〇〇年、一〇〇〇年で、去っていってしまう事、人のためにも町のためにもならない事、を熟知している。「その土地らしさ」とは、その土地が変わっていくのに、新しい姿に成っていくのに、ちょうどいいスピード、または、そのリズムだ、と僕は思う。そして、京都のリズムとは、川や通りのように、長く、細く、高い所から低い所へ、時に激しく、時に穏やかに。だが、過度に盛る事なく、決して衰えもさせず、"自分達の時間の刻み" を守っていく頑なさ——それが「京都らしさ」だ、と僕は考えた。

everything is foggy, and the only thing you see in the hazy darkness is the light from the lampposts dotting here and there. In the morning, it will be clear. The air crisp. You can ride your bicycle on the palace grounds but be warned: it is very hard to pedal on the gravel.

The capital was established in Nagaoka-kyo city in 784, and in 794, the capital moved to Kyoto, and remained there until 1869. Over the millennia, leaders came and went, so many battles were fought and places occupied so many times, that buildings were torn down and rebuilt. The city was burned to ashes, and along with it, many countless historical people were killed or fell from grace, disappearing from the city.

But the reason why Kyoto remained Kyoto was because of nameless men and women who stayed and protected the city, who stubbornly refused to give up their land and their culture. I wonder whether, at the base of what makes Kyoto what it is, the idea of evanescence lies at its root. No matter who wields power or money, no matter who comes to rule or govern them,

ときのあとさき

mama!milk 演奏会 at 京都

9/7 (Sat) 夕の部・法然院

9/8 (Sun) 朝の部・flowing KARASUMA

演奏 mama!milk　茶 graf tea salon

坂田 佐武郎　1985年、京都府宇治市生まれ。京都造形芸術大学卒業後、大阪府の「graf」でデザイナーとして勤務、2010
年に独立。現在、京都市を拠点に活動中。主な仕事に、文具メーカー「HIGHTIDE」の「hum products」のアイテム開発等
（2009年 -）、高野山ゲストハウス「Kokuu」のロゴマーク（2012年）、「アーツサポート関西」のロゴマーク（2014年）など。

Saburo Sakata　Born in 1985 in Uji-shi in Kyoto. After graduating from Kyoto University of Art and Design, he began working
at *graf* (Osaka), and went independent in 2010. He currently resides in Kyoto and has worked as product designer of "hum
products" for HIGHTIDE (stationary maker), designed the logomark for Kokuu, a Koyasan guesthouse (2012), and Arts
Support Kansai's logo mark in 2014.

"風流な" 京都

坂本大三郎
Daizaburo Sakamoto

僕が京都に抱いている印象をあらわすと、「風流」(=ふりゅう」とも)という言葉が思い浮かびます。その言葉は「上品で、よい雰囲気」の意味だ、と現代人は考えている人が多いと思いますが、かつての人たちは「人目を驚かせる奇抜な美」という意識を持っていたようです。

例えば、鞍馬寺の「火祭」、太秦の広隆寺の「牛祭」と並んで、京都の三大奇祭と言われている「やすらい祭」は、一一五四年に夜須礼(囃子詞)で、疫病を風流によって追い出す目的で、初めて行われたものと伝えられています。祭りの際に、思い思いの仮装をして行列を組み、悪霊を退散させようとしたのでした。雅で上品な風流では、あまり威力はなさそうですが、奇抜な風流であれば疫病も驚いて逃げていきそうです。

朝鮮半島のシャーマンが、神霊を招いて悪鬼を祓い農耕を祝する神事のことを「フリ」といい、日本と同じ「風流」の漢字を当てていることからも、風流の持つ性格には、アジア的な広がりを感じることができます。

This concept of *furyu*, by the time it reached the Kamakura Period, seems to have transformed itself in the culture of Kabuki, with its nomadic actors and shamans. Even in Kabuki theater, the aesthetics of *furyu* is still alive and well.

In the past, people who caused havoc were called "kabuki-mono," but they, too, embraced the concept of *furyu* by espousing unconventional ideas, such as violence and flashy clothing. That concept is still alive on stage as well as in movies' violence and sex scenes.

Many people think that the culture of Kyoto is too high class, but when you examine the city with *furyu* in mind, I think you will get another impression of Kyoto. The city does not just have a refined and sophisticated side; it has its roots in *furyu*—a side that surprises us by its unconventionality.

そして、この風流は、戦国時代頃になると、各地を漂泊する民間宗教者や芸能者が多く携えた「歌舞伎」という文化に変化していったと考えられています。たしかに、歌舞伎の中には、かつて風流が持っていたような美意識が、今でも残されているようです。

乱暴狼藉を働く者を「カブキモノ」とも呼びましたが、彼らの持っていた奇抜なものや乱暴で性的な様を好む美意識は風流から受け継いできたもので、それは芝居にも度々取り上げられ、濡れ場や殺し場として、現在も映画の中などに生き残っています。

京都の文化は、お高くとまっていいけ好かないと感じている人もいるかも知れませんが、風流という言葉を通して改めて見直してみると、それまでとは違う印象の京都が、あらわれてくるのではないでしょうか。京都には上品な面だけではなく、風流のように僕たちを驚かせてくれる、とても深い広がりを持った文化が根付いていると、僕は考えているのです。

KYOTO Prefecture's Long-Lasting Festival

Furyu: Kyoto as It Is

When I think of Kyoto, I think of the word *furyu*. People nowadays think that the word means "classy, refined" but in the past, people used it to mean "unconventional beauty that surprises people."

For example, at Yasurai-matsuri, one of the three major unconventional festivals in Kyoto (the two others being the Hi-matsuri Fire Festival at Kurama-dera temple and the Ushi-matsuri Cow Festival at Koryu-ji temple) started in the year 1154 as a way of "unconventionally" getting rid of plagues. People dress up in disguises to get rid of evil spirits. If people dressed up elegantly, it would surprise the evil spirits enough for them to flee away—or so the ancients must have thought.

"Furi," the ritual of Korean shamans calling on the spirits to get rid of evil spirits on the farmland, uses the same Chinese character as *furyu*, so we can see the basic idea of *furyu* as one that can be found throughout Asia.

Takao Takaki (Foucault)
高木崇雄（工藝 風向）

河井寬次郎の「仕事のうた」

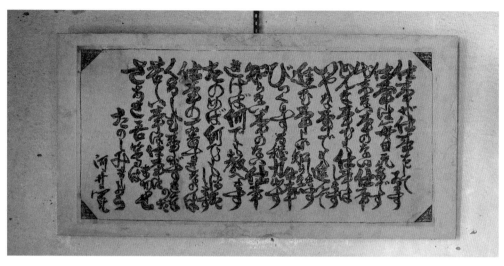

京都の東山五条を少し下って「河井寛次郎記念館」を訪ねると、故・河井寛次郎が自ら書いた額が掛けてある。

仕事が仕事をしてゐます
仕事は毎日元気です
出来ない事のない仕事
どんな事でも仕事はします
いやな事でも進んでします
進む事しか知らない仕事
びっくりする程力出す
知らない事のない仕事
きけば何でも教へます
たのめば何でもはたします
仕事の一番すきなのは
くるしむ事がすきなのだ
苦しい事は仕事にまかせ
さあさ吾等はたのしみましょう

（ルビは本誌編集部による）

「驚いてゐる自分に驚いてゐる自分」「物買って来る自分買って来る」といった、印象深い言葉を数多く生んだ河井らしい、リズムのよい詩だ。この「仕事のうた」を島根県の出西

One can see a calligraphy scroll by Kanjiro Kawai on the wall of KAWAI KANJIRO'S HOUSE near Higashiyama-gojo in Kyoto:

Work works itself to work
Work is happy each and every day
There's nothing work can't do
Work does anything and everything
Even work work doesn't want to do
Work only knows to move forward
Work surprises everyone with its unstoppable energy

There is nothing work doesn't know
It answers all if you ask
If you ask to do it work will do it
What work likes the most
Is to struggle with hard work
All the hard work work would do
Let us now work work work

As Kawai left interesting quotes like "I'm surprised at the surprised self" and "I make a purchase; I purchase (→p. 095)

窯では、毎日皆で唱うと聞く。このような詩文と作品の数々から、しばしば河井は「土と炎の詩人」と呼ばれる。

ただ、ロマンチックな「陶芸家」の印象とは異なり、もともと河井は東京高等工業学校（現在の東京工業大学）から京都市陶磁器試験所に入り、最先端の陶磁器研究を行っていた研究者、そして技術者だった。そのような近代的な技術者が、清水焼窯元の技術顧問を経て、個人作家となる。作家への転身当初すぐに「陶界の一角に突如彗星が出現した」と激賞されるも、やがて「創作」という行為自体が抱える矛盾（河井自身の言葉を用いるならば「追えば逃げる美、追わねば追う美」）に悩み、その矛盾を鋭く指摘した故・柳宗悦と衝突する。そして、年来の友人であり、職場の同僚でもあった故・濱田庄司を介した和解を経て〝民藝〟を生み出す原動力となっていった。このように、「近代化への反省がもたらした伝統への回帰」などといった、安易なまとめなどでは表しえない紆余曲折と矛盾を抱えているのが、〝河井寛次郎という人間〟であり、河井が柳や濱田たちと共につくり上げた〝民藝〟だった。

では、河井が、たびたび用いた言葉「仕事」

the everyday wares we have been using for generations were created to serve the spirit of "work;" there is no self or originality in the brands or the designers of these pieces.

Kanjiro Kawai was the kind of artisan who found work that was created out of necessity and lived his life by answering the call of the work. Every time I read this poem, it inspires me to work and to work harder.

"I work to discover a new self."

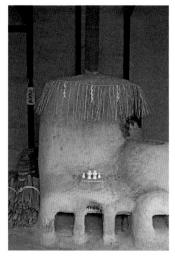

とは何なのか。それは「私」を追い出してくれるもの、である。河井は、「私」が仕事をしているのではなくて、「仕事が私に求める必然」こそが、仕事そのものを成立させている、と捉えた。だからこそ、「私」は仕事の求めに、ひたすら応じ、余計な手も口も出さず、一つ一つの工程をこなすしかない。美しい物を作りたい、人から認められたい、といった「私」の出る余地を与えないのが「仕事」だ。

そして、この、"「私」が含まれない物"こそ、他者にとってよい物となりうる、という河井の思いは、現代でこそ、よく理解されるだろう。「D&DEPARTMENT PROJECT」で紹介される品々のような、長く当たり前に使われてきた道具たちの魅力も、「仕事」に尽くすために生まれ、メーカーやデザイナーの「私」が消えた部分にこそ、感じられるから。

必然がもたらす仕事に惹かれ、ただ仕事に導かれるままに生きる──河井寛次郎とは、そういう人間だった。だからこそ、この詩を読むたびに、僕もまた、よし、仕事をしよう、と奮い立たされる。

新しい自分が見たいのだ──仕事する

myself," this rhythmical poem is just like him. I heard that in a Shussai pottery studio in Shimane, all the craftsmen sing this song every morning. Because Kawai often wrote about this theme, he is known as "The Poet of Earth and Fire."

Unlike the romantic image we have of pottery artists, Kawai was a scientist and a researcher who, after graduating from Tokyo Institute of Technology, went on to Kyoto Ceramics Research Institute. After learning about the most cutting-edge technology in ceramics, he became a technical advisor for Kiyomizu Pottery before he founded his own studio.

What does the word "work" mean to Kawai, who used it repeatedly in his poetry? For Kawai, work is something that pushes the self out; it's not he himself who is creating, but work itself pushes out into material reality through him. So he must answer to the needs of the work, answer its calling, and let it do its work through him without interjecting or projecting the self. *The desire to create beautiful work, works that touch people.* In that kind of demand, there is no place for an "I."

Today, Kawai's philosophy of work is finally being understood. The objects we introduce at D&DEPARTMENT as well as

long
life
design

左／1984年の「タカラ can チューハイ」
の発売当時パッケージデザイン。
上／現在の「タカラ can チューハイ」。
レモン 350ml 231円で発売中です。

ロングライフデザイン・ケーススタディ 24

宝酒造の「タカラ can チューハイ」

 2013年度 グッドデザイン・ロングライフデザイン賞 受賞

長く売れ続けている「デザイン性の高い商品」の一つ一つには、「長く売れ続けているデザイン以外の理由」があります。

京都市に本社がある宝酒造株式会社の「タカラ can チューハイ」は、一九八四年発売の世界初「缶入りチューハイ」。斬新なＣＭも話題となり、家庭で気軽に飲める人気のお酒になりました。高めのアルコール分八パーセントは、酒好きも納得のキレ味。新幹線の車内販売などの定番でもあり、旅のお供としても人気です。これ以上ないシンプルなネーミングに加え、製法を変えず、愛飲者に変わらぬ味を届け続けてきた事も、ロングセラーとなっている、もう一つの理由です。（前田次郎）

Long-Life Design Case Study　24
"Takara Can Chu-hi" by Takara Shuzo Co., Ltd.
There are numerous reasons why each long-seller products are loved by so
many people, and it's not just because of design. Takara Shuzo Co., Ltd.'s Takara
Can Chu-hi was the first canned Chu-hi (alcoholic drink) in the market, produced
in 1984. Clear taste and strong alcohol, even the drink-lovers approve of this
canned drink. Another reason why this is a long-seller is because they haven't
changed the ingredient or the process ever since the beginning. (Jiro Maeda)

 2013 Good Design Long Life Design
Award Recipient

Left: The package design from 1984
Right: Takara Can Chu-hi from
2015 (Lemon flavor, 350 ml, ¥231)

香・筆・墨・和風文具
株式会社
鳩居堂
京都市寺町姉小路角
TEL (075)231-0510

編集長が、バス・電車で行く

空閑トラベル II

京都駅周辺から左京区、北区を中心に

Osamu Kuga

空閑 理

天満宮

Kuga Travel 2: Editor's travel notes

京都駅周辺の楽しみ方

四月の京都は、冷たい雨の日が多く、そんな日の市内観光はバスが便利で、京都駅前の自販機で「市バス・京都バス一日乗車カード（大人五〇〇円）」を買って、よく利用した。京都駅での待ち合わせは、地下鉄改札前の「OGAWA COFFEE 京都駅店」。豆は二種類から、淹れ方はドリップかエアロプレスか、から選べ、「イッタラ」のカップで出してくれる。ラーメンが好きな人には、駅ビル中央口から徒歩約五分の「第一旭」本店が、朝五時から営業。夜行バスで早朝京都に着いたら、ここで食べて、七時から開く「京都タワー」の大浴場で朝風呂に浸かって、という事もできる。「第一旭」の隣は「新福菜館」本店で、こちらは、ラーメンと一緒にヤキメシを注文するのが常連。

バスに乗ったら、「東寺」こと「教王護国寺」へ。開祖・空海が入定した（つまり命日）四月二一日（新暦）が東寺の縁日で、現在、毎月二一日は「弘法さん」と呼ばれる「弘法市」が開かれている。広い境内は、屋台のテントで埋め尽くされて、歩けども歩けども尽きない骨董品のオンパレード。地元客も観光客も、本気でも冷やかしでも、欲しい物、気になる物を探して、グルグルと渦に巻き込まれるように、気がつけば、深い所に迷い込んでしまう。

メジャースポットを旅する。東山から岡崎公園、南禅寺へ

バスで、工事中、連日大渋滞の四条通りを抜け、八坂神社前を左折、知恩院前を通過、東山二条・岡崎公園口バス停で下車。「岡崎公園」には多くの巨大施設が建てられていて、その一つ、「平安神宮」は、平安遷都一一〇〇年事業として、明治になってから建てられた、当時の最先端のテーマパーク的神社。

Around Kyoto Station

April in Kyoto is often rainy and cold, and because of that, buses are quite convenient for sightseeing in the city. I often bought a Day Pass (¥500) at the vending machine in front of Kyoto Station on days I was sightseeing. If you are waiting for a friend, a great meeting place is "OGAWA COFFEE Kyoto Station"; you can choose two kinds of coffee from two kinds of beans, and they serve coffee in Ittala cups. If you like ramen noodles, "Dai-ichi Asahi" is situated about five minutes' walking distance from the Central Exit, and opens at 5am. You can ride the overnight bus to Kyoto, eat ramen here, and then take a morning bath at the Kyoto Tower public bath. Repeaters often order ramen and fried rice at "Shinpukusaikan Honten" next to Dai-ichi Asahi.

Ride the city bus to "Kyoogokoku-ji" temple, also known as "To-ji" temple. On the 21st of every month, the flea market known as "Kobo-ichi" opens at the temple. I shouldn't say this, but it is miles and miles of junk—or antiques, to some people— sold at miles and miles of stalls.

(→p. 101)

現在も観光客は多く、大鳥居の前には人力車がズラリと並ぶ。以前は、建築家の故・前川國男の傑作「京都会館」もあったが、すでに取り壊されていて、新しい劇場施設が建設中だった。気を取り直して「細見美術館」へ。見事な琳派のコレクションがあるそうだが、その時は写真展を開催中。木村伊兵衛「秋田おばこ」、林忠彦「文士シリーズ」の太宰治、植田正治「パパとママとコドモたち」、石元泰博「シカゴ」、森山大道「三沢の犬」、鋤田正義「母」――いつか実物を見てみたいと思っていた写真が、思いつく限り、全部あった。

岡崎公園を抜けて丸太町通りに出て、少し西に行くと、生活用品と器の店「ロク」がある。深緑色の表紙に「SKETCH BOOK」とだけ書かれた、ポケットサイズのノートが、何となく気になって、レジに持って行くと、店主の橋本和美さんが、測量士が屋外で使いやすいようにデザインされたメモ帳なのだと教えてくれた。薄くて軽く、パタンと完全に開く事ができ、表紙が硬いから立ちながらでも難なく書ける。取材にピッタリだと思って、三冊買った。

When we went, my friend and I also shared a *haishi rice* and *Chicken Bruxelles*.

Go along that road and you will come to Nanzen-ji temple, one of the most famous Kyoto tourist spot. I first came here as a small child, and have returned several times. There were so many spots in the temple where I was reminded of photos I took with whoever I was with at that particular time. However, if you go to "Konchi-in" temple within Nanzen-ji, it's less crowded. Ryuki Obara who used to work as a rickshaw driver, told me that this is the kind of places he wished he could have brought his customers to. There is also a tea shop and a garden designed by Enshu Kobori.

Books, books, books, Sakyo-ku: From Higashiyama to Kyoto University to Ichijoji

Go along Shirawaka Street, cross Marutamachi and turn right at the second light. There, you will find "HOHOHOZA", a bookseller and a publisher, in the building with a mural by Yuri

(→p. 103)

後日、「京都府土木事務所」を鴨川の取材で伺うと、担当の方が同じ物を使っていて、「これはね、本当に外でも使いやすいんですよ」と、彼も言っていた。

岡崎でランチなら、絶対、「グリル小宝」のオムライス。小、中、大があり、小でも十分、一人前の量だが、すごく美味しいので、大を二人で取り分けて、さらにハイシライスとチキンジクセルも食べた。琵琶湖疏水沿いを歩くと「京都市動物園」があって、低い柵の向こうにキリンやフラミンゴやヤギが見えて、とても、かわいい。この辺りまで来ると、やっとビルがなくなって、山が見えるようになる。その低山の一つに、一際奇抜で巨大な建築が見えたら、かつて京都随一のホテルと言われた旧「都ホテル」だ。大建築家・村野藤吾（故）が設計した数寄屋建築の傑作と言われた「佳水園」が、現在もあるのだが、経営が大型チェーン店に代わって「惨たんたる事になった」という村野の嘆きを、建築家・吉村順三（故）が著書で書いている。外観からは、その凋落ぶりは窺い知れず、一つ勉強だと思って、何とか予約を取ったのだが——

その授業料は高くついた。

「都ホテル」から歩いて直ぐ、京都観光の定番「南禅寺」へ。僕も、子供の頃、初めての京都旅行で来たし、その後も、何度も訪れている。そして「前にも、ここで写真を撮ったなあ。あの時は誰が一緒で、この時は誰で……」と思い出す場所が、いくつもあった。南禅寺の塔頭の一つ「金地院」は、観光客は、まばらで静か。嵐山で人力車を曳いていた「D&DEPARTMENT KYOTO」の小原龍樹さんは、「こういう所にこそ、お客さんを案内したい」と言う。境内の東照宮の天井には狩野探幽筆の「鳴龍」があり、京都三名席の一つ「八窓席」（茶室）と本堂の庭は小堀遠州によるデザインで、さらに、客は、まばらで静か。嵐山で人力車を曳いていた運良く特別拝観期間に遭遇した僕達は、長谷川等伯が描いた、テナガザルが湖面に映った月に触れようとする「猿猴捉月図」も見る事ができた。

Major tourist spot: From Higashiyama to Okazaki Park

The bus runs along Shijo Street, turning left at Yasaka Shrine past Chionin and I get off at Higashiyama-Nijo/Okazaki Park stop and enter "Hosomi Museum". When I was there, there was a photography exhibition with works by Ihei Kimura, Tadahiko Hayashi, Shoji Ueda, Yasuhiro Ishimoto, Daido Moriyama, and Masayoshi Sukita. These were photos I had always wanted to see, so I felt lucky to come across this show by chance.

Walk through Okazaki Park, you will see "Roku", a pottery and decoration shop on Marutamachi Street. I got curious about a notebook with *Sketchbook* written on the deep green cover, and when I asked about it to Kazumi Hashimoto, the owner, she told me that this notebook was made for surveyors working outside. It's light and thin, and with the hard cover, people can write standing up.

I highly recommend omelette rice at "Grill Kodakara" for lunch. It comes in three sizes, and the small is perfect for one person; but you can order large size and share it with a friend.

本・本・本の左京区。東山から京大、一乗寺へ

さらに北上すると、右手に見える如意ヶ岳の「大文字」が、次第に大きくなってくる。その麓にあるのは銀閣寺こと「慈照寺」だ。ちなみに送り火の「大文字」は二つあって、もう一つは「左大文字」とも呼ばれ、金閣寺こと「鹿苑寺」の大北山（大文字山）に点火される。壮大な光景だろう。

白川通りを進み、丸太町通りを越えて二つ目の信号で右に折れて路地に入ると、画家・下條ユリさんによる壁画が目印の「ホホホ座」がある。まるで劇団のような名前だが、北白川にあった新刊書と雑貨等の店「ガケ書房」（石垣のような外壁から、自動車が飛び出しているという、過激な外観だった）と、元々ここの二階にあった古書と古道具等の店「コトバヨネット」が一つになり、本等を売るだけでなく、自分たちで編集・制作までも手がけている。近くにある「安楽寺」を会場にライブイベントなども企画していて、何か面白い事がやりたくなったら、とりあえず「ホホホ座」に相談に行ってみよう、という感じの、頼れる兄貴的存在の店。二階店主が元「コトバヨ」の松本伸哉さん、一階店主が元「ガケ」の山下賢二さん。お二人に、それぞれ無理を言って、「京都の映画」「京都の本」、そして、一階店舗スタッフの、うめのたかしさんに「京都のCD」の、選定と原稿執筆をお願いした。

白川今出川の交差点を左に折れて、少し坂を下った左手の「古書 善行堂」へ。平積みされた本の束の隙間に、赤い髪を逆立て、褐色の肌に、ギラリとこちらを睨む女の子が見える。壁に貼られた「コム・デ・ギャルソン」のポスターだ。店主の山本善行さんは、元々は、本を「売る側」ではなく、「買う側」だったそう。山本さんが古書店を始めたのが、七年前。その前に何度も読んだのが、『昔日の客（関口良雄著、三茶書房版。夏葉社より復刻）』とい

（→p. 105）

"Café Shinshindo Kyodai Kitamon-mae" across from the northern gate of Kyoto University. I found out that the beautifully lacquered table and the matching benches, simple and sturdy, were designed by Tatsuaki Kuroda when he was 26 years old when I visited "KAWAI KANJIRO'S HOUSE" a few days later. Though this café is always crowded, it also has the quiet of a library.

If you go eastward from Hyakumanben crossing along Imadegawa Street, you can stand on the bridge at Demachiyanagi and view Kamo River split into two. Past that, if you see a long line along a shop in Kawaramachi Street, stop. That's "Demachi Futaba", the famous Japanese sweets shop. Stand in line with other customers. Be sure to buy "Mamemochi", then get on the Eizan Train from Demachiyanagi Station. The third station is Ichijoji Station, and there, you will find "Keibunsha Ichijoji", a bookstore with a big fan base all over Japan. They also sell decorations and knickknacks, and there, behind the shop, a building called Cottage which hosts varieties of

う、東京・大森の古書店店主（故）が著した、一冊の素晴（す）ばらしいエッセイ集。山本さんは、本が好きで、好きな本が増えていく事が好きで、そんな人がいる町や時代が好きで、そこで出会っていく人が好きなのだ。そして、そんな好きな物が溢（あふ）れる世界、つまり〝京都の扉（とびら）〟が、この店や「ホホホ座」や「恵（けい）文社（ぶんしゃ）」などで、一冊選んで買う度に、僕の前に、バーン！バーン！と、次々と扉が開かれていく気がした。

「善行堂」から坂道を下れば「京都大学 吉田キャンパス」だ。「京都大学の吉田寮には泊まれる」という情報が届いたのは、四月末。吉田寮は、鬱蒼（うっそう）とした茂みの中のボロボロの木造建築の旧棟と、完成仕立てのピカピカの新棟とが、隣り合って建っていた。電話で問い合わせると、「泊まれるには泊まれる」そう

Shimojo, the painter. When "Gake Shobo" (Cliff Bookshop—with the mural of a car flying out of the wall), a bookshop on the first floor, and "Kotobayo Net", a used books and furniture shop on the second floor, became one, they decided to not just sell but also to edit and produce books as well. It's the kind of place you go to when you want to do something interesting. I asked both Matsumoto, the former owner of Kotobayo, and Yamashita, the former owner of Gake, to write articles about Kyoto for this issue.

I turn left at Shirakawa Imadegawa and go down the hill to

"Kosho Zenkodo". From the piles of books, a girl with red hair glares at me—a Comme des Garçons poser. Yoshiyuki Yamamoto, the owner, says that he used to be a buyer of books, not a seller. He started this antique bookshop seven years ago. He loves books, he loves books increasing in numbers, and he loves people who loves books, and he also loves meeting other booklovers as well.

Go down the hill from Zenkodo and you will reach "Kyoto University Yoshida Campus". I drank a glass of iced coffee at

だが、新入生の対応期間中で、しばらくは難しいという事で、結局、最後まで泊まる機会がなかった。北門前の「カフェ進々堂京大北門前」でアイスコーヒーを飲む。シンプルでガッシリとした形と、拭き漆の色合いが、非常に美しい長テーブル、それにピッタリ合うように設計された長椅子は、当時二六歳だった木工家の故・黒田辰秋デザインだと、後日、「河井寛次郎記念館」で知った。いつも盛況で活気があるが、図書館のような静謐さも併せ持つ、素敵な居心地だ。

百萬遍交差点から今出川通りを西へ行くと出町柳で、橋の上から、鴨川が、賀茂川と高野川の二つに分かれる地点を眺められる。その先で、河原町通りのアーケードに行列が見えたら、そこが「出町ふたば」和菓子店だ。地元の人にも必ず喜ばれる、絶対的大名物「名代豆餅」を並んで買って、出町柳駅から叡山電車に乗った。

映画「スターウォーズ」に出てきそうな「国際会館」「宝ヶ池プリンスホテル」などがある宝ヶ池駅、延暦寺へ続く八瀬比叡山登山口駅、納涼床発祥の地・貴船山へ続く貴船口駅や、天狗と義経伝説の鞍馬駅などに、のんびりと出かける事ができる鉄道経路だ。出町柳から三駅目が一乗寺駅。ラーメン店が多く、全国的人気店「天下一品」の一号店も近くにある。そして、日本中からファンが訪れる書店「恵文社 一乗寺店」は駅から、すぐ。

雑貨店も併設され、店の裏口から入る「コテージ」では、様々なイベントも開催しているが、魅力は何といっても本だ。広々とした店内に、音楽はかかっているが、何となく静かな雰囲気で、用事がなくても時間をつぶしに、とりとめもなく立ち寄りたくなる書店だ。僕は未だに、アイデアに行き詰まった時や、やる事がなくて暇な時（最近、そういう時間は多くないけど）、何となくやる気が湧かない時（こういう時間は増えていっては困る）は、インターネットで検索、ではなくて、できることなら書店に行きたい、といつも思う。

「恵文社 一乗寺店」は、まさに、そんな理想形の書店だ。

shows. But the main attraction is books. It's the kind of shop where you want to stop by even if you are not looking for anything in particular; just browsing from one shelf to another is enough. Even with music played in the background, the shop is hushed. When I run out of ideas, or when I am bored (though that kind of time is so rare now) or when I don't feel like doing anything, I now know that I shouldn't do search on internet; instead, I should come to bookstores like this. For me, Keibunsha Ichijoji is an ideal and perfect bookstore.

Kyoto, the City
From Demachiyanagi to "Kitano Tenman-gu Shrine", it takes about 15 minutes by bus. I've already written that there's Kobo-ichi on every 21st of the month at To-ji temple, but on every 25th of the month, there's "Tenjin-san", or the flea market at "Kitanotenman-gu Shrine Antique Show".

(→p. 107)

住まば都

出町柳から「北野天満宮」までは、バスで約一五分。今出川通りを西へ直進、御所と同志社大学との間を通って、堀川通り、千本通りを越えて、北野天満宮ロバス停で下車。毎月二一日は東寺の「弘法さん」と先に書いたが、毎月二五日は北野天満宮の「天神さん」こと「北野天満宮御縁日」だ。よく晴れた土曜日だった事もあって、雨の平日だった「弘法市」よりも、さらに凄い人出。北野天満宮は、東寺よりも、「町の中にある」という事が、より強く感じられた。

北野天満宮から近い、七味唐辛子の専門店「長文屋」は、小辛・中辛・辛口・大辛から好みの辛さと量を伝えると、その場でパッパッと手際よく調合してくれる。山椒が苦手なら少なめにもできるし、その逆もできる。保存は冷蔵庫で。コーヒーと同じで、香りが命で鮮度が命。必要な量を小まめに買いに通えるといい。やはり、京都は、「住まば都」だ。

今出川通りから堀川通りを上って北大路通りを左に入ると、千利休と縁が深い「大徳寺」があり、その近くに、「興石・中村外二工務店」がある。市役所前の「俵屋旅館」や、大悲山の「美山荘」などを設計した、数寄屋建築の大家・中村外二（故）の工務店で、施主のためにデザインした家具、世界中から取り寄せた家具等を、広く一般の人も見て購入する事ができるショールームになっている。建物の奥に指物師の工房があって、そこでデザインされ、制作される照明器具は、実に精巧なつくりで美しく、そして、それが「照明器具である事」を忘れさせるような自然さを感じさせる逸品だ。

大徳寺から千本通りを上っていくと、琳派の祖・本阿弥光悦が芸術村を築いたとされる鷹ヶ峰に着く。バスは「源光庵前」で降りる。「源光庵」は非常に美しい寺だが、本堂の天井は伏見桃山城の遺構で、落城の凄惨さを伝える

which was taken from the former Fushimi Momoyama Castle which was destroyed in a battle. In the right hand wall of the main building, there are round and odd-shaped windows. I knew that one of them was called "the Window of Confusion" and another "the Window of Enlightenment" but I made a mistake. I kept staring out of what I thought was the "Window of Enlightenment", but in reality was "the Window of Confusion". I simply liked the view but maybe it was not coincidence but synchronicity. "Koetsu-ji Temple", just a few minute walk from Genko-an Temple, is the former house that belonged to Koetsu that was converted to a temple after his death. From here, the city was so far away, and the view of three mountains gave me a sense of contentment. Koetsu must have spent his life here with people he loved, full of inspirations, and died here happily. Even his grave was beautiful.

血天井がある。本堂の正面右の壁面には、正円の窓と、矩形の窓が、二つ並んでいる。どちらかが「迷いの窓」で、どちらかが「悟りの窓」、と呼ばれている事は知っていたが、僕は「悟りの窓」だと思い込んで、「迷いの窓」のほうを、じーっと見つめてしまっていた。「迷いの窓」から眺めた景色のほうが好きだった、というだけなのだが、何となく、心を見透かされたような気がした。そこから歩いてすぐの「光悦寺」は、光悦が住んでいた屋敷の跡地を、没後に寺としたもの。芸術村は遺らなかったが、京都市市街地は、はるか遠くにあり、モコモコモコと三つ連なる山の景色は、僕の気分を軽やかにしてくれた。光悦は、ここで伸び伸びと、気の知れた仲間たちと、清廉な気持ちで、創作に没頭し、生涯を終えたのだろう。光悦の墓は、とても美しかった。

There's "Chobunya" which sells mixed spice near Kitano Tenman-gu Shrine. They will mix the spices according to your preference in front of you; they can also change the quantity of each spice as well. Be sure to refrigerate the spices; like coffee, freshness is important. Best way to shop here is to buy in small quantity, but you can only do that if you live in this city.

Go north on Horikawa Street and turn left at Kitaoji Street. You will find "KOHSEKI", a carpenter and furniture shop and studio led by Sotoji Nakamura who designed several beautiful and classical buildings in Kyoto. He is most known for designing traditional Japanese homes. In the shop, you can buy lighting fixtures and furniture he designed for people. The studio in the back is where these lightings get designed and produced. You will be amazed by their beauty.

If you go up Senbon Street, you will reach Takagamine, a former artist colony founded by Koetsu Honami. The bus stop is Genkoan-mae. "Genko-an Temple" is a beautiful temple but you can see its bloody past on the blood-splattered ceiling

ガイセ キキさん（丸久小山園）

Photo: Mai Narita
Hair Styling: Yoshihiro Mitsumori（OTAKU PROJECT）
Make-up: TOMATO（OTAKU PROJECT）
Special Thanks to: Marukyu Koyamaen Makishima Factory

※このページは2015年発刊当時に取材・撮影したもので、現在は茶道家
として活動しており、丸久小山園のアドバイザーも務めています。

京都府の本

"やけに本が多い、お土産もの屋"と称し、京都を題材にした本の編集もする「ホホホ座」。座長の山下賢二さんが選んだ、"京都らしさを感じる"4冊。

ホホホ座 浄土店
京都府京都市左京区浄土寺馬場町71
ハイネストビル1階
075-741-6501（1階、書籍・雑貨）
hohohoza.com

1. 映画館
中馬聰 著
三九五八円（リトルモア）

日本全国で数が少なくなってきている、単館映画館をモノクロ撮影した写真集。客席はもちろん、映写室から売店や廊下、看板まで、まるで昭和の時代に撮影されたかのような錯覚を起こさせる。著者も映写技師として、映画館で働いていたという。京都の現存している映画館も写っている。シネコンの健康的な雰囲気と違い、妖しげな暗闇に潜り込むような感覚は、これからの時代も、僕は必要だと思う。

2. わたしがカフェをはじめた日。
ホホホ座 著
一三七五円（小学館）

京都には、たくさんのカフェがあって、女性が一人で切り盛りしている店も、他の地方都市に比べれば多い。この本は、そんな女性店主たちに、その開業までの物語を聞き書きした本だ。『理想の暮らし』を切り売りした本が溢れる昨今、その理想に映るライフスタイルの裏側には、誠実な紆余曲折が存在するのだということを、七組の女性たちの群像劇として紹介。

3. 京都の市電 昭和を歩く 街と人と電車と
福田静二 著
一六五〇円（トンボ出版）

かつて京都の町中のそこかしこに、路面電車が走っていたのをご存じだろうか？僕が子供の頃は、まだ車が、ガンガン走っていた。僕の家の前の大通りの中央分離帯あたりに停留所があって、親に手を引かれながら、線路の上を歩いて渡るのは、なかなかスリリングだった。この写真集には、道のど真ん中を、車を押しのけて走る、優雅で嘘みたいな世界が収められている。

4. 京都の音楽家案内
山下賢二 著
六三〇円（ガケ書房）

京都では、毎日どこかのカフェやライブハウスで、音楽家たちが演奏している。かつて「ガケ書房」という本屋があって、そこでも、たくさんの音楽家たちが、自分の音を鳴らした。店主であった僕が、創業時から関わってきた、京都発の音楽家たちのエピソードをまとめたミニエッセイ集。ちなみに、ここに登場する音楽家たち全員が、「ガケ書房」最終日に、店内で順番に歌ってくださった。感謝。

Books of Kyoto

Kenji Yamashita, a leader of HOHOHOZA which edits and publishes books about Kyoto, selected four books that best capture the essence of Kyoto:

1. *Eigakan* (Movie Theaters) By Satoshi Chuma ¥3,958 (Little More)

2. *Watashi ga Café wo Hajimeta Hi* (The Day I Opened a Café) By HOHOHOZA ¥1,375 (Shogakukan)

3. *Kyoto no Shiden Showa wo Aruku Machi to Hito to Densha* (Kyoto City Rails: The Journey through Showa—City, People and Trains) By Seiji Fukuda ¥1,650 (Tonbo Shuppan)

4. *Kyoto no Ongakuka Annai* (A Guide to Composers in Kyoto) By Kenji Yamashita ¥630 (Gake Shobo)

URBAN RESEARCH
DOORS

京都府のCD

ホホホ座　浄土店
📍京都府京都市左京区浄土寺馬場町71
ハイネストビル1階
☎075-741-6501（1階、書籍・雑貨）
🏠 http://hohohoza.com

「ホホホ座」のスタッフであり、五条楽園にある、改築した5店舗が入る「五条モール」内の、本と紙の店「homehome」も運営する、うめのたかし氏がセレクトした"京都らしいCD"。

1.
イキテル・ソング
～オールタイム・ベスト～
高田渡

日本フォーク界伝説シンガーの高田渡は二〇歳の頃、京都に在住。今年は、没後一〇年。それを記念したベスト盤だ。亡くなる直前、京都ヘライブに来ていた渡さんに、ライブ交渉をした。「僕は難しいよ」と渡さんは答えた。同時発売の本『マイ・フレンド 高田渡青春日記1966—1969』（河出書房新社）を読んだ後は、コーヒーを飲みに、「三条へいかなくちゃ」。

💰二七五〇円（KING RECORDS）

2.
ドキソワーズ
安藤明子

故・高田渡は京都・河原町通三条にある喫茶店「六曜社」へ通っていたという。ここの地下店マスターのオクノ修はフォークシンガーでもあるのだが、ここで働く"六曜ガール"の安藤明子も、また歌いたい、である。ほんわか切ない言葉と歌声に、僕らはドキドキしてソワソワし、恋をする。ミュージシャンの小西康陽やバンヒロシらもまた、彼女の音楽に恋をした。ド、ド、ドキソワーズ！

💰二四二〇円（SOFTTOUCH RECORDS）

3.
さみしいだけ
前野健太

東京を拠点に活躍するシンガーソングライターの前野健太がブレイク前深夜バスで京都・紫野にある[SOLE CAFE]へライブへ来た時鴨川で生まれた名曲が、二曲目の「鴨川」だ。そこに歌があった、とマエケンはよく語っているが、登場の大学生達がライブに行くとしたら、それは歌とギターの不定形ユニット「ラヴラヴパーク」のような音楽だと思う。本作は「くるり」のファンファンも参加の、愉快に、体が心が、踊りだす八重奏。

💰二〇九四円（romance records）

4.
ラヴラヴスパーク
サンキュー

京都は、学生の街だ。それ故、何もかも許されるような、ゆるい空気がある。柴崎友香原作の京都が舞台の映画『きょうのできごと』は、そんな雰囲気を、よく物語っている。この場のような音楽だと思う。"太古から流れ続けている歌"がある。

💰二〇〇〇円（39レコード）

CDs of Kyoto

Takashi Umeno, the manager of homehome, a stationary-and-book shop in Gojorakuen, and also a staff at HOHOHOZA , selected CDs that best embodied the spirit of Kyoto for us:

1. Ikiteru Song – All Time Best　Wataru Takada　¥2,750 (King Records)

2. dokisoise　Akiko Ando　¥2,420 (SOFTTOUCH RECORDS)

3. Samishiidake　Kenta Maeno　¥2,094 (romance records)

4. Love Love Spark　Thank you　¥2,000 (39 records)

© KADOKAWA

ガメラ3 邪神〈イリス〉覚醒

松本伸哉(しんや)(ホホホ座)

Shinya Matsumoto (HOHOHOZA)

『ガメラ3 邪神(じゃしん)〈イリス〉覚醒(かくせい)』
1999年／103分／東宝
監督：金子修介(本編)、樋口真嗣(ひぐちしんじ)(特技)
脚本：伊藤和典、金子修介
出演：中山 忍、前田 愛、藤谷文子、山咲千里、
　　　手塚とおる、小山 優、他
DVD／Blu-ray 発売中 発売元・販売元 (株)KADOKAWA

debate among people, but I am not sure what the right answer is—to keep or to renovate old buildings. I would imagine that the Gojunoto (five storied pagoda) in To-ji temple probably caused quite a stir when it was first built, because of its unconventional shape. Every time I think about these things, I think of *Gamera*, the movie.

Gamera 3: Iris Awakens

1993 / 103 min / Toho
Director: Shusuke Kaneko, Shinji Higuchi (Special Affect)
Screenplay: Kazunori Ito, Shusuke Kaneko
Actors: Shinobu Nakayama, Ai Maeda, Ayako Fujitani, Senri Yamazaki, Toru Tezuka, Masaru Koyama

一九九七年、新しくなった「京都駅ビル」の評価は大きく分かれ、暗く、無機質な姿を「墓石」と喩える者もいた。そして、その完成から二年後に公開された本作で、京都駅は、廃墟と化した。京都駅構内が舞台の、ガメラ対イリスの最終決戦。ガメラ起死回生の一撃で、イリスは爆発し、「京都駅ビル」も全壊。ガメラから放たれた火球は市街地を直撃し、一帯を火の海と化した。三部作からなる平成版のガメラは、地球の守護神として登場する。子供を助けるようなシーンもあるが、自らの繁栄のために地球環境を破壊する人類を、ガメラは味方と見なしていない。寺院などを建造し、タテヨコ都合よく道路を造り、山に火を放ち「大」の文字で夜空を焦がす。約一二〇〇年にわたり築かれた「京都の文化」も、ガメラにとっては、守るべき対象ではなかったのだろう。

現実の京都では、価値ある遺産も、さまざまな理由によって失われ、新しく変わって行く事も多い。時に、それは、揉め事に発展もするが、正解はない、と思う。東寺の五重塔でさえ、完成当時は、異質な物だったのだろう。そんな思いにとらわれた時、私はいつも、この映画の事が頭に浮かぶ。

京都府を舞台にした、主な映画
『羅生門』監督：黒澤 明（一九五〇年）／『御法度』監督：大島 渚（一九九九年）／『パッチギ！』監督：井筒和幸（二〇〇四年）／『オリヲン座からの招待状』監督：三枝健起（二〇〇七年）／『マザーウォーター』監督：松本佳奈（二〇一〇年）／『堀川中立売』監督：柴田 剛（二〇一〇年）

Movies Set in Kyoto

Gamera 3: Iris Awakens

People are divided in their opinions about Kyoto Station Building, which was built in 1997. Some have even described it as a tombstone because of its dark and sterile façade. Two years after it was built, this building lay in complete ruins in *Gamera 3* after the last battle between Gamera and Iris, which took place inside Kyoto Station. Gamera, in the last offensive, shot a fireball at Iris, blowing it up and with it, Kyoto Station Building. The fireball shot by Gamera set the entire city ablaze. Gamera, who stars in this series, appears as the protector of Earth. There are scenes where he helps children, but he is unforgiving toward humanity, which destroys nature for the sake of financial prosperity. For Gamera, Kyoto is full of temples, shrines, and grid-shaped streets that are not worth protecting.

In Kyoto today, many old buildings have been torn down for one reason or another. In some cases, this has caused fierce

113

京都府の、ロングライフデザインの産地を巡る旅

野口忠典
Tadanori Noguchi

嵐山にある京座布団の店「プラッツ」は、一八九四（明治二七）年に、京都市上京区の西陣で「加藤ふとん店」として創業し、製綿から、布団の製造、卸、小売りまで手がけていた。数年ぶりに代表の加藤就一さんにお会いして、工場で、小座布団の工程を見せてもらった。一つの小座布団に必要な綿の量は六〇〇グラム。綿は手作業で詰め込んでいく。手の感覚を頼りに、綿を四隅に詰め、荷重のかかる所を厚く、盛り上がるように仕上げていく。その日の綿の質や繊細さや、その日の湿度などを考慮して、手作業による微妙な調整が必要になる。だが、機械だと、綿を均等に入れるだけの座布団になってしまい、真ん中からへたっていく。だが、「プラッツ」は、世界遺産でもある嵐山の名刹「天龍寺」をはじめ、寺院や料亭など、府内一〇〇軒以上の座布団を、それぞれの要望のサイズで納めていて、今日まで、ずっと手作業で作り続けている。

西陣の「かみ添」の入り口の扉には、鋭い緊張感が感じられた。「かみ添」は、「型押し」という、すべて手摺りで行う、古くからある印刷技術で、紋様を紙に写し、襖紙や便箋、封筒などを手がけている。「かみ添」の嘉戸浩さ

I became nervous at the entrance of Kamisoe, the paper studio, into the Nishijin neighborhood. It prints crests, using an embossing technique, onto papers and stationery. Ko Kado told me that by embossing crests onto paper, what was once a flat surface becomes three dimensional, and it turns into an object that can change the interior space. He also told me of an elementary-school-aged girl who came to the shop to ask for some nice stationery to write a letter for her mother for Mother's Day. I was touched by his desire to create papers for special occasions that best express people's feelings. Maybe I became nervous because I could feel this passion.

I always thought *kyoyaki* pottery to be something that was beyond my reach, but at Tosai, every piece of pottery had a little note next to it saying, "Please feel free to touch the pottery." I interviewed Yoshio Yamada (the Second Tosai Yamada), the owner. Tosai creates and sells *kyoyaki* pottery. After designing the piece, the clay is mixed by one artisan, then, depending on the shape, each piece is handmade by a specialist, and there is a painter who draws the design. Tosai studio is responsible for the final coloring. Each step of the process is highly (→p. 116)

んは、紙に紋様を刷る事で、紙という平面が、襖となって立ち上がり、空間を構成する物へと、形と意義を変えていく、それが面白いと話してくれた。また、小学生の女の子が、母の日に、いい紙で母親に手紙を書きたいから、とお店に来てくれた事があると嘉戸さんから伺った。いつもより、ぐっと気持ちを込めたい時に、その気持ちに添えられる物として、選んでもらう物でありたいという、屋号に込めた嘉戸さんの想いが伝わっている事に、私は感動した。扉を開ける前の緊張感は、その強い想いから生まれているのかもしれない。

「京焼」の老舗「東哉」。「京焼」というと、私は、敷居が高い印象を持っていたのだが、店内に並べられた器の横には「お手に取って、ご覧ください」と書かれた短冊が添えてあった。当代の山田悦央（二代目 山田東哉）さんに、お話を伺った。「東哉」は、「京焼」の制作、小売り・販売をしている工房。企画した物を、職人に依頼して生地をつくってもらい、皿物、袋物（徳利や花器）、盃など、それぞれに専門の生地職人がいて、絵付けには、下絵専門の絵付け職人がいて、「東哉」では、上絵付けを専門に行っている。かなり細分化され、洗練された

A pilgrimage tour of Kyoto Prefecture's long-lasting designs

NIPPON VISION

Ever since Platz opened its door in 1894 in Kamigyo-ku, Kyoto, as the Kato Futon Shop, it has been involved with the whole procedure of making futons: from wadding cotton to making the futon cover to selling it. I met with Shuichi Kato, the president, who showed me the futon-making process at the factory. It takes 600g to make a small *zabuton* (floor cushion). Cotton is stuffed into the cover by hand. Workers have been doing this for a long time: relying only on their experience, they stuff the cotton to the four corners, thicken the area that will take the most weight, and fluff them. Depending on the quality of the cotton, as well as the humidity of that day, they have to readjust the cotton slightly. You might imagine that with machines, the cotton is stuffed evenly, but it inevitably flattens in the middle. Platz has made cushions for Tenryu-ji, the world-heritage temple, as well as nearly 100 customers, including renowned temples and restaurants, making cushions by hand according to the specifications of each customer.

専門職である。驚いたのは、個人客からの、「この器の形で、あの器の紋様を入れてほしい」「もう少しサイズを小さめに」などといった要望にも応えてくれるという事。「あくまで、作品ではなく商品である」という、「東哉」の、ものづくりの姿勢は「京焼」を身近な物として感じつさせてくれる。器をつくるのに、一日で幾つつくれるか、上絵付けに金などをどのくらい使うかを計上し、そこに職人の創意工夫まで付加した価値を、きちんと商品の値段に反映させる。あくまで、美術品ではなく、日々、使う器としての価格の付け方だ。

今回訪れた場所は、いずれも、神社・仏閣や料亭、そして、個人の要望に応える事で、技術を受け継ぎ続けている。別注や誂えに対応する事は、機械ではできない技術であり、その需要が多いのも京都ならでは、だ。職人を守り育てるためには、それぞれ専業で行われる個々の仕事に敬意を表して、協業し、一つの物をつくり上げる。他の産地とは異なる、独特の世界観が生まれ、産地としての京都に興味を惹かれるのだ。何より「ほんまもん」をつくる人たちに出会えた事が、私は嬉しかった。

specialized. What surprised me most was that customers can request changes if they want a particular piece of pottery with the design from another piece, or if they want a different size. Tosai believes that what it sells is not works of art but products, which makes *kyoyaki* more accessible to us. The staff members think carefully about how many pieces they can make each day and how much it might cost to make it, while at the same time adding originality to each piece; all of this is rightly reflected in the price. These are not museum pieces; they are priced with the knowledge that the pieces will be used every day.

Each place I went this time worked with shrines and temples, as well as restaurants and individual customers, to keep their traditional crafts going. Machines sometimes cannot be used to create custom work. Of course, they can keep their businesses running because of Kyoto, where there is demand from customers, and because the city fosters the tradition of protecting and nurturing its artisans by revering each step of the process and cooperating with each other to create one thing. Kyoto is like no other place in Japan when it comes to production. This is where *honmamon*—authentic people and objects—can thrive and flourish.

プラッツ　小座布団むら糸
上・う金色　中・麻紫　下・木賊
42 × 45 cm　各4,950円
Platz　Small cushion Muraito
Top: Ukon（turmeric）color
Middle: Asamurasaki（hemp-purple）
Bottom: Tokusa（scouring rush）color
¥4,950 each

東哉　皿 染付 線・梅
左・4寸 3,300円　中・5寸 4,950円
右・6寸 6,600円
Tosai Blue and white ceramic dish, Ume drawing
Left: 12 cm ¥3,300
Center: 15 cm ¥4,950
Right: 18 cm ¥6,600

お問い合わせ
d47 design travel store
☎03-6427-2301

Yuki Aima
相馬夕輝

京都定食

何度も通いたくなるのは"京じゃない暮らし"の見える京都

京都市には、卵や餡をかけた料理が多い。京都の伝統野菜である九条ネギと、お揚げさん(油揚げ)を卵でとじた「衣笠丼」や、ピリッと生姜が効いた卵と餡を絡めた「鶏卵うどん」、椎茸や蒲鉾など具沢山うどんにドバッと餡かけした「のっぺいうどん」。卵や餡を使った、これらの料理は、どこか中華風で、僕は、それが気になって、「鳳飛」「芙蓉園」「平安」など、"京都風とされる中華料理店"を数軒、食べ巡った。「パリッ」でも「サクッ」でもない独特の食感の皮(卵が使われているらしい)の「春巻」や、辛子が麺に和えられた餡かけの「からしそば」など、あっさり味で、これまで味わった事がない、和食のような、とても美味しい中華料理だった。

中でも「芙蓉園」の、玉葱とかしわ(鶏肉)に、とろとろ卵の入った餡かけ「鳳凰蛋」は、ふわふわとした食感の卵と、きれいな金色の餡が、ほんのり甘く、ひと口食べると、何とも懐かしい味わい。その味が忘れられず、連日通い、『鳳凰蛋』を、ご飯にかけて、丼にして食べてみたいんですが」と、女将さんにお願いしてみると、

sweet memory of childhood went through my mind. I could not forget the taste, so I went back to the restaurant ever day; one day, I asked for the same dish, but over rice, and the chef happily obliged my request. Egg and thick starch sauce must be what Kyoto people have been eating for generations, a necessary dish not found in any guidebooks.

I went to taste Fucha cuisine at a temple in Uji. Fucha means, "to eat and drink tea with many," and just like its meaning, the cuisine involves the eaters sharing food out of a big plate. What used to be a monastery food from China became Kyoto cuisine, which then spread all over the country. Many Kyoto dishes made at home were originally taught by monks, so you can see how involved and familiar Buddhist temples have been in everyday life of Kyoto.

I then went to Iio jozo, a vinegar brewery, in Miyazu-shi, by the Sea of Japan. The best-known label from this brewery is Fujizu. The company works with the local rice producers to grow organic rice, which it distills to sake then ferments to make into vinegar. The rice is bought above the market price from the farmers while offering training and new equipment to them, protecting their livelihood.

Shibakyu, a pickle shop, grows its own shiso, (→p. 122)

「それは時々、この店の、まかない飯で、山椒を振って食べるのよ」と快諾してくださり、やはり美味しく、常連気分で平らげた。「卵に餡かけ」は、京都の人達の胃袋を支えてきた、不可欠の料理の一つなのかもしれない。

宇治市の、ある寺へ、「普茶料理」を食べに行った。「普茶」とは「普く大衆と茶を共にする」という意味があり、大皿料理を皆で囲んで、それを箸で突き合い、和気藹々で食べる物。開祖の隠元禅師が日本に伝えた食材には、さやいんげん、西瓜、蓮根、孟宗竹（筍）などがあり、どれも日本の季節を感じさせる食材だ。中国の精進料理から影響を受けた料理が「和食」として、京都から全国に広まった。「おばんざい（お惣菜）」も、お坊さんが教えた料理が家庭料理になった物が多いというから、京都の暮らしには、昔から、お寺は身近な存在だったのだろう。

日本海に面する宮津市の「飯尾醸造」へ。ここは酢の醸造元で、代表銘柄は「富士酢」。地元農家の棚田に、無農薬の米づくりを依頼し、その米から酒を造り、さらに発酵させて酢を造っている。景観保全のために自社でも米づくりに取り組む。できた米は、市価よりも高い値段で買い取る。また、有効な技術指導や、最新

Kyoto's "Home Grown" Meal

Going Back Again and Again to Restaurants that Serve Unstereotypical Kyoto Local Dishes

In Kyoto, there are quite a few dishes that serve eggs and thick starch sauce. There is Kinugasa-don, Kujo green onion and fried tofu cooked with eggs; Keiran Udon, a noodle dish with raw ginger cooked with eggs and thick starch sauce; or Noppei Udon, shiitake mushrooms and other ingredients cooked in thick starch sauce over noodles. For me, dishes that use eggs and thick starch sauce remind me of Chinese food. I began to wonder whether there was any connection, so I stopped by several Kyoto-influenced Chinese restaurants in the city, such as Houhi, Fuyouen, and Heian. They had spring rolls that used a unique textured skin (which may use eggs) or Karashi-soba, a mustard noodle dish that had mustard on the side of the thick starch sauce noodle dish. All of them were quite simple in flavor, like no other Chinese food I have ever tasted.

My favorite was a Hououtan dish served at Fuyouen, a dish of onion and chicken cooked with egg and thick starch sauce; the egg was so airy, and the sauce amber colored. One bite and a

※左横から、時計回りに

【柴漬け】
「志ば久」の茄子の柴漬けと、らっきょうの紫蘇巻き。

【さやいんげんのゴマ和え】
今となっては誰もが和食だと思っている、普茶料理が起源の、おばんざい。

【酢ばす】
「富士酢」を使った蓮根（蓮）の甘酢漬け。

【寿免（唐揚げ汁）】
普茶料理の一つで、豆腐の唐揚げを浮かべた澄まし汁。

【かしわ（鶏肉）入り餡かけ卵焼き丼】
かしわと、とろとろ卵を使った、中華料理店まかない飯の親子丼。

料理　岡竹義弘（d47食堂）
写真　安永ケンタウロス

鋭の機器の導入などを、経費や時間を惜しまず自社で取り組む事で、農家の方々の暮らしも守ろうとする徹底ぶりに、僕は深く感銘した。大原三千院の参道沿いにある「志ば漬（柴漬け）」の命である紫蘇を、毎年、自家採種して栽培している。紫蘇を自分達で栽培するから、たっぷりと「志ば漬」に仕込む事ができる、四代目の久保統さんは言う。昔ながらの製造方法を守り、大原の環境と伝統を深く理解して、生業にして暮らしている生産者達。誰がつくっているのか、その顔が見える事は、こんなにも落ち着ける事なのだ、と改めて感じさせてくれた。

旬の食材を、蒸したり、和えたり、漬け込んだりと、四季折々の野菜を使った暮らしが、京都には、とうの昔からあったのだ。「京」といえば、これ！という料理の数々より、むしろ、卵と餡かけにこそ、今に続く京都の暮らしを感じることが、僕にはできた。ふわふわの卵、たっぷりの餡かけ――食べなきゃ、暮らさなきゃ、通わなきゃ、それらの大事な中身を見せてはもらえない。通い詰めると、ほんの少しだけ見えてくる。それが、"京じゃない京都"の魅力で、「京の定食」じゃない、「京都の定食」だ。

Japanese basil, which is the main ingredient for Shibazuke, the shop's flagship organic pickles. While the company has been carrying on the traditional pickling process, it has also been living in harmony with the environment and the traditions of Ohara neighborhood. Kyoto has a long tradition of preparing dishes using only seasonal vegetables. For me, this trip was not about eating familiar Kyoto dishes, but eating egg and thick starch sauce dishes that have been supporting the lives of Kyoto residents quietly. This, for me, is true Kyoto cuisine, which makes great Kyoto teishoku.

Photo, clockwise from the left side:
Shibazuke: Salt-pickled eggplants with red perilla and pickled scallion wrapped with Japanese basil from Shibakyu; String beans marinated with sesame: A dish that people think is Japanese food, but which has its origin in Fucha cuisine; Subasu: Lotus pickled in Fujizu; Sume (Fried tofu soup): A Fucha cuisine—clear soup with fried tofu; Rice bowl with eggs and Kashiwa (chicken) cooked in thick starch sauce: Off-the-menu chicken-and-egg rice bowl served only to staff in Chinese restaurants

編集長が、車で行く

空閑トラベル **III**

宇治、嵐山、美山、そして日本海へ

Osamu Kuga

空閑 理

Kuga Travel 3: Editor's travel notes

京都府南部へ。酒の伏見区、茶の宇治市

「その土地らしさ」をモットーとする本誌の取材では、お酒といえば地酒、地酒といえば日本酒、となる事が多いわけだが、実は、僕はウイスキーが好きである。そして、京都といえば、そう「山崎」がある！と思って、大阪府との境の、ギリギリ向こう、大阪側に位置している事を知り、残念ながら本誌「京都府号」の取材対象にはできず、近くの「アサヒビール大山崎山荘美術館」（こちらはギリギリ京都府）へ。大阪と京都を繋ぐ水陸の要所で、羽柴秀吉が明智光秀を破った「山崎の合戦」の舞台でもある天王山の登山口から坂道を上がっていく。「サル出没注意」という看板が、いくつも続いた後に、「秀吉の道」という説明板があったが——意図しない事だろう、たぶん。美術館はその先にあり、本館の二階はカフェになっていて、ビールを飲める。テラスからの眺めは素晴らしくて、宇治川、木津川、桂川が眼下に見える。

その下流で合流して、淀川と名前が変わり、大阪へ、海へと流れてゆく。

山崎から、日本酒「月桂冠」「黄桜」で有名な酒処の伏見は、車で東へ走って約二〇分。伏見を歩いていて興味深いのは、内陸である、この土地が、鴨川、宇治川、木津川、桂川の水運が発達していたため、古くは「港町」「京の南の玄関口」として紹介されている事。大きな蔵が建ち、それらの杉板の壁と漆喰壁のコントラストが美しい街並みで、「月桂冠大倉記念館」には歴史展示室があり、「黄桜カッパカントリー」には、そこの限定酒が飲めるレストランなどがある。その近くに「ブルーノ」などの自転車や自転車用品の、輸入・製造・卸を手がける「ダイヤテックプロダクツ」の本社がある。その建物は、元は

To the southern Kyoto: Fushimi and sake, Uji and tea

I am a whiskey lover. And when I remember that Yamazaki is in Kyoto, I headed toward "Suntory Yamazaki Distillery", only to see that it was across the border in Osaka. So instead, I went to "Asahi Beer Oyamazaki Villa Museum of Art", which was on this side of the border. The view from the terrace was beautiful—I could see Uji River, Kizu River, and Katsura River below me.

From Yamazaki, it's nearly 20 minutes by driving to get to Fushimi, known for sake companies like "Gekkeikan" and "Kizakura". "Gekkeikan Okura Sake Museum" has an archive, and "Kizakura Kappa Country" has a restaurant which sells limited edition alcohol.

Nearby, there's the headquarter of "Diatech Products", an import and production company of bicycles such as Bruno as well as bicycle goods. The building used to be a traditional Japanese house that a sake master used to live and had, for some years, lay in ruin but now is converted to an (→p. 129)

127

酒樽職人が住んでいた古民家で、廃墟だったが、見事に改築してオフィスに。土間の奥は庭に通じていて、自転車を整備できるように道具が揃っていた。「藤岡酒造」には、貯蔵タンクをガラス越しに見える「酒蔵Barえん」が併設されていてユニーク。代表銘柄「蒼空」が美味しい。

伏見から宇治へ。京都市出身の建築家・若林広幸氏設計の宇治駅から、激流の宇治川沿いにある「朝日焼 作陶館」で陶芸体験。型を使った初心者向けのコースで、他の人達はキレイな器をスイスイと完成させていったが、僕は、自分でも唖然とするほど不器用で、先生の四元由佳さんに手とり足とり教えてもらって、やっとの思いで体験を終えると、他の人達は、「平等院」の博物館を見学して、帰りに抹茶のソフトクリームを食べて、すでに戻って

are considered "gods"; he pointed out all four "gods" as we passed them.

Miyama: the Land of Folktales

I rented a car from "Orix Rent a Car Shijo Nishino-toin" and drove for an hour and half to Miyama. But I stopped by Ayabe on the way to Miyama because it's the home of "GUNZE", a textile company founded in 1986. "GUNZE Museum" is closed on Tuesday and "GUNZE Memorial Hall", an archive, is open only on Friday.

I ate lunch at "Takematsu Udon-ten" (¥450). Every time a new order comes in, they make a new udon noodle from scratch. It seems that people order two bowls on average. People come from all over Japan to sample the udon.

The iconic tourist spot in Miyama must be "Kayabuki no Sato", a neighborhood composed only of thatched roof houses. There are, in total, 38 thatched roof houses. There are archives and inns, restaurants and souvenir shops in these (→p.130)

やっぱり凄い、嵐山

きていた。一か月半後、焼き上がった物が自宅に届いたが、素敵に仕上がっていました。家で毎日使っています。四元さん、ありがとうございました。

宇治といえば銘茶で有名だが、宇治から、さらに車で三〇分走った和束町まで足を延ばしてほしい。これぞ「茶の里」という、斜面に茶畑の段々が広がる、本当に美しい景色を見る事ができる。

五月に入り、世間はゴールデンウイーク。そのまっただ中、しかも絶好の天候の下、嵐山に出かけると、覚悟はしていたものの、本誌取材史上最高の人出だった。ギッシリとバスと乗用車と人力車が犇めく渡月橋を徒歩で渡る。左手には美しい岩田山、キラキラと輝く桂川には無数のボートが浮かんでいる。右手には遠く如意ヶ岳の大文字山まで見えた。天龍寺を過ぎ、嵐電嵐山駅を過ぎた先で左に折れると、有名な「竹林の小径」への入り口。

「竹林は見るものじゃない。浴びるものだ！」とガイドしてくれるのは、もちろん、嵐山で人力車を曳いていた小原龍樹さん。竹林を抜けて、トロッコ嵐山駅を過ぎると人もまばらになっていき、ここら辺りから奥は、俥夫に連れてきてもらわないと、なかなか、わからない嵐山の隠れ処的スポットだそうで、JRのテレビCM「そうだ 京都、行こう。」のロケ地・常寂光寺や、落柿舎（元禄の俳人・向井去来の家）などがある。ちなみに、小原さんによると、嵐山の人力車の俥夫には、脚力、話術、知識、すべてに卓越した"四天王"がいるそうで、小原さんが「あ！ ほら！ あそこに！」と、見つけて教えてくれるので、僕は四人とも、お目にかかる事ができた。

office space.

At "Fujioka Shuzo", you can watch the distillery tanks from the bar called "Sakagura Bar En".

From Fushimi to Uji. I spent some hours at "Asahiyaki Sakutokan" a pottery studio along Uji River making pottery. Other beginners, using molds, made beautiful pottery but I'm all thumbs: Yuka Yotsumoto, the pottery master, had to help me every step of the way. A month and half later, my ware arrived; thanks to you, Yuka, I am using it every day.

Arashiyama: Of course, speechless

One day I went to Arashiyama on a beautiful day, and walked on Togetsukyo congested with cars and rickshaws. Once passed Tenryu-ji temple and Arashiyama Station, I turned left to face the famous bamboo forest. Ryuki Obara, former rickshaw driver, told me, "You don't go into bamboo forest just to see it, you have to experience it with your senses." According to Obara, there are drivers who have excellent strength, conversation skill, and knowledge of the area who

今は昔。美山へ

四条西洞院の「オリックスレンタカー」※を出発して五条通りを西へ直進、沓掛インターから京都縦貫自動車道を通って、約一時間の美山町へ向かう。

その途中、綾部市へ。一八九六年創業の繊維メーカー「グンゼ」の創業の地。その経営姿勢を知れる「グンゼ博物苑」は火曜定休で、「グンゼ記念館」は金曜日のみ開館。当時の本社事務所や蔵などを改築して資料館にしている。隣接する「あやべ物産館」で、綾部で製造される「アカツキ製作所 KOD」の水平器を売っていて、シンプルだが、用途に合わせて、実に多種多様、使う予定もなかったが、思わず買ってしまったほど魅力的。

ランチは「竹松うどん店」。注文毎に手打ちの、コシの強いうどんは一杯四五〇円から。皆、だいたい二玉ずつ食べるみたいだ。遠方から、この店を目当てに来る人も多いそう。美味しいし、空気も気持ちがいいから。

美山町は、京都市街地より二、三週間ほど遅れて桜が見頃を迎え、僕が訪れた時は満開で、密集して咲くのではなく、若葉をつけた新緑の広葉樹林の中、ところどころに、淡い桜色が見え、それらの近くには茅葺き屋根の民家が建ち、幻想的で、うっとりするほど美しかった。

美山観光のド定番は、茅葺き屋根の民家が建ち並ぶ集落「かやぶきの里」。三八棟が茅葺き屋根で、一九九三年に「重要伝統的建造物群 保存地区」に選定された。資料館や民宿、食堂や土産物店などがあり、民家はほとんど現役で、今も人が暮らしている。お伽話の世界のような風景で、集落のすぐ裏には低い山があり、きっと、その森の中には、鹿がいて、猿がいて、貂がいて、狸も猪も熊もいるだろう。高畑勲監督の映画『かぐや姫の物語』の、主人公の姫が生まれ育った場所に、そっくりだ。日本最古の物語とさ

※現在閉業

houses, and people are still living them. In the mountain behind the hamlet, there must be deer and monkeys and boars and raccoons, it's almost like a scene out of a folktale. It looks exactly like the setting of "The Tale of The Princess Kaguya" directed by Director Isao Takahata. There are many fairy tales and folk tales like "The Tale of Bamboo Cutter", the oldest fairy tale in Japan, which originated in Kyoto.

Ten minutes by car from Kayabuki no Sato, I came across "Tautasha", a proud carrier of *d mark*, thirty minutes from

Tautasha is "Ashiu Research Forest", an affiliate of Kyoto University. Yoshida from Tautasha took me into the forest. We crossed the stream, down the valley, and when it started raining, we pitched a tent and had our lunch. We made miso soup there and ate food made out of ingredients made at Tautasha including rice, miso, deer meat, and pickles (except, of course, the seaweeds wrapped around the rice ball).

(→p. 133)

131

れている『竹取物語』のように、長く語り続けられている昔話や、お伽話には、京都で創作された物が多い。都から離れ、権威からも、四神からも逃れた、この美山のような環境に、昔の都人も、今の僕達も、同じように、美と自由を見出して、憧れるのだ。

「かやぶきの里」から一〇分ほど車で走るとdマーク記事の「田歌舎」で、「田歌舎」から、さらに三〇分ほどで、京都大学付属「芦生研究林」がある。「田歌舎」の吉田佑介さんにガイドしてもらって、森の中に入ってすぐ、白骨化した鹿が、道の真ん中に横たわっていた。吉田さんによると、冬の間に自然死したのだろうという事で、きれいに他の動物に食べられていた。沢を渡って、峠を越えて、雨が降ってきたところで、テントを張ってランチにした。味噌汁はその場でつくって、お弁当を食べた。米も味噌も鹿肉も漬け物も、おにぎりの海苔以外は全部、「田歌舎」でつくっている。参加者の希望や体力に合わせて、限りなく自由に歩かせてくれ、ありのままに、自然を体験させてくれた。

海へ。宮津市、伊根町

再度、沓掛インターから京都縦貫自動車道などを経由して、宮津天橋立インターから宮津港へ。日本海だ。幹線道路沿いにある、「カネマスの七輪焼き」でランチ。朝獲れの新鮮な魚をすぐ捌いて、昆布や煮干しなどの薄塩出汁に漬け込んで、短時間で干し上げた一夜干しを、この店では「一刻干し」と名付けて出していて、炭火で焼いて食べるのだが、これが絶品。地魚の美味しい食べ方を学びながら、さらに美味しく頂けます。

ここから日本三景「天橋立」は車で、すぐ。車を駐めて、ケーブルカー

people moving about, living their everyday lives. It's a beautiful atmospheric seaside town.

"Mukai Shuzo" (distillery) is in the town, and this is, perhaps, the distillery closest to the sea. All around the distillery it smells of rice malt. Even the sea began to look like sake. No one has studied the relationship between the taste of scotch whiskey and the sea wind in Islay Island, but I have a sneaking suspicion that where it is has affected the taste of sake from this distillery.

At "Funaya no Sato Ine" atop the hill, a roadside shop selling local produces, you can view the entire Bay of Ine at one glance. The view from here is magnificent.

I highly recommend staying at "Kagiya", an inn converted from traditional Japanese houses. At night when you go out in the wooden deck, you can watch sea urchins and anemones and turbos crawling at the bottom of the ocean. When they turned off the light after midnight and swirl the surface with a deck broom handle, the sea began to twinkle: sea (→p. 135)

で山裾（やますそ）に登って、上の展望台から、一直線に湾を横切っている天橋立を眺めるのが、一般的な天橋立観光の楽しみ方らしいが、それだけでは、あまりに勿体（もったい）ないと僕は思う。ぜひ、海に向かって歩いてほしい。「天橋立」そのものには、何か特別な施設があるわけではない。ただ、人が少なく、ゴミがとても少なく、砂浜は真っ白で、青く透き徹った海は凪いでいて、水面がキラキラと白く輝いている。とても静かで、とても明るく、遠くから風が渡ってくるのが海面に見え、心も身体も何もかも浄化してくれそうなほど、きれいだ。周りには何の観光地化もされていない民家や水産物店が、沖縄の離島みたいに密集していて、堤防にはナマコが笊（ざる）に干してあった。

「天橋立」から、さらに北へ車で約三〇分、伊根町（いねちょう）の「舟屋（ふなや）の里」を目指す。途中、京都出身のロックバンド「くるり」の傑作「THE PIER」のCDカバー写真の撮影地もあるので、興味がある人は探してみてください。苦労したけど、僕は四度目で見つけた。

伊根湾は絶景だ。クルッと丸まったような鉤形（かぎ）の湾は南側に開かれて、しかも外海（そとうみ）との間に、湾に蓋（ふた）をするように「青島（あおしま）」が一つ浮かんでいる。湾内は、まったくと言っていいほど波がない。鏡のような海面で、しかも、その水は透き徹っている。湾岸（わんがん）には、静かな静かな波の上に、舟屋、つまり舟のガレージが、ぐるりと見渡す限り建っていて、そこで人々が生活をしている。この上なく風情ある、海の町だ。心が、しんみりとする。

「向井酒造（むかい）」は、その舟屋群の側にあって、杉戸（すぎと）の一枚向こうは海、多分、日本一海に近い酒造の一つだろう。あたりには、麹（こうじ）のいい香りが漂っていて、ほとんど風のない真っ青な海が酒に見えてくる。アイラ島のスコッチみたいに、潮風が日本酒の風味に影響するかは、立証されてはいないそうだが、この景色を知った僕らにとっては、「影響ない」とは、もう思えない。

To the sea: Miyazu, Amanohashidate, Ine.

I drove over Kyoto-Jukan Expressway and headed toward Miyazu Harbor and the Sea of Japan. I had lunch at "Kanemasu Shichirin-yaki (Kanemasu Barbecue Pit)" along the expressway which serves slightly sun-dried fish dipped in fish stock, and served barbecued over coal. This is very delicious.

"Amanohashidate", considered as one of the best three sights in Japan, is just a drive away. I parked my car; people say that the best view is from the top of the mountain via cable car, but in my view, the best view is to head toward the sea. Amanohashidate has no special facilities but the beach is white sand and clean, and the ocean stark blue, dappled with light from the sky. It's so beautiful I felt rejuvenated after standing there for a while.

Thirty minutes north from Amanohashidate is the Bay of Ine in a shape of a C with Aoshima Island position as if to put a lid in the bay. There is absolutely no wave, and the surface of the transparent water is like a mirror. And on land, you can see

実に、美味そうである。

道の駅「舟屋の里 伊根」は、小高い丘の上にあって、伊根湾全体を見渡す事ができる。ここからの眺めも、実に素晴らしい。

伊根まで来たなら、ぜひ泊まりたい。お薦めは、舟屋に泊まられる「舟宿 鍵屋」。夜、舟屋のデッキに出たら、すぐ足下の、キレイな小さな波の下に、ウニやサザエや、イソギンチャクとかカニが、ゆっくりと動いている。じっと眺めていると、ガラスの鎖のような透明な筋状の物が、何本も漂っているのを見つけた。何だろうと思って、手ですくい上げたら、重力に耐えきれずにバラバラになって海に落ちてしまい、その一つ一つが、それぞれ自由に泳ぎ去ってしまった。宿主の鍵賢吾さんに訊くと、その不思議な生物は、ホヤの集合体「群体ボヤ」の一種だそうで、個体が繋がり合って動くのだという。

深夜過ぎに、デッキの明かりを消して、ほぼ完全な闇をつくり、デッキブラシで水を掻き回すと泡や飛沫がキラキラ光った。夜光虫（ウミホタル）が、外部からの刺激で光るのだ。タイミングよく雨が降ると夜光虫が雨粒に刺激されて、湾全体が星空のように輝く夜もあるのだそうだ。ぜひ見たい。

朝になって、食べた朝食のレンコダイの塩焼き（とても美味しい！）の、骨やお頭を海に放り投げると、ウミネコとカモメが、すぐに飛んで集まってきて、それらを空中や海面でキャッチして、残さず全部食べてくれた。

波穏やかな静かな町で、「景気・不景気の波もなく、近くにある物、周りにある物で、きちんと自分の生活や仕事を続けられたら、自分も楽しいし、誰かを楽しませる事もできる」と鍵さんは笑って話していた。ウミネコ達も嬉しそうに鳴いていた。

京都滞在中、最も気持ちのいい朝だった。

fireflies, awaken by the water movement, lit brilliantly. If you are lucky and it begin to rain, the bay itself can light up like the night sky.

In the morning, as I threw the leftover bones from the breakfast into the sea, seagulls swooped down to catch them in midair. Kengo Kagi, the owner of the inn, told me, "If I can continue to work with what is around me, to use what is local and regional, I will be happy, and I can keep making other people happy. If I can run a business unaffected by recession, I am doing the right thing."

Out of all the mornings in Kyoto, this was, by far, my favorite.

京都の美味しい手みやげ

宇治茶ミニ缶セット 私は、京都ですっかり日本茶党に。新茶の季節の茶園は美しく、毎年訪れてお祝いしたい(佐々木)。 玄米茶・煎茶・ほうじ茶 各30g 1,296円 丸久小山園 ☎0774-20-0909 ♀京都府宇治市小倉町寺内86 **Ujicha Mini Can Set** Brown Rice Tea, Sen Tea, Houji Tea 30g each ¥1,296 Marukyu Koyamaen ♀Ogura-cho Terauchi 86, Uji, Kyoto

和く輪く京美山(無濾過生原酒) ラベルに描かれた茅葺き屋根の葺き替えで出た古茅を、酒米の肥料に再利用。ぜひ、ロックで(神藤)。 500ml 2,000円 和く輪く美山酒店 ☎0771-75-9081 ♀京都府南丹市美山町内久保下カルノ54-1 **Waku Waku Kyo Miyama (Non-filtered raw unprocessed sake)** 500ml ¥2,000 Waku Waku Miyama Liquor Shop ♀Miyama-cho Uchikubo Shimokaruno 54-1, Nantan, Kyoto

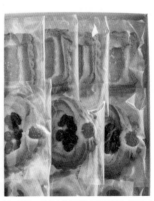

伊根満開 赤米酒 若手の女性杜氏が生み出した、伊根の赤米から造った淡い赤色の日本酒。濃厚な味の料理との相性もいい(前田)。720ml 2,090円 向井酒造株式会社 ☎0772-32-0003 ♀京都府与謝郡伊根町平田67 **Ine Mankai Red Rice Sake** 720ml ¥2,090 Mukai Shuzo ♀Ine-cho Hirata 67, Yosa, Kyoto

阿闍梨餅 1922年から製法を変えない、あじろ笠を象ったモチモチ半生菓子。竹籠を使った贈答用のパッケージも秀逸(前田)。10個箱入り 1,296円 阿闍梨餅本舗満月 ☎075-791-4121 ♀京都府京都市左京区鞠小路通今出川上ル **Ajari Mochi (Sweets)** 10 pieces ¥1,296 Ajari Mochi Honpo Mangetsu ♀Marikoji-dori Imadegawa Agaru, Sakyo-ku, Kyoto, Kyoto

ロシアケーキ 全種類を買いたい、ブローチのような素朴な焼き菓子。クラシカルな店舗デザインには、ほっとする(神藤)。10個入り 2,130円 村上開新堂 ☎075-231-1058 ♀京都府京都市中京区常盤木町62 **Russian Cake** 10 pieces ¥2,130 Murakami Kaishindo ♀Tokiwagi-cho 62, Nakagyo-ku, Kyoto, Kyoto

Tasty Souvenirs from KYOTO

生麩饅頭 ぷるんとした食感が癖になりました。包みの笹の葉づかいがお洒落で、パッケージも素敵(佐々木)。5個入り 1,204円 麩嘉 ☎075-231-1584 ◉京都府京都市上京区西 洞院通 椹木町上ル東裏辻町413 **Namafu Manju (Sweets)** 5 pieces ¥1,204 Fuka ◉Nishinotoin-dori Sawaragi-cho Agaru Higashi-uratsuji-cho 413, Kamigyo-ku, Kyoto, Kyoto

果実酢 鮮やかな暖色が、見た目も美味しい果実酢。使い分けは、その日の気分によって(神藤)。各120ml 756円〜 株式会社 飯尾醸造 ☎0772-25-0015 ◉京都府宮津市小田宿野373 **Fruit Vinegar** 120ml each ¥756〜 Iio Jozo ◉Odashukuno 373, Miyazu, Kyoto

中辛、六味 注文後、目の前で調合してくれる、風味絶佳の七味。唐辛子を抜いた六味も、一度味わったら手放せない(空閑)。5匙 340円(山椒多めは、390円) 長文屋 ☎075-467-0217 ◉京都府京都市北区北野下白梅町54-8 **Seven Flavor Spice (Medium-spicy), Six Flavor Spice** Five Spoonful ¥340 (w/ extra sansho pepper ¥390) Chobunya ◉Kitanoshimohakubai-cho 54-8, Kita-ku, Kyoto, Kyoto

漬け物各種 素敵な包装の漬け物を、お好みで。大原で育った赤紫蘇を使った「志ば漬」は、必ず(空閑)。130g 486円〜(写真は「しそ巻らっきょう」100g 864円) 志ば久 ☎075-744-4893 ◉京都府京都市左京区大原勝林院町58 **Pickled Vegetables** 130g ¥486〜 (Photo: "Shiso-maki Rakkyo" 100g ¥864) Shibakyu ◉Ohara Shorinin-cho 58, Sakyo-ku, Kyoto, Kyoto

珈琲豆 シーズン毎に移り変わる、お薦めの珈琲豆。店主の業を盗んで、ぜひ、ネルドリップで(神藤)。200g 1,512円 FACTORY KAFE工船 ☎075-211-5398 ◉京都府京都市上京区河原町通 今出川下ル梶井町448 清和テナントハウス2FG号室 **Coffee Beans** 200g ¥1,512 FACTORY KAFE KOSEN ◉Kawaramachi-dori Imadegawa Kudaru Kajii-cho 448 2F Room G, Kamigyo-ku, Kyoto, Kyoto

アラビアの真珠(珈琲豆) 京都を離れたら、なかなか三条へは行けないので、定番の味をお土産に。砂糖とミルクを入れるのが超定番(空閑)。200g 1,250円 イナダコーヒ本店 ☎075-221-0507 ◉京都府京都市中京区 堺町通 三条 下ル道祐町140 **Arabian Pearl (Coffee Beans)** 200g ¥1,250 Inoda Coffee ◉Sakaimachi-dori Sanjo Kudaru Doyu-cho 140, Nakagyo-ku, Kyoto, Kyoto

hokka

金沢に生まれ愛されて90年

米蜜ビスケット

京都府の、編集部が取材抜きでも食べに行く店

京都府の市街地を、自転車や歩きで取材した本誌編集部。小腹(こばら)を満たす甘味。疲れを忘れさせる名店の逸品(いっぴん)。「あっさり薄味」のイメージとは裏腹に、「濃い味」も人気の京都。歴史ある名飲食店が多い京都の、文句なしに美味い、お薦めの八品をご紹介。

Kyoto's Delicious Local Foods

Our editorial team went all over Kyoto, on foot as well as on bicycles, to get this issue out on time. Here and there, we stopped to snack on sweets, eat lunch, and dine at both famous and not so famous restaurants during our two months' stay here. We would like to introduce the eight best local foods from Kyoto, the city known for its historical restaurants.

1
ラーメン
Ramen

朝5時開店！ 夜行バスで京都駅に降りたら、"第一は朝日"と共に、「第一旭」。特製ラーメンは麺大盛り、肉モリモリ、スタミナつきます(空閑)。700円
京都たかばし 本家 第一旭
📍京都府京都市下京区(しもぎょうく)東塩小路向畑町(ひがししおこうじむかいはたちょう)845
☎075-351-6321
🏠www.honke-daiichiasahi.com
Dai-ichi Asahi
📍Higashishiokoji Mukaihata-cho 845, Shimogyo-ku, Kyoto, Kyoto

2
オムライス
Omelette Rice

本誌「空閑(くが)トラベル」紹介の「オムライス」は、これの事だ！「美味(おい)しい卵料理」をもう一つ選ぶなら、間違いなく、これ(神藤)。中1,050円
グリル 小宝(こだから)
📍京都府京都市左京区(さきょうく)岡崎北御所町46
☎075-771-5893
🏠www.grillkodakara.com
Grill Kodakara
📍Okazakikitagosho-cho 46, Sakyo-ku, Kyoto, Kyoto

3
コロッケ各種
Croquettes of various kinds

揚げたて俵型(たわらがた)コロッケが、ワインのおつまみ。ブルーチーズやバジルなど、創作コロッケメニューが、ずらり(佐々木)。1個170円〜
NISHITOMIYA
📍京都府京都市東山区西町126 1F
☎070-8513-0452
NISHITOMIYA
📍Nishimachi 126, Higashiyama-ku, Kyoto, Kyoto

4
清酒 燗(かん)
Seishukan (blend of six hot sakes)

料理は何を注文しても美味(うま)いけど、酒は、こればかりを何合も。灘の酒6種(なだ)をブレンドした、ここだけの燗酒(かんざけ)(空閑)。650円
神馬(しんめ)
📍京都府京都市上京区(かみぎょうく)千本通(せんぼんどおり)中立売上ル(なかたちうり)西側玉屋町(にしがわたまや)(ちょう)38
☎075-461-3635
Shinme
📍Senbon-dori Nakatachiuri Agaru Nishigawa Tamaya-cho 38, Kamigyo-ku, Kyoto, Kyoto

5
フレンチ
トースト
French Toast

表面はカリカリ、中は厚焼き卵のようにフワフワ。苦味の利いた珈琲と、交互に食べるのが最高。ホットケーキやプリンも美味（神藤）。700円
スマート珈琲店
📍京都府京都市中京区寺町通三条上ル天性寺前町537
☎075-231-6547
🏠www.smartcoffee.jp
Smart Coffee
📍Teramachi-dori Sanjo Agaru Tenseijimae-cho 537, Nakagyo-ku, Kyoto, Kyoto

---

6
抹茶ソフトクリーム
Maccha ice cream

W抹茶（抹茶アイス＋抹茶）づかいの贅沢ソフト。お土産には、増永明子さんデザインのギフトボックスがお薦め（佐々木）。400円
ますだ茶舗
📍京都府宇治市宇治蓮華21-3
☎0774-21-4034
🏠masudachaho.jp
MASUDA TEA STORE
📍Ujirenge 21-3, Uji, Kyoto

7
モーニングセット
Morning Set

創意ある盛りつけの、野菜たっぷりトーストセット。パンの耳まで平らげて、お腹も満足。いざ、賀茂川散策へ！(神藤)
680円
COFFEE HOUSE maki（出町店）
📍京都府京都市上京区河原町通今出川上ル青龍町211
☎075-222-2460
🏠www.coffeehouse-maki.com
COFFEE HOUSE maki（Demachi-ten）
📍Kawaramachi-dori Imadegawa Agaru Seiryu-cho 211, Kamigyo-ku, Kyoto, Kyoto

---

8
さばずし
Saba zushi
(mackerel sushi)

褐色の竹壁カウンターが趣深い。注文後、丁寧に作られる「名代さばずし」は、肉厚で、ぺろりと完食した。お土産用の包装紙も◎(神藤)。1/2本（6切れ）2,120円
京のすし処 末廣
📍京都府京都市中京区寺町通二条上ル要法寺前町711
☎075-231-1363
🏠sushi-suehiro.jp
SUEHIRO
📍Teramachi-dori Nijo Agaru Yohojimae-cho 711, Nakagyo-ku, Kyoto, Kyoto

美味しい卵料理

にしん蕎麦、ちりめん山椒、八ツ橋などが、"ザ・京都の食文化"だと思っていたのは、実際に取材に行くまで。京都の人は、京都が内陸の都だったため、鶏肉や卵などを、昔からよく食べていたそう。そして、本誌編集部も、出汁巻き卵、鶏卵うどん、オムライスなど、数多くの卵料理に出会いました。そんな京都府の数ある卵料理の中から、編集部が本気でハマった絶品の三品を一挙に、ご紹介。

【きんし丼】京極 かねよ
「か・ね・よ」と書かれた赤提灯が目印の鰻料理専門店。名物「きんし丼（並二六〇〇円）」は、丼から食み出した大きな卵焼き（出汁割り焼き）の

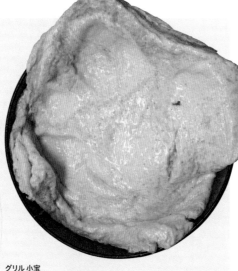

京極 かねよ
- 京都府京都市中京 区六角通 新 京 極東入ル松ヶ枝町 456
- ☎ 075-221-0669
- 🕐 11:30–15:30(L.O.) 17:00-20:30(L.O.) 　無休
- 🚉 京都市役所前駅から徒歩約 5 分

Kyogoku Kaneyo
- 📍 Rokkaku-dori Shinkyogoku Higashi-iru Matsugae-cho 456, Nakagyo-ku, Kyoto, Kyoto
- 🕐 No regular holidays
- 🚉 Approximately 2-minute walk from Kyoto Shiyakusho-mae Station

グリル 小宝
- 📍 京都府京都市左京 区岡崎北御所町 46
- ☎ 075-771-5893
- 🕐 11:30–21:00(L.O.) 火曜、第 2 第 4 水曜休（臨時休業あり）
- 🚉 東山駅から徒歩約 15 分

Grill Kodakara
- 📍 Okagazaki Kitagosho-cho 46, Sakyo-ku, Kyoto, Kyoto
- 🕐 Closed on Tuesday, as well as 2nd and 4th Wednesdays
- 🚉 Approximately 15-minute walk from Higashiyama Station

[Chicken Bruxelles] Grill Kodakara

Their most famous dish, without question, is rice omelet, but what we want to recommend, instead, is the Chicken Bruxelles (¥2,290). Underneath a big sunny-side-up egg and homemade sauce, there it is: a whole roasted leg! The first bite will take you back to your mother's kitchen.

[Kinshi-don] Kyogoku Kaneyo

Look for the red lantern with the word, "Ka Ne Yo," the sign for the eel restaurant. Their famous dish, Kinshi-don (¥2,600 for a normal portion), consists of roasted eel marinated in a 100-year-old secret sauce underneath an egg, sunny side up, overflowing from the bowl. First, eat the egg and the eel as appetizers with a glass of beer or a cup of sake, then eat the rice underneath!

下に、一〇〇年超えの秘伝のタレが
かかった鰻丼が! 最初は、卵と鰻
を肴に日本酒かビールで。そして丼
持って"三昧の絶妙"を掻き込んで!

【チキンジクセル】グリル 小宝
この店の不動の人気は、オムライス。
それは、間違いなく美味いが、編集
部が、ぜひ、お薦めしたいのは「チ
キンジクセル(二二九〇円)」。自家
製ソースがかかった、大きな卵焼き
の中に、肉汁たっぷりの鶏モモ肉一
枚が丸ごと入っていて超美味。懐か
しい味わいでもあり、皆でシェア。

【玉子サンドイッチ】喫茶 マドラグ
二〇一二年に閉店した洋食の名店「コ
ロナ」の「玉子サンドイッチ」を受け
継いだ、ここも歴史的な名店。天
丼の高い、お洒落な空間で、夜、
ゆっくり小瓶ビールを飲みながらが、
いい。「コロナの玉子サンドイッチ
(八〇〇円)」は縦にして、端から食べ
ていけば、具は飛び出さないでグッド。

喫茶 マドラグ
京都府京都市中京 区上松屋町 706-5
075-744-0067
11:30– 売り切れまで 日曜休
烏丸御池駅から徒歩約 5 分

La Madrague
Kamimatsuya-cho 706-5, Nakagyou-ku, Kyoto, Kyoto
Closed on Sundays
Approximately 5-minute walk from Karasuma-Oike Station

The Recommended Dish by the Editorial Team

Fabulous Egg Dishes

Until I went to Kyoto, the only image I had of Kyoto's cuisine was its familiar dishes: Nishin soba, *chirimen* peppers, *yatsuhashi*. However, in reality, because its citizens are landlocked, they have traditionally eaten quite a variety of egg and chicken dishes. Our Editorial Team encountered quite a few egg dishes for this issue, so we have chosen the three best Kyoto egg dishes.

[Corona Egg Sandwich] La Madrague

When Corona closed its doors in 2012, its most famous dish, the Egg Sandwich, was inherited by La Madrague, an equally famous restaurant. The sandwich should be eaten at night while drinking a cocktail. The way to eat this sandwich (¥800) is by eating it vertically—that way, you will be able to eat it without making a mess.

LIST OF PARTNERS

008

よーじやグループ／株式会社 國枝商店　花街の芸妓さんや舞妓さん、歌舞伎役者、映画関係者等のための舞台化粧品メーカーとして、一九〇四年に創業。「よーじや」の代名詞ともいえる、あぶらとり紙は、発売当初、顔を覆うくらい大きなサイズだったが、肌への使用感にもこだわり、気軽に持ち歩ける現在のサイズに改良した後、大流行を経て、一般の女性に定着。また、男性の愛用者も多い。基礎化粧品や化粧筆などのオリジナル商品が充実していて、「柿渋」「牡丹」など、口紅やフェイスカラーには、日本の伝統色が数多く使われています。トレンドではなく、"京おんなの美意識"を集約した商品は、祇園店や三条店をはじめ、京都市内の一〇店舗・二コーナーで、購入できます。
▲ www.yojiya.co.jp

012

むす美／山田繊維 株式会社　一九三七年、京都市中京区で創業。「人と人の心を結ぶ」「日本人の知恵と文化を世界へ結ぶ」伝統を現代の暮らしに活かし、未来へ結ぶと、強く意識し、約八〇年、風呂敷の製造・卸業を営んでいます。オリジナルの風呂敷は、現在、五〇〇種類近いデザインがあり、オンラインショップやアンテナショップ（東京都渋谷区）では、ユニークな達磨や招き猫の柄の「COCHAE」シリーズ、また、ファッションブランド「ミナ ペルホネン」とスタートさせた「ちょうむすび」シリーズなど

014

が、とても人気。同社広報の山田悦子さんの著書『ふろしきハンドブック』等では、基本の「真結び」「一つ結び」から、シーンに合わせた使い方までを楽しく学ぶ事ができます。
▲ www.ymds.co.jp

BRUNO／有限会社 ダイアテックプロダクツ　京都市伏見区に本社を構え、自転車の製造・卸会社。自転車レースの出場経験が豊富な、スイス人のブルーノ・ダルシー氏と共同開発したオリジナル自転車「BRUNO」の小径車「Ventura Drop」と「Minivelo 20 Road」に乗って、縦横無尽に京都市内を走り回った本誌編集部。普段着でも乗りやすい高性能の自転車があると、移動するという行為が、格段に充実します。そう実感して、京都の自転車旅の中で、特に印象的だった道やサイクリングロードを、広告の中で紹介しました。次号は、「滋賀県号」。「BRUNO」を輪行バッグに運んで「ビワイチ（琵琶湖一周ロングライド）」に、私は挑戦する予定です。

016

有限会社 昇苑くみひも　一九四八年、創業。宇治市の本社工場では、一九五八年に導入された複数の製紐機の音が、ガシャンガシャンと鳴り響き、複数の細い糸の束が、幾つもの工程を経て、組紐へと組み上がっていきます。組紐は、古くから茶道具や着物の帯締め等に使われ、留

▲ www.brunobike.jp

018

める事や括る事を、美しく見せてきました。「昇苑くみひも」は、現在、ストラップやブレスレットなどのアクセサリー類も製造し、本社併設の店舗に入ると、木造の古い組台を見る事ができ、アクセサリー類や、欲しい長さの組紐を購入できます。広告は、同社の組紐の実物を構成して、染めた紐の色の美しさ、組み合わせの多彩さを、グラフィカルに表現しました。
▲ www.showen.co.jp

IKEUCHI ORGANIC KYOTO STORE／IKEUCHI ORGANIC 株式会社　愛媛県今治市に本社を構える、「風で織るタオル」で知られる、オーガニック・テキスタイルブランド。「東京ストア」に続いて、二〇一四年に「京都ストア（京都市中京区富小路通三条、上ル福長町一〇一）をオープン。「SACRA ANNEX」一階奥にあり、レジカウンターと一体の大きなシンクで手を洗い、好みのタオルを選んで手を拭いて、使い心地を試す事ができます。私達編集部は、「京都号」取材中に共同生活を送った賃貸マンションでも「IKEUCHI ORGANIC」のタオルを愛用しました。「ピローケースを連れていくと、旅先でも快眠できますよ！」という、店長の益田晴子さんのアドバイスを、次号「滋賀県号」から実践したいと思います。
▲ www.ikeuchi.org

071, Back Cover

オリックスレンタカー／オリックス自動車 株式会社　京都市市内から、日本海側の宮津市「天橋立」や伊根町「舟屋の里」へは、レンタカーの利用が、とても便利です。二〇二五年七月一八日には、京都 縦貫自動車道が全線開通し、さらに行き来が楽になります。南丹市の美山町「かやぶきの里」は、京都市市内から車で約一時間の、美しい自然に囲まれた集落です。その他の車旅にお薦めの魅力的なエリアは、主に「空閑トラベルⅢ（一二六ページから）」で、ご

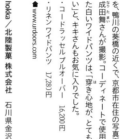

138

110

紹介します。掲載各地を巡って、オリジナルスタンプを集める、本誌恒例のイベント「ぐるぐる」では、「オリックスレンタカー」の京都駅前新幹線口店や、京都南店など、府内六店舗を出発点にして、快適・愉快な旅を、ぜひ、満喫してください。

▶ caronix.co.jp

URBAN RESEARCH DOORS／株式会社 アーバンリサーチ 「アーバンリサーチ」のライフスタイルショップ「DOORS」とつくるシリーズ広告で、毎号、その取材県で出会った美しい女性をモデルに撮影する「In-Town Beauty」。宇治市の「丸久小山園」に勤務するガイセキキキさんを、鴨川の葵橋の近くで、京都市在住の写真家・成田舞さんが撮影。コーディネートで使用した白いワイドパンツは「穿き心地が、とてもいいと、キキさんもお気に入りでした。

・コードラッセルプルオーバー 16,200円
・リネン ワイドパンツ 17,280円

▶ www.urdoors.com

hokka／北陸製菓 株式会社 石川県金沢市生まれの「hokka」のお菓子が、毎号、取材中に出会った物と共演する、シリーズ広告。今回は「米蜜ビスケット」です。麴 料理研究家の小紺有花さんが監修した、金沢市の老舗「俵屋」の米飴、玄米甘酒、国産の大麦粉などを使用した、自然な甘さの「hokka」の新製品。一枚ずつの個包装の表面は、数十年前に使用していた型を使用した、欧風の花柄の文様が可愛らしい。本誌編集部が京都取材から持ち帰った、「かみ添」の唐紙や、清水焼「龍豊窯」の器の柄と合わせて、コーディネートしました。

▶ www.hokka.jp

193

152

COMME des GARÇONS／株式会社 コム デ ギャルソン 「強いクリエーションは永久。また、定番として長い支持を受けている物も、強いクリエーションである」とする「コム デ ギャルソン」の考えに、「D&DEPARTMENT PROJECT」は賛同。本誌「東京号」の表紙は、「コム デ ギャルソン」が一九八八年から一九九一年まで発刊していた、イメージマガジン「Six」の表紙を使用しています。「コム デ ギャルソン 京都店」は御幸町通 御池上ルにあり、「KYOTOGRAPHIE 京都国際写真祭2015」の会場の一つでした。

▶ www.comme-des-garcons.com

株式会社 丸久小山園 園祖・小山 久次郎 現在の宇治市小倉町で、茶の栽培と製造を始めたのは、江戸時代の元禄年間 五月、「新茶見学会」(一一〇ページ)に参加させていただく小山元治社長や小山俊美専務、そしてスタッフの皆さんが、新茶の季節の到来を心から喜んでいるのが、ひと目で実感できました。その嬉しさは、茶の味や技術とともに、きっと、創業時から変わらず受け継がれてきた、小山園の魅力の大きな一つだ、と私は思いました。一年かけて、自社農園で大切に育てた茶葉を、一枚ずつ手で摘み、手間を惜しまず碾茶にして、そして、「ミクロン単位の粉末にし」「雲鶴」「又玄」などの抹茶に仕上げていきます。久」を丸で囲んだ「丸久印」には、「品質本位の茶づくり」という同社のモットーと、宇治茶の誇りが込められています。

▶ www.marukyu-koyamaen.co.jp

宿はなし 今日も川のそば
暮れゆく夕凪を眺めれば
飛び石のほら真ん中で
笑う顔 泣く顔 日も暮れた
宙ぶらりん 千のこころは
さざれ石すら動かせず
べんがら格子の街を背に
暮れゆく日々に ただ悔やむだけ

見つめ合う事に飽きたらば
慕情の落ち穂 拾い集め
燃やそうか ほら流そうか
遊ぶ幼子の目に問うか
鈴の音は抱いた体の腫れた傷だけを
癒そうぞ

「宿はなし」くるり
『図鑑』SPEEDSTAR RECORDS（二〇〇〇年）より（ルビは、本誌編集部による）

JASRAC 出 1507492-501

連載 36

ふつう

「川の景色」

深澤直人
Naoto Fukasawa

京都の鴨川に架かる荒神橋から上流の方を見た景色が、私は好きだ。一見、どこの都市にもありそうな、ふつうの川の景色なのに、やはり雄大で美しい。確かに人工的に整備された河原だが、自然のままのような感じがする。周りに人が住んでいるので、借景の感じもする。出町あたりから二手に分かれた上流の彼方に連なる山々の背景も、川と融け合っていて美しい。川の分かれた所に下鴨神社の緑が見える。川の両側には、もこもこした緑と、美しい桜の並木がある。

京都に住む友人は、これはきっと人工的に造られた細く長い公園なんだ、と言う。日本庭園の中の小川のせせらぎが実世界になって、京都自体が巨大な、お庭になったようにも見える。川を含む都市計画のデザインの極みが、ここにある。

鴨川は、初めから、このように整備されていた訳ではないらしい。川底をさらい、流れを緩やかにしながら、両脇に大きな平地を造り、そして公園にした。以前は葦が生い茂った鬱蒼とした河原だったと聞く。

私は、五年前から京都にアパートを借りて、鴨川に、よく行くようになった。お寺やお庭

Futsuu (Normal)：The Riverscape

One of my favorite views is looking upstream from Kojin Bridge, which lies across Kamo River in Kyoto. At a glance, it's an ordinary view that one can find in any city, but to me, it's beautiful. The riverbanks are obviously manmade although they are designed to look natural. The view looks like a painting. The mountain range near Demachi, where the river splits, also contributes to the beauty of the view. There I can see the green wooded area of Shimogamo Shrine. Cherry blossom trees line both sides of the river.

My friend who lives in Kyoto says that this artificially designed park is long and narrow. The river is like a stream in a Japanese garden, and the city of Kyoto itself becomes, in my imagination, a big garden. This is, I think, an example of very successful urban planning: the inclusion of natural elements enhances the plan. In the past, Kamo River did not look like this, but with time, generations of urban designers calmed the speed of the river by making the river bottom deeper and created wide, flat river banks, making them into parks. People tell me that the river banks used to look untamed with wild reeds.

I started renting an apartment in Kyoto five years (→p. 151)

を、よく見に行った訳ではない。いつも鴨川沿いを散歩した。自転車で川を通って、二条あたりのカフェに、よく行った。川を渡って出町桝形商店街で、小さな天ぷらと、うどんの玉を買って、家に持ち帰ってよく食べた。なんだか質素だけど、私には豊かな暮らしだった。どこに行くのも、川沿いを通った。川が、私の生活の中心にあった。川端のベンチで、おにぎりを食べていたら、トンビが手かから、それをさらっていった事もあった。

鴨川は、京都の人の憩いの場だと思う。川の景色が、いつも京都の日常の背景にあったと思う。川の流域に人が住み始めて、やがて、小さな都市になっていった。鴨川に、ほど近い京都御所の地下には水系があって、その水脈を毎日管理する管理番のような家系があって、その家には代々引き継がれた池が庭にあり、その池の水位で御所の地下水を管理していたと聞いた事がある。京都は、川と地下水系の上に造られた街だったのだ。

昔の人の都市計画は、自然の摂理に逆らわないやり方で出来上がっていた事がわかる。京都は、日本の中でも自然災害の少ない場所だ。盆地の縁の連なる山々を背景に、お寺な

temples built along the sides of the mountains. *Shakkei*—borrowed landscape—is just that: no one owns it. It is part of nature. No one owns Kamo River. I suspect that the reason that I feel relaxed when I walk along the river is that people who designed the city around the river knew that human beings are part of nature, and the best city planning allows us to live harmoniously with nature. The body fits into the environment.

Students and other people are always having parties on the river banks. The left side of the split along the river is a running course for joggers. Both serious and amateur joggers run along this path. I do think that being able to live by Kamo River is quite

an astonishing thing. When I walk downstream along the river and gaze at Kyoto Botanical Garden to the left, I am always struck by how beautiful this view is. I want to own it. The river is full of bounty. What a rich and enriching life I have because of this river. These are my thoughts as I take my daily walk along the river.

深澤 直人　プロダクトデザイナー。ヨーロッパ、北欧、アジアを代表するブランドのデザインや、国内の大手メーカーのコンサルティング等を多数手がける。ロイヤルデザイナー・フォー・インダストリー（英国王室芸術協会）の称号を授与されるなど、国内外での受賞歴多数。著書に、『デザインの輪郭』（TOTO出版）など。2012年より、「日本民藝館」館長。

Naoto Fukasawa　Product designer. Fukasawa has designed products for major brands in Europe and Asia. He has also worked as a consultant for major domestic manufacturers. Winner of numerous awards given by domestic and international institutions, including the Royal Designer for Industry Award, honored by the British Royal Society of Arts. He has written books, most importantly *An Outline of Design* (TOTO). Since 2012, he is the Director of Nihon Mingei-kan (Japan Arts and Crafts Museum).

どが建っている。借景は、その名の通り「借りてきた景色」だから、自分の物ではない。みんなが分け合っている自然の景色の中に、鴨川も流れている。川辺を歩いていると心が落ち着くのは、この川を造った人々が、人間も自然の一部であるという事を理解していて、人間の身体の周囲としての環境のデザインが、きっと、よくできているのだろう。

川辺の緑の上では、いつも大学生などが集って楽しくパーティーなどをしている。Y字の左側（西）の鴨川の上流の賀茂川から交わった下流（南）の鴨川に至る川沿いは、ランニングに恰好な場所として有名だから、いつも人が走っている。マジなランナーも、多くここに集まるらしい。日本の中でも、世界の中でも、鴨川沿いに住める事は、かなりの贅沢で豊かな事だと思う。賀茂川の上流から下流へ歩きながら、左手（東）に「京都府立植物園」の緑が見えるあたりの景色は本当に美しく、この景色が欲しいと、私は、いつも思う。「ああ、なんて豊かな川なんだろう」「なんて"豊か"で、ふつう"に美しい生活の景色なんだろう」いつも、私は、そう思いながら、鴨川を歩いている。

ago and began visiting the city quite often. I don't often go to temples and gardens; I just walk along the Kamo River. After bicycling over the river, I often go to cafes in the Nijo neighborhood. I go across the bridge and buy small *tempura* and udon noodles at Demachimasugata Shopping Arcade to cook at home. It may sound like a simple life, but for me, it is very rich. Anywhere I go, I travel alongside the river; the river dictates my life in Kyoto. Once, when I was eating *onigiri* on a bench along the river, a kite flew down and stole my food right out of my hand.

Kamo River is a place of rest for residents of Kyoto. The view of the river has always been part of their daily lives. A long time ago, people started to live along the river, eventually forming a small town. I heard that there is an underground water source somewhere underneath the Kyoto Palace, and a family has been looking after it for generations. The family has a pond in their garden so they can keep an eye on the quality and quantity of the underground water. Kyoto was built around a river and atop an underground water source.

The city planning of the past was based on living harmoniously with nature. Kyoto is one of the very few cities in Japan that does not experience many natural disasters. There are

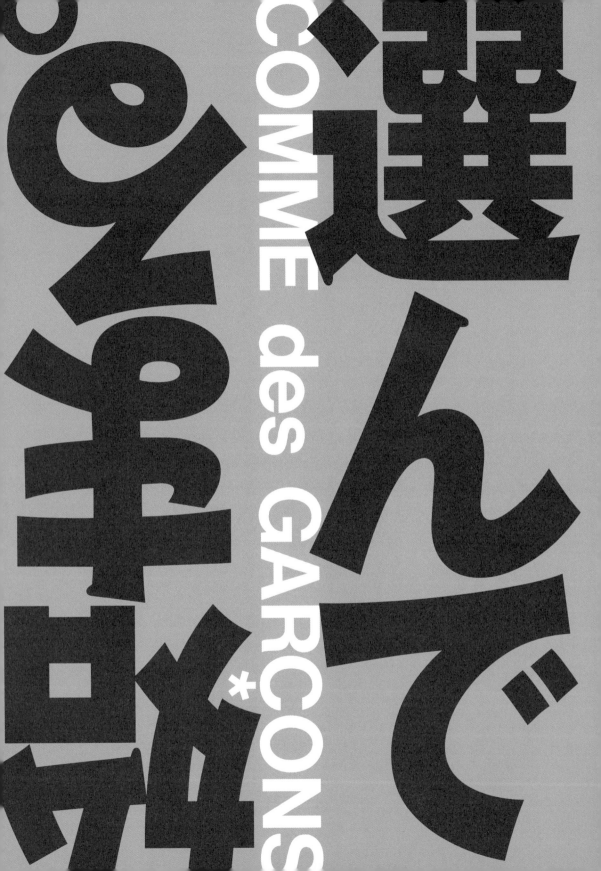

選んでみせ

COMME des GARÇONS
*

D&DEPARTMENT PROJECT
FRIENDS

47
REASONS
TO
TRAVEL
IN
JAPAN

わらはんど
📍 青森県弘前市千年4-3-17
☎ 0172-87-2747
🏠 kimumoku.jp/warahand/
Warahand
📍 Chitose 4-9-24, Hirosaki, Aomori

GRIS(グリ)
📍 北海道札幌市中央区南2条西8-5-4 4F
☎ 011-206-8448
GRIS
📍 4F, Minami 2-jo Nishi 8-chome 5-4,
Chuo-ku, Sapporo, Hokkaido

県産木材を使った、安全で楽しい木製玩具 弘前市を中心とする木工職人たちの合同会社「わらはんど」。「子供たち」を意味する津軽地方の方言から名付けられた(また、童と手の造語)。その代表的な玩具の一つが「うづくり積み木」。青森杉の夏目(木目の白く軟らかい部分)を削って凹凸を付けた、シンプルな積み木。温かい色あい、よい手触り、組む時の木の音の優しい響きが、親子をリラックスさせ、より和やかなコミュニケーションを生む。代表社員の木村崇之さんは「この積み木は、どんな半端な素材からも作れる。戦後に植林し、今、伐採のピークを迎えている青森杉の、究極の活用方法です」と胸を張る。(齋藤 望/NPO法人「弘前こどもコミュニティ・ぴーぷる」)

中華と和食と、お酒の名店 狸小路のアーケードの先、白いビルのドアを開け薄暗い階段を4階まで上がると、飲食店「GRIS」がある。店主の小野城碁・理恵子さん夫妻が、地元「トロッコ一級建築士事務所」と共にリノベーションした店内は、エゾマツの床、グレーの壁、磨りガラスの窓に、裸電球の明かりがマッチして、こころからほっとできる。看板メニューの「グリのシュウマイ」を、ぜひ。少し大きめで、十勝産の豚肉が、ぎっしり、からし醤油を付けて一口で。もちろん、ビールは北海道限定の「サッポロクラシック」。食後には「高橋工芸」の「Kami グラス」(薄い木のコップ)で、ほうじ茶が頂ける。(宮越葉子/D&DEPARTMENT HOKKAIDO)

Safe and Fun Wooden Toys Made Out of Locally Produced Lumber   Named after a Tsugaru word that means "child" (also a neologism combining *warabe* [child] and "hand"), "Warahand" is a limited liability company comprising woodworkers mainly working in Hirosaki. One of its representative products is "Udukumi Blocks". They are simple building blocks shaped by shaving the soft white parts of Natsume, an Aomori cedar. Their warm color, great feel in the hand, and emission of a gentle sound when stacked relaxes families and promotes friendly conversation. The company representative Takayuki Kimura proudly says, "These blocks can be made with any remnant wood. It is the ultimate use of Aomori cedar that was planted after the war is now ripe for harvesting." (Nozomu Saito, NPO Hirosaki Child Community "People")

A great restaurant serving alcoholic drinks and Chinese and Japanese food   The restaurant "GRIS" is located past the Tanukikoji arcade, through a white door, and up four flights of a dark staircase. Its owners Shiroki and Rieko Ono renovated the space with local architectural office "Studio 1065". GRIS' calming interior features naked light bulbs, which perfectly match its Yeddo spruce floors, gray walls, and ground glass windows. "GRIS Shumai" is the signature dish. It's slightly larger than average, and filled with Tokachi pork. Take the whole thing in one bite with mustard and soy sauce. It should of course be eaten with "Sapporo Classic" beer, which is only available in Hokkaido. After the meal, you can enjoy a cup of roasted green tea in Takahashi Kougei's thin walled wooden "Kami Glass". (Yoko Miyakoshi, D&DEPARTMENT HOKKAIDO)

Cara
www.takahashikougei.com

004

宮城
MIYAGI

仙台光原社
こうげんしゃ
📍 宮城県仙台市青葉区一番町1-4-10
☎ 022-223-6674
🏠 kogensya.sakura.ne.jp
Sendai Kogensha
📍 Ichiban-cho 1-chome 4-10, Aoba-ku,
　Sendai, Miyagi

003

岩手
IWATE

盛岡市ごみ分別早見表
📍 岩手県盛岡市菜園1-8-15 B1F(homesickdesign)
☎ 019-613-6479
🏠 homesickdesign.com
Morioka Quick Guide to Trash Organization
📍 B1F, Saien 18-15, Morioka, Iwate

季節の変化が楽しめる民芸品店　1968年に開店した「仙台光原社」。古くからの蔦が外壁を覆い、その葉の色が新緑、紅葉と四季折々で、とても変化が美しく、故・芹沢銈介デザインの看板や鉄行燈が際立つ。玄関口の水色の大谷焼の睡蓮鉢には、ブチの金魚が泳ぎ、陽が射すと、とても綺麗。店主の及川陽一郎さんは、「伝統、民芸、モダン、新しさなどの枠に囚われず、良い物だけを紹介したい」と、各地から様々な生活雑貨類を厳選。柚木沙弥郎さんの仙台玩具の型染めポストカードは、この

店オリジナルで、私も大好き。季節毎の催しや展示会も楽しく、2004年の「初春の市」の記念品で頂いた、中国の小皿も素敵で、お揃いのレンゲも私は、買った程だ。(伊藤愛／マフラー制作)

見える所に貼りたい、自慢の「ごみ分別早見表」　デザイン事務所「homesickdesign」の「盛岡市ごみ分別早見表」は、デザイナーの清水真介氏自身が、公式の物より、わかりやすくて美しい物を、と企画し、約1年かけて制作した。2013年に完成して、それ以降、毎年新しい物が、市内各所で好評・販売されている。田上たか氏の水彩のイラストは、新聞紙の記事や食品のパッケージなど、盛岡らしい物が描かれていて楽しい。視覚的に美しいだけでなく、地区の回収指定曜日が書き込めるマスや、分別に迷うリサイクルのごみの欄が大きく詳しく見やすい事など、様々な工夫がある逸品だ。この表は他所の人々に羨ましがられて、その度に私も嬉しい。(田代淳／「うるしぬりたしろ」)

A folk craft shop, where you can enjoy seasonal changes

"Sendai Kogensha" opened in 1968. Its building walls have long been covered in ivy, the color of which changes beautifully with the seasons. The ivy-covered walls also highlight the Keisuke Serizawa-designed shop sign and steel lantern. At the entrance is a light blue colored Ootani-yaki ceramic water lily bowl, which has spotted goldfish swimming inside. It's beautiful when the sunlight hits it. Owner Yoichi Okikawa explains, "I want to show good things, regardless of whether they're traditional, modern design, or folk craft works." I love Samiro Yunoki's postcards, which are stencil-dyed with traditional Sendai toy patterns and made exclusively for Sendai Kogensha. The store also organizes fun events and exhibitions seasonally. I liked the small Chinese plate I received as a commemorative gift at the 2004 "Early Spring Market" event so much that I bought a matching spoon. (Ai Ito, scarf maker)

A favorite trash guide to be promnently displayed

Shinsuke Shimizu of the design office "homesickdesign" spent approximately a year designing the "Morioka Quick Guide to Trash Organization," which he made to be more beautiful and easier to understand than the official one. Since its completion in 2013, it has been sold annually in various places in Morioka. Taka Tagami's fun watercolor illustrations depict Morioka-like objects such as newspaper articles and food packaging. The Guide is not only beautiful, but also filled with practical features such as a space for writing in the local trash collection days and a large column of trash items that people often find difficult to categorize. It makes me happy whenever people living outside of Morioka express envy for the trash guide. (Jun Tashiro, Urushi-nuri Tashiro)

006
山形
YAMAGATA

もりのばんさん ── 採集と火
📍 山形県鶴岡市周辺
🏠 atotsugi.inc
Banquet in the Forest
📍 Tsuruoka City, Yamagata

005
秋田
AKITA

ババヘラ・アイス
📍 秋田県男鹿市角間崎下屋長根12-1
（有限会社 進藤冷菓）
☎ 0185-46-2066
🏠 babahera.net
Babahera Ice cream
📍 Kakumazaki Geyanagane 12-1, Ogashi,
Akita（Shindo Reika Inc.）

森を食べる、究極の晩餐　森に入り、食材を見極め採集し、調理して食べるというプログラム「森の晩餐」。運営するのは、地域の食や手仕事の「アトツギ（後継ぎ）」をテーマに活動するリトルプレス「アトツギ編集室」の4名と、狩猟や山菜採り、それらの調理等の熟練者。彼らと参加者が力を合わせれば、森は、たちまちフルコース料理に変わる。2014年の第2回は、月山山系・朝日連峰周辺の山に入り、クルミのデュカやキノコオイルなどの素材の野性味を活かした調理を行った。しかし、次回も同じメニューを作るのかは、全く不明。何が採れるのか、そもそも採れるのか、それを楽しむのが「森のテーブルマナー」の主題。要参加費。（岩井 巽／東北芸術工科大学 学生）

1950年代から続く、郷土の絶品アイス　秋田の夏の風物詩「大曲の花火」会場に向かう途中、広く青い空の道端に、鮮やかな黄色とピンクのパラソルが開いていた。イメージイラストの青・黄・ピンクのコントラストは、子供が描いた絵か、トイカメラの写真のようで、今もハッキリと目に浮かぶ。そして、売り場に黄色いほっかむりをした「ババヘラ・アイス」売りのお姿ちゃんが、ちょこんと座っていた。ババ（お姿ちゃん）がヘラで、ピンク（イチゴ味）と黄色（バナナ味）の2色のシャーベットを、交互に盛るので、「ババヘラ・アイス」。春から秋にも県内各地で出会える（通信購入可）。（薗部暁子／d47 design travel store）

The ultimate supper made of the forest　"Banquet in the Forest," is a program in which participants go into the forest, forage ingredients, then cook and eat them. It is operated by the four members of "Atotsugi Editorial Room," a small publisher that focuses on the theme of carrying on regional cuisine and handiwork, and foraging and hunting experts. With the help of these experts, participants transform the forest into a full-course meal. For the second "Banquet in the Forest" of 2014, participants entered the Asahi mountain range of the Gassan mountains and cooked with mushroom oils and walnut duqqa made with wild ingredients. Whether participants will make the same dishes next time is unknown. "Forest table manners" dictate that you cook with and enjoy what's available in the forest. Participation fee required.（Tatsumi Iwai, Tohoku University of Art and Design）

Exquisite local ice cream introduced in the 1950s　While I was heading to "Oomagari Fireworks," an Akita summer tradition, under the huge blue sky and on the side of the road, I saw a bright yellow and pink parasol. The high contrast illustration on the parasol, executed in blue, pink, and yellow, looked like it was drawn by a child or shot on a toy camera. I remember it clearly to this day. Under the parasol was an old woman with a yellow towel wrapped around her head was sitting and selling "Babahera Ice Cream." The name comes from the fact that an old woman [baba] alternately scoops pink and yellow sherbet with a spatula [hera]. It's sold between spring and autumn in various areas throughout the prefecture（and through mail order）.（Akiko Sonobe, d47 design travel store）

www.tendo-mokko.co.jp

008
茨城
IBARAKI

ちょっ蔵 新酒を祝う会
📍 茨城県笠間市稲田2281-1
☎ 0296-74-2002
（磯蔵酒造内 実行委員会 Isokura Shuzo）
🏠 isokura.jp/event/iwaukai/2015
Chokkura—New Sake Celebration
📍 Inada 2281-1, Kasama, Ibaraki

007
福島
FUKUSHIMA

FOR 座 REST 2015
📍 福島県福島市大町9-21 ニューヤブウチビル 1F（FOR 座 REST 2015 実行委員会）
🏠 www.ankaju.com/forzarest/
FOR ZA REST 2015
📍 New Yabuuchi Bldg. 1F, Omachi 9-21, Fukushima, Fukushima

地元で愛される酒蔵の、年に一度の新酒祭り　創業明治元年の笠間市稲田「磯蔵酒造」が、毎年新酒の季節、4月下旬に開催する新酒祭り。2015年で、9回目となる。「いろいろありますが、今年も生きて酒が呑める。こんなに有難い事はありません」という蔵主の言葉通り、決して広いとは言えない酒蔵に、2000人以上の“酔っ払いが溢れている様”は圧巻。大小2つのステージでのライブパフォーマンス、落語家による寄席、きき酒選手権など、酒席に華を添えるイベントが、1日中行われる。入蔵料には、代表銘柄「稲里」の新酒の4合瓶1本に、笠間焼のぐい呑みが付いてくる。焼物の産地ならではの、おもてなしの心が、とても嬉しい。(沼田健一／「trattoria blackbird」)

New sake celebration organized by locally loved sake brewery
Established in 1868, "Isokura Shuzo" sake brewery organizes an annual new sake celebration event at the end of April. In 2015, it will hold its ninth new sake celebration event. As the brewery owner says, "Many things happen in life, but we're grateful to be alive and drink sake." The brewery is by no means big, and to see over 2000 drunks in it is an amazing sight. There are two stages, on which live performances, storytelling, sake-tasting championships, and other sake-related events that make drinking more fun are held all day. Admission includes a bottle of the brewery's best-known "Inasato" and Kasama-yaki sake cup, an expression of hospitality unique to a region known for its pottery. (Kenichi Numata, trattoria blackbird)

祝10周年！　僕が、初めて福島県に行ったのは、2012年4月。福島市の飯坂温泉「旅館 清山」で開催された「FOR 座 REST 大学」のライブで、会場から溢れるほどの地元の人々と一緒に、細野晴臣と高田漣の素晴らしい演奏を聴いた。そこで福島市のセレクトショップ「Pick-Up」の田中栄さんら、よき友人を得る事もできた。そして2015年7月、ついに「FOR 座 REST」が復活。会場は10年前の第1回と同じ「福島市民家園」。アン・サリー、大友良英など常連組の他に、本誌「山形県号」取材で出会った、山伏・坂本大三郎さん、東北芸術工科大学の宮本武典さん、デザイン事務所「アカオニデザイン」もワークショップで参加する。再会が楽しみだ。(空閑 理／d design travel 編集部)

Tenth anniversary!
In April 2012, I saw a wonderful live performance by Haruomi Hosono and Ren Takada at the Seizan Inn in the Iizaka hot spring region. The local audience was so large that it was barely contained at the inn. It was also at that show that I became friends with Sakae Tanaka, the staff of the multi-brand store "Pick-Up" in Fukushima city. In July 2015, "FOR ZA REST" will be revived and held again at "Fukushimashi Minkaen," where it was first held 10 years ago. In addition to regulars Ann Sally and Yoshihide Otomo, the mountain ascetic Daizaburo Sakamoto, whom I met while researching the *d design travel Yamagata*, Takenori Miyamoto from Tohoku University of Art and Design, and the design office "Akaoni Design" will participate in workshops. I'm looking forward to the reunion. (Osamu Kuga, d design travel Editorial Team)

 マルヒの干しいも
www.maruhi.co.jp

 野沢民芸
NOZAWA MINGEI
www.nozawa-mingei.com

010

群馬
GUNMA

小阿瀬 直
📍 群馬県高崎市田町 53-2 2F
（小阿瀬直建築設計事務所 [SNARK]）
☎ 027-384-2268
🏠 www.snark.cc
Sunao Koase
📍 2F, Tamachi 53-2, Takasaki, Gunma
（SNARK）

009

栃木
TOCHIGI

風間 教司
📍 栃木県鹿沼市上材木町 1737（根古屋路地）
☎ 0289-60-1610
（日光珈琲 カフェ 饗茶庵 本店 Café Kyo-Cha-an）
🏠 nikko-coffee.com
Kyoji Kazama
📍 Kamizaimoku-cho 1737, Kanuma, Tochigi

"今の視点"に、ずっと愛せる心地よさをプラス　小阿瀬直さんは、建築設計事務所「SNARK」の代表だが、活動は建築のみに留まらない。自家用家具づくりを発展させ、プロダクトレーベル「Lodge」を起ち上げたり、2015年春には、事務所2階をコーヒースタンド兼シェアオフィスとして開放。そこには、一緒に「モノづくり」に励む仲間が、たくさん集まる。こういった環境がある事が、家を建てる施主を心強く、また、楽しみにさせるのだろう。オープンハウスに行くと、その色や造りの印象が強く記憶に残った。外観は独特な中間色に覆われ、職人手づくりの金具が随所に使われるなど、愛着に繋がる濃やかな心遣いが多くて実に嬉しい。(土屋裕一／本屋業「suiran」)

鹿沼市の兄貴　風間教司さんは、自宅一部を自ら改築、1999年に「カフェ 饗 茶庵」を開店。最初は10席。他も改築し、一軒カフェになったのは10年目。美味しい「かぼちゃのプリン」を味わう時には陽が射し込む部屋、読書をしたい時には薄明るい居間、と空間を選べる。「試行錯誤は当前。始める事が大事」と、カフェの支店も出し続ける。月に1度開かれる市「ネコヤド商店街」は、店を持ちたい若者が客商売の経験ができるように、と彼が仲間達と共に9年前に始めた。今では開業した若者達と一緒に商店会を結成し、街を盛り上げている。この夏、ゲストハウスも開業する予定の彼は、「まずは始める事です」と、頼もしく笑って語った。(佐々木晃子／d design travel 編集部)

Adding everlasting comfort to contemporary perspectives
Sunao Koase is the president of the architectural office "SNARK." He also launched the product label "Lodge" for his furniture line and, in 2015, opened the second floor of his office as a shared office and café. The space now draws a variety of people who are interested in "object making." Such an environment is sure to entertain and reassure Koase's architectural clients. When I went to an open house event there, I was struck by the structure and color of the building. The exterior was covered in unique neutral tints and handmade metal fittings were used thoughtfully throughout the interior to cultivate deep personal attachment. (Yuichi Tsuchiya, Book Seller "suiran")

The brother from Kanuma　Kyoji Kazama renovated a part of his home to open "Café Kyo-Cha-an" in 1999. It started out with just 10 seats. After more renovations, it became a standalone business in 2005. You can choose the room you want to be in—the well-lit room for enjoying the delicious "pumpkin cake" and the darker room for reading, for example. "Experimentation is the norm. The important thing is to start," Kazama explains. He's opened several branch cafes since. Nine years ago, he also started, with friends, "Nekoyado Arcade," where a market is held monthly to allow young people, who want to start a shop, to gain business experience. He has since organized a shop association with young people who've opened up businesses to vitalize the local city. This summer, he will also open a guesthouse. "The important thing is to start," he reiterated with a confident smile. (Akiko Sasaki, d design travel Editorial Team)

012
千葉
CHIBA

omusubi 不動産
おむすび
📍 千葉県松戸市常盤平陣屋前1-13
☎ 047-710-0628
🏠 www.omusubi-estate.com
Omusubi Fudosan
📍 Tokiwadaira Jinyamae 1-13, Matsudo, Chiba

011
埼玉
SAITAMA

ホーケン化粧品
📍 埼玉県川口市芝新町11-10
☎ 0120-83-99-83
🏠 www.ho-ken.co.jp
Hoken
📍 Shibashin-machi 11-10, Kawaguchi, Saitama

町と、町の自然を活性化させる不動産屋 「おこめをつくる不動産屋」を標榜する「omusubi 不動産」は、八柱駅の「さくら通り」にある、殿塚建吾さんが営む不動産会社。空き家の古い家やマンションを、DIY（自分でやろう）可能物件として紹介するほか、居住者と一緒にお米を作る体験や、DIY ワークショップを開催するなど、居住者それぞれに合った、町の暮らしの提案を楽しく行っている。丁寧な紹介の物件情報も、ユーモアに溢れていて楽しい。縁側と庭がある平屋の家は、「庭で穫れたトマトを、そのまま外で洗ってムシャリ」などと紹介。そして、そんな生活に憧れて、私自身、現在、平屋で野菜とハーブを育てていて、収穫の夏が待ち遠しいのだ。(三枝里夏／ライター)

親から子、孫へと使い続けられる、ロングライフ化粧品 1927年創業の「ホーケン化粧品」。以前は、多くの百貨店等で販売されていたが、第二次世界大戦の悲劇をきっかけに「良質な物を、必要な分だけ作って届けたい」と、主に通信販売に。私のお薦めの石鹸「ハニックスソープ」は、60日間丁寧に天日干しされ、無香料・無着色。ロングセラー「ハニックスクリーム」は、川口市の工場で少量生産。創業時から変わらぬデザインで、共に首都圏で大人気。広報の古屋和美さんは、「化粧品会社ではあるけれど、商品を通した人と人との繋がりを大切にしていきたい」と言う。創業者の祖父から受け継いだ大切な想いなのだ。(中村千晶／d47 design travel store)

A real estate company vitalizing the city and its natural environment "Omusubi Fudosan" advertises itself as "a real estate company that makes rice." It's located on Sakura Dori near Yabashira Station and is run by Kengo Tonozuka. The company specializes in DIY (do it yourself) properties, such as old houses and apartments, and organizes DIY home repair and rice-making workshops to propose a lifestyle that fits individual tenants and the city they live in. Its property listings, which are carefully written, are also full of humor. For example, the description of a one-storied house with a yard and a verandah reads, "Pick the garden-grown tomato, wash it outside, and eat it in one go." I aspired to such a lifestyle, and I currently live in a one-storied house and grow herbs in my garden. I can't wait till summer harvesting season. (Rika Saegusa, writer)

Long-lasting design cosmetic products that can be passed down generations "Hoken" was established in 1927. It was previously available in many department stores, but after the tragedy of World War II, the company decided to "produce quality products in only necessary quantities" and shifted its primary business to mail order. I recommend "HONEYX SOAP," which is sun dried carefully for 60 days and made without color or fragrance additives. Its long-selling "HONEYX CREAM" is made in small batches at its Kawaguchi factory. Both are popular primarily in the Tokyo Metropolitan area and their designs have not changed since 1927. Company publicist Kazumi Furuya says, "We are a cosmetics company, but we value the connection made through people through our products." It is a philosophy, she says, which was passed down from the company founder's grandfather. (Chiaki Nakamura, d47 design travel store)

DIC川村記念美術館 http://kawamura-museum.dic.co.jp

SUZUKOU PEWTER www.takumi-suzukou.com

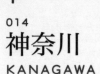

014
神奈川
KANAGAWA

神奈川県立近代美術館 鎌倉
📍 神奈川県鎌倉市雪ノ下 2-1-53
（鶴岡八幡宮境内）
☎ 0467-22-5000
🏠 www.moma.pref.kanagawa.jp
The Museum of Modern Art, Kamakura
📍 Yukinoshita 2-chome 1-53, Kamakura,
Kanagawa

013
東京
TOKYO

首都高速道路
☎ 03-6667-5855
（首都高お客様センター Customercenter）
🏠 www.shutoko.jp
Metropolitan Expressway

故・坂倉準三設計の、国内初の公立近代美術館 こじんまりとした地元の美術館が、2016年初春に閉館が決まって、その存在の価値が多くの人に注目されて、私は驚いている。私が、県立近代美術館「鎌倉館」の好きな所は、展覧会を見てから、階段を下りたテラスからの平家池の素晴らしい自然。あるがままの自然だからこそ、季節毎の花や草木の色などが移ろう様子が美しい。2006年の「山口勝弘展」は、雨の降る日で水面の波紋がきれいだったと、約10年前に訪れた日を、ありありと思い起こす。エレベーターもない昔ながらの美術館が、世界中の芸術や文化を発信する場所として、これまで残ってくれていた事を、私は県の誇りと思う。（黒江美穂／d47 MUSEUM）

体感ハイスピードの東京観光 2013年度「グッドデザイン・未来づくりデザイン賞」の目黒区の「大橋ジャンクション」から、首都高速3号渋谷線で、ガラス張りのビル群に映る、たくさんの「東京タワー」を抜けて、都心環状線を皇居に沿うように、三宅坂から竹橋へ、次から次へと現れるカーブを車で走る。ジェットコースターのような道路のねじれとアップダウンが続き、コンクリートの空間を、高速で走る車の群れと、僕は、心地よい並走を楽しむ。速度に合った道路幅、標識の配置など、安全性も緻密にデザインされた"超巨大迷宮ハイウェイ"。この疾走感と恍惚感は、車の少ない日曜日の夜が特によい。ただし安全運転で。（神藤秀人／d design travel 編集部）

Japan's First Public Modern Art Museum Designed by the Late Junzo Sakakura To my surprise, after a modest, local art museum was scheduled for closure in early spring of 2016, the value of its presence has been drawing a lot of attention. What I like about the Museum of Modern Art, Kamakura is the wonderful view of Heike Lake from the terrace, which you can reach by descending the stairs after seeing the exhibition on display. Because the view is of nature as is, the trees, flowers, and colors of leaves change beautifully with the seasons. I vividly recall going to the 2006 Katsuhiro Yamaguchi exhibition on a rainy day and seeing beautiful ripples on the surface of the lake. I'm proud that this old art museum, which doesn't even have an elevator, survived this long as a place that transmits art and culture from around the world. (Miho Kuroe, d47 MUSEUM)

High-speed sensory Tokyo tours From the Ohashi Junction in Meguro, which received the 2013 "Good Design Award for Future-Making Design," take the Metropolitan Expressway 3 Shibuya Line and take in the many Tokyo Towers reflected in skyscraper windows. Then take the curvy Tokyo Metropolitan Expressway Ring Route along the Imperial Palace from Miyakezaka to Takebashi. The continuously bending expressway goes up and down like a roller coaster. I enjoy driving alongside the cars traveling at high speeds through the concrete space. This is an enormous labyrinth-like highway that's precisely designed with road widths and signage appropriate to the driving speed and with safety in mind. The intense thrill of driving through this highway is best enjoyed on a Sunday night, when there isn't a lot of traffic. Make sure you drive safely. (Hideto Shindo, d design travel Editorial Team)

016

富山
TOYAMA

新とんかつ（総曲輪店）
📍 富山県富山市総曲輪3-6-15-21
☎ 076-424-4536
🔗 shintonkatsu.com
Shintonkatsu (Sogawa Branch)
📍 Sogawa 3-chome 6-15-21, Toyama, Toyama

015

新潟
NIIGATA

ぽんしゅ館 新潟駅店
📍 新潟県新潟市中央区花園 1-96-47
　　CoCoLo 西館 3F
☎ 025-240-7090
🔗 ponshukan-niigata.com
Ponshu:kan Niigata
📍 CoCoLo Nishikan 3F, Hanazono 1-chome
　　96-47, Chuo-ku, Niigata, Niigata

アートに囲まれて食べる、絶品とんかつ　私が、初めて「新とんかつ」の暖簾を潜った時、その空間の雰囲気に、とても驚いた。高岡市出身画家の故・古川通泰さんの絵画や、親交のある陶芸家の器などが飾られた薄暗い店内と、それらとは対照的に明るくライトアップされ、ずらりと皿が並んだ厨房。「食べる事は、その店の雰囲気を味わう事でもあります」。1945年の創業時から受け継がれてきた信念だそう。ジュワッと揚げる音、サクッと切る音、そして、常連客の富山弁の会話。五感を刺激する店内で、美術品を眺めながら、揚げ立ての、とんかつを待つのは、とても斬新な時間だ。運ばれてきたアツアツの「ロースかつ」を、私は急いで、頬張った。（石井 唯／D&DEPARTMENT TOYAMA）

越後の日本酒文化と、そのデザインを楽しめる店　新潟市に来たら、ぜひ立ち寄ってほしい「ぽんしゅ館」。「利き酒番所」に県内全ての酒蔵（何と93！）の酒が集められ、500円で5蔵の利き酒ができる。酒蔵の特長、銘柄の解説が添えられた、壁一面の試飲マシンが見た目以上に大圧巻。たくさんのラベルを眺めているだけでも、とても楽しく、本当に迷ってしまうが、それがいい。全て個性があって、新潟の日本酒の面白さ、そして、丁寧な酒造りを続ける酒蔵の凄さに気づかされた。店内には、県内から選ばれた、味もパッケージも魅力ある食品も競い合うように並べられていて、それらが購入できるのも嬉しい。1号店は、「越後湯沢駅」構内。（迫 一成／クリエイト集団「hickory03travelers」）

Eating exquisite pork cutlets while surrounded by art　The first time I entered "Shintokatsu," I was amazed by its ambiance. The dimly lit restaurant features the late Michiyasu Furukawa's paintings and pottery by artists, who are acquaintances of the restaurant owner. In contrast, the kitchen is brightly lit and filled with plates. "To eat at a restaurant is to take in its ambiance," explains the owner. It's a philosophy that has been carried on since the establishment of the restaurant in 1945. The restaurant is filled with various sounds—of the fryer, of the cutlets being cut, and of the regulars and their Toyama dialect. Looking at the artworks while waiting for the freshly fried pork cutlet was a novel experience. All five senses were stimulated as I hurriedly ate the steaming pork loin cutlet. (Yui Ishii, D&DEPARTMENT TOYAMA)

Enjoy Echigo's sake culture and design　"Ponshukan" is a must-see for anyone traveling to Niigata. "Kikizake Bansho," the sake-tasting section of the shop offers sake from all the sake breweries in the prefecture (of which there are 93!) and a selection of five to taste for ¥500. The tasting machine, which takes up an entire wall and offers descriptions of breweries and their sake is rather awe-inspiring. Just looking at the uniquely designed sake labels is very enjoyable. The entire presentation showed me the joy of Niigata sake and the care with which the prefecture's breweries continue to make sake. The store also offers foods that taste great and are superbly packaged. The first store is located inside Echigo Yuzawa Station. (Kazunari Sako, hickory03travelers)

セイアグリー健康卵
www.ferver.co.jp

新潟市美術館
ミュージアムショップ

018
福井
FUKUI

☕

Cafe Chotto　※現在休業中
📍 福井県吉田郡永平寺町東古市9-36
☎ 050-7520-2645
🏠 7864e1a73af58c93.lolipop.jp
Cafe Chotto
📍 Eiheiji-cho Higashifuruichi 9-36, Yoshida, Fukui

017
石川
ISHIKAWA

🛍

二三味珈琲 shop 舟小屋
📍 石川県珠洲市折戸町木の浦ハ-99
☎ 0768-86-2088
Nizami Coffee Shop Funagoya
📍 Orito-machi Kinoura Ha-99, Suzu, Ishikawa

永平寺参拝の時に、ぜひ行きたい、素敵なカフェ「永平寺」は、修行僧の日常を間近に見る事ができる曹洞宗の大本山。県外からのお客様をお連れすると、必ず感動される。福井市内から、「えちぜん鉄道」と「京福バス」を、「永平寺口駅」で乗り継いで行くのだが、その、静かな駅前にある、青みがかった越前瓦が目印の「Cafe Chotto」を、お薦めしたい。酒井和美さん・恵さん姉妹が、祖父母が暮らしていた築100年以上の古民家を改築。帯戸（幅広の戸）や囲炉裏のある白壁の室内で、珈琲と季節毎の自家製菓子で、もてなしてくれ、「京福バス」運転手も寛いでいる。（新海康介／アネックスホテル福井「二の丸グリル」）

最果ての珈琲豆焙煎所　能登半島先端に「二三味珈琲 shop 舟小屋」がある。二三味葉子さんが、祖父の舟小屋を改築し開店させた珈琲豆焙煎所（販売のみ）だ。「たまたま実家に帰り、舟小屋を見た時にインスピレーションが閃いた」と葉子さん。地元に珈琲文化を根付かせ、珠洲市観光の大きな切っ掛けの場所となった「二三味珈琲」。金沢市内に住む僕でも、車で約3時間は正直大変だったが、辿り着いた時に、目の前に広がる日本海の絶景に、とても感動してしまった。市街地にある支店の「cafe」では珈琲が飲めるが、ぜひ、舟小屋で、焙煎し立ての豆の香りに酔ってほしい。（村井一気／「life is beautiful」実行委員）

A pleasant café on the way to Eiheiji Temple　Eiheiji is the main temple of the Soto school of Zen Buddhism and visitors can get a firsthand look into the daily lives of monks training there. Whenever I take anyone from outside Fukui Prefecture there, they're always moved. From Fukui, you take the "Echizen Railroad" and "Keifuku Bus" to Eifukuji Station to get there. In front of the quiet station is "Café Chotto." You'll notice its bluish Echizen tiled roof right away. Owner sisters Kazumi and Megumi Sakai renovated an over-100-years-old home, which their grandparents lived in, to house the café. The white walled café, which features a traditional hearth and doors with a lock rail, is a great place to enjoy coffee and seasonal sweets. The "Keifuku Bus" drivers can often be seen relaxing in the café. (Kosuke Shinkai, Ninomaru Grill, Annex Hotel Fukui)

The remotest coffee roaster　"Nizami Coffee Shop Funagoya" is located on the tip of the Noto Peninsula. Owner Yoko Nizami renovated her grandfather's boathouse [*funagoya*] and opened the coffee roaster and beans shop in it. "I happened to be back at my parents' home and was inspired by the boathouse," Nizami explains. "Nizami Coffee" established a coffee culture in Suzu and became a big tourist attraction there. I live in Kanazawa, and it took me three hours to drive there. Honestly, it was a long journey, but when I arrived, I was moved by the expansive view of the Sea of Japan in front of me. "Nizami Café" in the downtown Suzu serves coffee, but I recommend taking in the robust aroma of coffee beans roasting in Funagoya. (Kazuki Murai, life is beautiful exeecutive committee)

✛ GENOME REAL STORE

Qui boon

020
長野
NAGANO

くらもと古本市
📍 長野県諏訪市 上諏訪街道（酒蔵5か所）
☎ 0268-75-9377（株式会社バリューブックス くらもと古本市係 Value Books）
🏠 www.valuebooks.jp
Kuramoto Furuhon Ichi
📍 Kamisuwa Kaido Street, Suwa, Nagano（Five Sake Breweries）

019
山梨
YAMANASHI

BEEK
📍 山梨県北杜市大泉町西井出 8240-6550 B（BEEK DESIGN）
☎ 090-7946-9512
🏠 www.beekmagazine.com
BEEK
📍 Oizumi-cho Nishiide 8240-6550 B, Hokuto, Yamanashi

お気に入りの酒と書店に出会えるイベント　歴史ある「酒蔵の町・上諏訪」は、「信州舞姫」「麗人」「本金」「横笛」「真澄」といった老舗酒蔵5蔵が、約400メートルに建ち並んでいる。「くらもと古本市」は、それら5蔵を会場に、長野県と山梨県の書店等が、20店近く出店する。私は、全蔵で試飲できるクーポン券（1800円）を買い、出来立ての新酒を呑み比べてみた。各会場の本棚に並ぶ、食や暮らしの本、絵本、アートブックなどに、それぞれの書店の個性が明確に表われ、こんなに面白い古本市が地元にあったのかと驚いた。「真澄」の蔵元「宮坂醸造」で、中庭の立派な松を眺めながら、ほろ酔いで、買ったばかりの本を読んだ。本当に幸せだった。（進藤仁美／d47 design travel store）

Uターン編集者が発信する、山梨の魅力　土屋誠さんは、都内で10年間のデザイナー業の後、山梨県に帰郷し、フリーマガジン「BEEK」を制作。第2号は本をテーマに「春光堂書店」や「不二御堂」など、県内の様々な書店を巡り、第3号は「山梨の週末」をテーマに、その場所や人々、出来事を取材し、紹介。編集からデザインまで、制作は、全て一人。また、山梨生活を、県外の人にも体感してほしいと、「BEEK Life Style」とイベントを名付け、第1回は名古屋に出店し、幻の米と呼ばれる「武川48」で炊いた、ごはん等を販売する予定。山梨出身の私も、この「BEEK」で紹介された余暇を満喫している。（廣瀬智也／D&DEPARTMENT YAMANASHI）

An event where you might find your new favorite books and sake　Kamisuwa is a historical town known for its sake breweries. Within 400 meters of the city are the renowned breweries "Maihime," "Reijin," "Honkin," "Yokobue," and "Masumi." "Kuramoto Furuhon Ichi（Used Book Fair）" is held in the five breweries and features nearly 20 booksellers from Nagano and Yamanashi Prefectures. I bought an ¥1,800 coupon for sake tasting in all five breweries and compared the fresh sakes. I also looked at the books on food and living, picture books, and art books and could see that each bookseller had a distinct personality. I was amazed by how interesting the book fair was. At Miyasaka Jozo, which makes "Masumi," I, slightly drunk, took in the beautiful pine trees in the garden and read my newly purchased book.（Hitomi Shindo, d47 design travel store）

Yamanshi's attractions presented by an editor who returned to the prefecture　Makoto Tsuchiya returned to Yamanashi Prefecture after working as a designer in Tokyo for a decade and launched the free magazine *BEEK*. The theme of its second issue is "books," and it features a variety of bookstores in the prefecture, including "Shunkodo Shoten" and "Fujimido." The third issue's theme is "weekend in Yamanashi," and it includes articles on relevant places, people, and events. Tsuchiya handles all aspects of the magazine's production, from editing to design. He also organizes an event called "BEEK Life Style" with hopes of letting people living outside Yamanashi experience the prefecture's attractions. For the first "BEEK Life Style" event, he will set up shop in Nagoya and sell meals featuring Yamanshi's legendary "Mukawa 48" rice. I'm a Yamanashi native, but I enjoy taking part in the leisure activities recommended by the magazine.（Tomoya Hirose, D&DEPARTMENT YAMANASHI）

SINCE 1935
HADACHU ORIMONO
info@hadachuorimono.jp

022
静岡
SHIZUOKA

お抹茶 こんどう
静岡県静岡市駿河区津島町5-9
054-282-4222
omaccha.blogspot.jp
Omaccha Kondo
Tsushima-cho 5-9, Suruga-ku, Shizuoka,
Shizuoka

021
岐阜
GIFU

京や
岐阜県高山市大新町1-77
0577-34-7660
www.kyoya-hida.jp
Kyoya
Oshin-machi 1-77, Takayama, Gifu

擂り立てとろろと、挽き立て抹茶の郷土料理店　私は、「d47 食堂」で「静岡定食とろろ汁」を出すために、とろろ汁の作り方を学びに、近藤雄介さんの店に行った。カウンター席に座ると、目の前で地元特産の「ほんやま自然薯」が、すり鉢で見る見る擂られていく。作務衣姿に精悍な顔立ち、緊張感がある近藤さんの仕事ぶりは美しかった。本山地区で自然薯を栽培する事になった経緯や、静岡が発祥のワサビ漬けの話、抹茶を挽くために厳選して石臼を買った姿勢などを語る彼に、私は、つい前のめりになって聞き入ってしまった。カウンター越しで挽かれ立ての抹茶の「泡立ち冷やし抹茶割り」や、黒豆きな粉の「古代米入りの長皿団子」も美味しい。(内田幸映／d47 食堂)

飛騨高山の歴史ある郷土料理店　越後の古民家を移築した郷土料理処「京や」の店内には、炭の囲炉裏席があり、飛騨の昔の暮らしの光景を彷彿とさせてくれる。女将さんの西村京子さんの1日は、手作りの赤かぶらの漬け物を器に盛る事から始まる。西村さんの母の味の「鶏ちゃん」は、鶏の肉、皮、肝に、内卵も入れ、「鶏の全部を入れる事で、とてもジューシーになるのよ」と、西村さん。「平瀬酒造店」の純米酒「久寿玉」とよく合い、私はご飯も進んだ。漬け物を、いったん水に浸してから半日煮る「煮たくもじ(くもじ＝漬け物)」は、漬け物が傷んでくると、昔は、どこの家でも作って、町中、各家から、その香りがしていたそうだ。「京や」の、それは絶品。(中山小百合／d47 食堂)

A restaurant serving local cuisine of freshly grated yam and freshly ground green tea　I visited Yusuke Kondo's restaurant "Omaccha Kondo" to learn how to make grated yam soup for a "Shizuoka Style Grated Yam Meal" for "d47 Shokudo." I sat at the counter and watched the locally produced Japanese yam being grated right in front of me. Watching Kondo, who has a tense, but fearless expression and was dressed in a monk's work clothes, prepare the yams was a beautiful sight. He told me of how the yams are produced in Honyama; wasabi pickles, which originated in Shizuoka; and how he carefully selected and purchased a stone mortar for grinding matcha tea. Riveted, I found myself leaning over the counter. The cocktail "frothy iced matcha with shochu" made with matcha ground behind the counter, and "sweet rice cake with wild rice on a long plate," served with black bean powder, are both also delicious. (Yukie Uchida, d47 SHOKUDO)

A historical restaurant in Hidatakayama serving local cuisine　"Kyoya" is housed in a renovated old home, which was moved from Echigo. It features seating surrounding traditional charcoal hearths and evokes the traditional Hidatakayama lifestyle. Its proprietor Kyoko Nishimura starts her day by serving pickled red turnips on plates. "Keichan," a chicken dish modeled after her mother's cooking, is made with chicken meat, skin, innards, and ovaries. Nishimura explains that putting in all of the chicken makes the dish extra juicy. The dish goes perfectly with rice and "Hirase Shuzoten's" "Kusudama" sake. "Nitakumoji," which is made by stewing pickles for half a day after soaking them in water, is a dish that all families in the area used to make. In the past, Nishimura says, the whole neighborhood smelled like the dish. Kyoya's version is exquisite. (Sayuri Nakayama, d47 SHOKUDO)

CAMBRIDGE-NO-MORI.COM
SPACE DESIGN STUDIO

The Libretto
Books & Furniture

024
三重
MIE

丸川竜也
⌖ 三重県津市中央6-2
（株式会社ドラゴンブルームス）
☎ 059-253-7845
🌐 dragonblooms.jp
Tatsuya Marukawa
⌖ Chuou 6-2, Tsu, Mie (DRAGONBLOOMS, INC.)

023
愛知
AICHI

TOKONAME
⌖ 愛知県常滑市原松町6-70-2
（TOKONAME STORE）
☎ 0569-36-0655
🌐 tokoname.com
TOKONAME
⌖ Haramatsu-cho 6-chome 70-2, Tokoname,
Aichi (TOKONAME STORE)

これからの世代が大きな夢が得られる故郷に 私が、丸川竜也さんに初めてお会いしたのは、5年前。当時の江東区清澄白河の事務所で、自身が手がける松阪木綿の現状や展望を熱心に話してくれ、私は彼に感銘を受けた。彼は、作務衣姿で売場に立つ事が多く、松阪木綿の織元の若旦那と思われがちだが、デザイン事務所「ドラゴンブルームス」の代表であり、デザイナーだ。親子三代受け継ぐ「丸川商店」の屋号を守り、松阪木綿を使った新商品や、伊勢うどんのパッケージデザイン、フリーマガジン「ミエノコ」の編集長を兼ね、衣食住にわたるデザインを手がける。現在は松阪市に事務所を移し、地元の若者を鼓舞して、邁進し続けている。（野口忠典／d47 design travel store）

常滑焼の伝統を更新するチャレンジ パステルカラーが可愛らしいティーポットを買った。急須などを作ってきた、日本六古窯の一つの常滑焼の、素材と技術を活かした「TOKONAME」シリーズ茶器は、濃やかな土のサラサラとした質感。ポットは注ぎ口の形がよく、湯切れもよい。持つと見た目以上に軽く、繊細な印象だが、しっかりと焼き締められているので、とても丈夫。使いやすくて、僕は毎日使っている。「TOKONAME」プロジェクトは、常滑焼の窯元「山源陶苑」の鯉江優次さんの呼びかけで始まった。2015年4月に直営店をオープンさせ、新しいアイデアで常滑焼を広めようとする鯉江さんの熱意が、県内外から来店客を集めている。（山田藤雄／「DEAN & DELUCA」）

Making his hometown a place future generations can realize their dreams I first met Tatsuya Marukawa five years ago at his office in Kiyosumi Shirakawa. His passionate discussion of the current state and his hopes for Matsuzaka cotton impressed me. He often works in monk's work clothes, and is perceived as the young master of a cotton manufacturer, but he is in fact designer and president of the design office "DRAGONBLOOMS." He designs products for all aspects of life. Preserving the trade name of "Marukawa Shoten," which has been passed down three generations, he creates new Matsuzaka cotton products in addition to designing packaging for Ise udon noodles and editing the free magazine *mienoko*. He is currently based in Matsuzaka, where he continues to realize his dreams. (Tadanori Noguchi, d47 design travel store)

The challenge of updating the Tokoname ware tradition I bought a cute pastel colored teapot. The "TOKONAME" series of tea ware, which uses the materials and techniques of Tokoname ware, known for its traditional Japanese teapots, is made of fine clay giving it smooth texture. The teapot's spout is exquisitely designed and does not drip. It appears delicate and feels even lighter than it looks, but is fired tight for durability. I use it daily. Yuji Koie of the "Yamagen Togen" pottery started the TOKONAME project and its first directly operated store opened in April 2015. Koie's passion for spreading Tokoname ware through innovative ideas draws customers from within and outside Aichi Prefecture. (Fujio Yamada, DEAN & DELUCA)

www.shovelz.jp

www.karimoku60.com

027
大阪
OSAKA

ゼー六（堺筋本町店）
📍 大阪府大阪市中央区本町1-3-22
☎ 06-6261-2606
Ze-roku (Sakaisuji Honmachi)
📍 Honmachi 1-chome 3-22, Chuo-ku, Osaka, Osaka

025
滋賀
SHIGA

丸中醤油
📍 滋賀県愛知郡愛荘町東出229
☎ 0749-37-2118（蔵元 Brewery）
🏠 www.s-marunaka.com
Marunaka Shoyu
📍 Aisho-cho Higashide 229, Echi, Shiga

商人の拘りも挟んだ、アイス最中　大阪には「贅六」という言葉が残り、商人には無用の贅物6つ（禄、閥、引、学、太刀、身分）の事を指し、本町橋手前の趣ある木造の喫茶店「ゼー六」の元祖の店名由来になった。店の一番人気はテイクアウトできる、掌サイズ八角形の「アイス最中」。最中の中心の「ゼー六」の文字の周りに「ICECREAM」の文字があり、見た目も可愛く、味はあっさりで美味い。夏には近所の主婦、ちびっ子、仕事合間の会社員等が汗を拭きながら並ぶ。ドライアイスは使わず新聞紙で包むので、持ち帰り時間は30分以内でないと購入不可。「時間、ずるしたらあかんで」と言う、店主の笑顔の奥に、美味しさへの拘りを感じる。（万城目絢子／d47 食堂）

創業寛政の歴史が守る、極上醤油　琵琶湖の東、愛知郡にある「丸中醤油」の醸造蔵は、現在まで、できるだけ修復する事なく受け継がれてきた。なぜならば、天井、床、壁、桶や樽などに棲みつく微生物（醸造菌）が、昔から変わらぬ味を守ってくれているからだ。毎日、作務衣姿の職人が、五感を研ぎ澄ませ一心不乱に櫂入れし、今では大変珍しい手動式での「舟絞り」などの工程から生み出される醤油は、驚くほど旨みがあり、私は虜になった。作務衣の背の、麦の穂で「中」の字を囲んで描かれた「丸中醤油」のロゴや、「丸中醤油」の力強い筆文字デザインのよさ。この醤油だけで味付けする出汁巻き玉子は、とても美味しい。（大塚麻衣子／d47 食堂）

Ice cream and merchant's obsessions sandwiched between wafers　In Osaka, there a term called *zeiroku* or the "six extravagances." They refer to the six extravagances that a merchant doesn't need—stipend, clan, backroom dealings, education, weapons, and status. It is also the origin of the café Ze-roku's name. Located in at the foot of Honmachi Bridge, its most popular item is the palm-sized ice cream sandwich, which can also be ordered for take out. The tasty sandwich is cute and mildly flavored. In the summer, housewives, children, and company employees all line up in the heat to buy the ice cream sandwiches as they wipe the sweat off their brows. The shop offers no dry ice. Simply wrapped in newspaper, the sandwiches must be eaten within 30 minutes. The owner smiles as he warns, "You can't cheat time, you hear." And the warning shows his determination to provide a delicious product.（Ayako Makime, d47 SHOKUDO）

A superior soy sauce protected by its 200-year history　"Marunaka Shoyu," a soy sauce brewery located on the east side of Lake Biwa in Echi, has been preserved with as little repairs as possible because the microbes (i.e. malt) living in the casks and tubs and the building's roof, floor, and walls ensure that the soy sauce tastes the same as it always has. Artisans dressed in monk's work clothes single-mindedly stir the soy sauce daily. The soy sauce, made using traditional, and now rarely used manual techniques, has astonishing *umami*. I was hooked the first time I tasted it. The Marunaka Shoyu logo, which comprises the character for "naka" encircled by ears of barley and the brush-written logotype is exquisitely designed and exudes strength. Delicious Japanese omelettes can be made flavored with Marunaka Shoyu alone.（Maiko Otsuka, d47 SHOKUDO）

kami·mon
http://www.kami-mon.net

www.ebisuya.com

京都・唯一の村　みなみやましろむら
むらびと
http://mura-kyoto.com/murabeat/

www.is-kki.com

京小座布団プラッツ
Platz
www.kyoto-platz.jp

www.kuradailystore.com

庵 Iori 　京都 町家 暮らすように旅する
-Machiya Stay- Living like a Local

8175inc. 　made in kyoto GOSHUIN-CHO
8175-kyoto.com

026
京都
KYOTO

えびす屋 京都嵐山總本店
📍京都府京都市右京区嵯峨天龍寺
　芒ノ馬場町3-24
☎075-864-4444
🏠ebisuya.com/branch/arashiyama/
Ebisuya
📍Saga Tenryuji Susukinobaba-cho 3-24,
　Ukyo-ku, Kyoto, Kyoto

嵐山のランドマーク　京都府を代表する観光地、嵐山。その嵐山の魅力を伝えるのに一役買っているのが、人力車の「えびす屋」である。渡月橋から竹林を通って、嵯峨天皇も住まわれたと言われる嵯峨野へと案内してくれる。俥夫の中山大督さんは、「何もかも、全て自然なのが嵐山の魅力。お客さんに、それに気づいてもらえる瞬間が嬉しい」と言う。俥夫は人力車の楽しさを伝えるのと同時に、嵐山や京都の素晴らしさを伝える観光大使でもある。乗るには、ちょっと勇気が要るかもしれないが、ぜひ、勇気を出して乗ってみてほしい。今まで経験した事のないような景色を見れる事だろう。(小原 龍樹／D&DEPARTMENT KYOTO)

An Arashiyama landmark　Arashiyama is one of the best-known tourist destinations in Kyoto. The rickshaw business "Ebisuya" plays a major role in communicating the area's attractiveness. Ebisuya's rickshaws will take you from Togetsu bridge, through Takebayashi, and to Sagano, where the Saga Emperor is said to have lived. Daisuke Nakayama, a rickshaw driver, says, "Everything is natural in Arashiyama. That's the best part. And I love it when my customers have that realization." Rickshaw drivers are ambassadors of tourism. They not only convey the joy of riding a rickshaw, but also of the wonders of Arashiyama and Kyoto. It might take a bit of courage to ride a rickshaw, but try it. You will see amazing sights, the likes of which you've never seen before. (Ryuki Obara, D&DEPARTMENT KYOTO)

029
奈良
NARA

奈良ホテル ティーラウンジ
📍 奈良県奈良市高畑町1096
☎ 0742-26-3300
🌐 narahotel.co.jp
Nara Hotel Tea Lounge
📍 Takabatake-cho 1096, Nara, Nara

緊張なく楽しめる、一流の、おもてなし　「奈良ホテル」は、故・辰野金吾と故・片岡安が設計し、「関西の迎賓館」として、1909年に開業した、日本を代表するクラシックホテルの一つだ。「奈良公園」内にあり、庭やロビー等は自由に見学できる。私は、奈良に来る知人とゆっくり話をするなら、ここのティーラウンジで、と決めている。檜造りの優雅な本館にあり、元は屋外テラスだった部分を改築してあって、天井までの大きな窓から、庭の四季の風景が楽しめる明るい空間。私は、いつも「ケーキセット（1544円から）」を注文する。アップルパイやチーズケーキと共に、定番メニューになっている、松の実がたっぷり使われたケーキが、私のお薦め。（喜多和夫／カフェ「工場跡事務室」）

A relaxing lounge with first-rate service　Opened in 1909, "Nara Hotel" was designed by the late Kingo Tatsuno and Yasushi Kataoka as a hotel for welcoming foreign dignitaries to Kansai. It is one of Japan's best-known classic hotels. Located inside Nara Park, the hotel's garden, lobby, and other common spaces can be accessed freely. Whenever I need a place to talk to visitors in Nara, I bring them to the Nara Hotel Tea Lounge. It is located in the Japanese cypress-made main building in what used to be the outdoor terrace. The floor-to-ceiling windows provide great seasonal views and I always order the "cake set (¥1,544 and up)." I recommend the pine nut cake, which is part of the regular menu alongside the apple pie and cheesecake. (Kazuo Kita, cafe Kojoato Jimushitu)

028
兵庫
HYOGO

弁当と傘
📍 兵庫県豊岡市戸牧8-10
（ヒグラシコーヒー内「弁当と傘」編集室）
🌐 bentoutokasa.com
Bento to Kasa
📍 Tobera 8-10, Toyooka, Hyogo（Hirugashi Coffee）

2011年創刊の、但馬地方発のリトルプレス　「弁当忘れても傘忘れるな」——晴れと雨、天気がよく変わる日本海側の地方で、よく使われる諺だ。兵庫県北部の但馬地域で暮らす女性4人による、自費出版の小冊子「弁

当と傘（愛称は「べんかさ」）」の名は、この諺から取ったそう。創刊号ではコウノトリ（但馬地域は但馬最後の野生のコウノトリの生息地）、第2号では地場産業の鞄を特集し、それらの思い出を地元の人々に聞き、彼女たち自身が好きな物を見に行き、会いたい人に会いに行き、そして、等身大の但馬の素敵さを知る事で、記事は出来上がっている。発行は不定期。B5変形判、32ページ、600円（税込み）。（佐藤 晶／d47 design travel store）

A small press based in Tajima and established in 2011　In the regions facing the Sea of Japan, there's a popular saying: "You can forget your lunchbox, but you can't forget your umbrella." The independent, small magazine *Bento to Kasa* [lunchboxes and umbrellas] is published by four women who live in Tajima, Hyogo Prefecture and takes its name from the popular saying. The premier issue had a feature on storks (Tajima is the last Japanese habitat of wild storks) and the second had a feature on the local industry of bags. The articles are researched and written by the four women, who talk to locals about their memories pertaining to the topic, interview people they want to meet, go see what they want to see, and learn about Tajima's accessible attractions. *Bento to Kasa* is published irregularly. The magazine, 32 page customized B5 format, costs ¥600. (Akira Sato, d47 design travel store)

工場跡　CAFE & GALLERY

多鹿治夫鋏製作所
takeji-hasami.com

031
鳥取
TOTTORI

大因州製紙協業組合附属
山根和紙資料館
📍 鳥取県鳥取市青谷町山根128-5(本社)
☎ 0857-86-0011
🏠 www.daiinshu.co.jp/yamane_library.html
Daiinshu Seishi Yamane Japanese Paper Library
📍 Aoya-cho Yamane 128-5, Tottori, Tottori

030
和歌山
WAKAYAMA

寺田商店
📍 和歌山県和歌山市和歌浦東1-2-29
☎ 073-446-5087
🏠 www.eonet.ne.jp/~teradasyoten/
Terada Shoten
📍 Wakaura-higashi 1-chome 2-29,
　Wakayama, Wakayama

「変わらない和紙づくりの心」 木造の小学校を、日置川の畔に移築し、改築した空間に、国内はもとより、アジアやアフリカなど、紙の装飾品や衣服等が並ぶ資料館。中でも、浄土真宗の妙好人の一人の因幡の源左の言葉が刷られた型染めを、ぜひ見てほしい。「人が取つても やつぽり 家の者が 余計食ふわいや」と鳥取弁で書かれた、寛大な源左の言葉に、身につまされる思いがする。「紙の技術が伝承され、発展してきたのは、山や川、先人たちのおかげ」と、館長は作り手の心について話してくれた。その心と、手触りに魅かれ、僕は大因州 和紙を名刺に使用している。資料館は無料で一般公開され(要予約)、売店では、和紙の文具等を購入できる。(田中信宏/「COCOROSTORE」)

世代を超えて愛される、素朴な銘菓 サクッと軽い口どけのよい玉子煎餅に、万葉集にも詠まれた風光明媚な景勝地・和歌浦の風景などが焼き印された「和歌浦せんべい」。地元の人には、それぞれ好きな図柄があり、私が子供の頃は「不老橋」が出ると嬉しかった。「寺田商店」では、煎餅に最適な小麦粉、風味の強過ぎないレンゲ蜂蜜、地元産の卵など、約70年前に初代が試行錯誤して行き着いた材料と配合を、三代目の寺田憲司さんが受け継いでいる。オリジナルのオーダー煎餅は、地元企業のノベルティなどに使われ、手がけた物は130種以上にもなるそう。当寺

も、受け取る人の顔を綻ばせる"チャーミングな名刺代わり"として、オリジナル煎餅を愛用。(宇治田沙季/善称寺)

Unchanging heart of Japanese papermaking The "Daiinshu Seishi Yamane Japanese Paper Library" is housed in a wooden schoolhouse, which was moved and renovated at its current site. Inside are paper ornaments and clothes from Japan, as well as Asian and African countries. Of particular note is a block-dyed paper printed with these words from Genza of Inaba, the devout worshipper of the Jodo-Shin sect: "Even if others take it, those in the house will eat a lot." The generous sentiment, written in Tottori dialect arouses one's sympathy. In regards to the thoughts of the object's maker, the library director explained, "The development of papermaking techniques is indebted to the mountains, the rivers, and our ancestors." Struck by his passion and the feel of the paper, I use Daiinshu Japanese paper for my business card. The library is free and open to the public (reservations are required). There is also a gift shop that sells Japanese paper stationery. (Tanaka Nobuhiro, COCOROSTORE)

A simple, but great cake loved by customers of all ages The "Wakaura Senbei" is a light, crisp egg cracker that melts in your mouth and is printed with various beautiful Wakaura sceneries, which were written about in *Manyoshu*, Japan's oldest poetry anthology. Locals tend to have a favorite image. When I was a child, I was always happy when I got a cracker with a picture of the Furo Bridge. At "Terada Shoten," third generation owner Kenji Terada continues to use the cracker recipe devised through trial and error by the first owner 70 years ago. The cracker is made with the best flour, a not too fragrant lotus honey, and locally produced eggs. Crackers can also be custom printed and local companies order them as novelty items. To date, Terada Shoten has produced over 130 custom crackers. Zenshoji Temple also uses customized crackers from Terada Shoten as a charming stand-in for a business card, which brings smiles to their recipients. (Saki Ujita, Zenshoji Temple)

ウメボシ8
www.kinpachimikan.com/ume/

033
岡山
OKAYAMA

吉備津土人形
Kibitsu Tsuchi Dolls

稀少な郷土玩具　大分県の民芸店「ぶんご」で、体に水玉模様があるユニークな猿の置物を見つけた。「真ん中の、小さいのを下さい」と店主に言うと、「3つ並べて飾る物なんですよ。岡山県の『吉備津土人形』の『吉備津猿』と言うの」と教わった。「吉備津土人形」は、岡山市の吉備津神社参道などで、明治の初め頃まで、主に、春秋の大祭の前後に売られていた縁起物。地元の伝説に因んだ物の制作をしていた、郷土玩具研究家の故・東隆志が制作を再開したという。また、「吉備津達磨」も、親子3体セットで夫婦円満や安産を祈願する物。彼の人形は、現在、倉敷市の「日本郷土玩具館」等で実物を見る事ができる。ぜひ、見てほしい。(針谷 茜／D&DEPARTMENT PROJECT)

A scarce local toy　While traveling to Oita Prefecture, I found a unique polka dotted monkey object at the folk craft shop "Bungo." I told the owner I wanted the small one in the middle and he responded, "They're meant to be displayed in threes. They're called 'Kibitsu monkeys.' They're a type of 'Kibitsu tsuchi doll,' which are made in Okayama Prefecture." "Kibitsu tsuchi dolls" were auspicious toys sold before and after the main spring and fall festivals on the paths leading to Kibitsu Shrine and others in Okayama during the early Meiji era. It's said that the late local toy researcher Takashi Azuma, who had been producing objects related to local mythology, resumed their production. "Kibitsutsuchi Daruma" is also sold in a family of threes and is believed to help realize happy marriages and safe and easy births. Azuma's dolls can now be seen in the Japan Rural Toy Museum in Kurashiki.　(Akane Hariya, D&DEPARTMENT PROJECT)

引両紋　HIKIRYOMON

032
島根
SHIMANE

ウエダの洋菓子(南田町店)
島根県松江市南田町32-13
0852-27-5689
Ueda no Yogashi (Minamitamachi branch)
Minamitamachi 32-13, Matsue, Shimane

茶好きの町のソウル手土産　松江藩七代藩主・松平不昧公が、町人にお茶文化を根付かせたという歴史的背景もあり、松江の人々は、よく家で抹茶を飲む。そんな松江の町には、和洋問わず菓子店が多い。和菓子銘菓は多々あるが、洋菓子の代表格は「ウエダの洋菓子」のワッフルだ。六代目の上田晃久氏しか焼く事ができない、もちっとした厚手のワッフル生地に、たっぷり包まれたカスタード。これが溢れ出るのを手で押さえながら頬張るのだ。僕は甘い物を好んで食べないが、これだけは、いつもペロリ。パッケージも晃久氏が自らデザイン。「何でも自分で作っちゃうのよ、職人だから」と妻の章子さんは言う。手土産の超定番。(売豆紀拓／「シマネプロモーション」)

Soulful souvenir from a city that loves tea　Fumai Matsudaira, the Matsue feudal lord of the Edo Period, established tea culture among Matsue's citizens. To this day, the people of Matsue drink a lot of *matcha* tea at home. And due to the popularity of tea there, Matsue also boasts many sweets shops, of both the Japanese and Western variety. There are many great Japanese sweets shops, but among Western sweets, the waffles from "Ueda no Yogashi" is one of the best known. The thick and chewy waffle, which only sixth-generation owner Akihisa Ueda can make, is filled with custard. You have to try to keep the custard from spilling out as you bite into the waffle. I don't usually like sweets, but these waffles are an exception. Ueda also designed the packaging. His wife Akiko says, "He makes everything himself because he's a craftsman." The waffles are a standard go-to souvenir.　(Taku Mezuki, SHIMANE PROMOTION)

YUTTE　ご縁の国のおくりもの。
yutte.com

035

山口
YAMAGUCHI

澄川酒造場
📍 山口県萩市中小川611
☎ 0838-74-0001
Sumikawa Shuzojo
📍 Nakaogawa 611, Hagi, Yamaguchi

034

広島
HIROSHIMA

天心閣
📍 広島県廿日市市宮島町413
☎ 0829-44-0611
🏠 www.sarasvati.jp
Tenshinkaku
📍 Miyajima-cho 413, Hatsukaichi, Hiroshima

全国民待望の銘酒蔵復活　「地酒のまえつる」の店主・前鶴健蔵さんに連れられ、私が萩市の「澄川酒造場」を訪ねたのは、2014年10月だ。前年の水害で、蔵の1階が流され、しばらくは酒造りは難しいと言われていたが、全国からの支援があり、見事に再建を果たした。仄暗い約90年前の土壁は、真新しい板壁に換えられ、その壁には、蔵を訪れた全国の酒店主やファンからの応援メッセージが手書きで、びっしりと書かれていた。それを見て、蔵が築いてきた歴史を、私は強く感じた。翌月、東京に戻り、出来立ての「東洋美人 生酒 原点」を呑み、栗のような麹の味に、蔵に充満した甘い酒の香りと、壁のメッセージを思い出し、私は嬉しくなった。(菊地妙子／D&DEPARTMENT TOYAMA)

宮島の新名所、絶景カフェ　私は、毎年、何度も行く大好きな宮島で、土産物店などが並ぶ「町家通り」沿いに、今まで入った事のない路地を見つけた。その奥の石階段を上がっていくと、高台に古い一軒家のカフェ「天心閣」があった。かつては貴族の別荘として使われていた建物を改築し、カフェに生まれ変わらせたのは、島内にある「伊都岐珈琲」のオーナー佐々木恵亮さん。敷地には日本庭園。眼下に、鮮やかな朱塗りの五重塔と、どっしりとした風格の千畳閣と厳島神社がある、美しい入江を眺めながら、濃厚な「チョコレートのテリーヌ」と、自家焙煎珈琲を頂いた。この店と景色に、今年も、私は通う。(岡本友紀／女性鍛冶屋)

The revival of a famed sake distillery that all Japanese waited for　Kenzo Matsueru, owner of "Maetsuru Liquor Shop", took me to "Sumikawa Shuzojo" in Hagi in October 2014.　The distiller had closed for a while due to water damage it suffered in 2013, but it was reconstructed with nationwide support.　The approximately 90-years-old dusky earthen walls have been replaced with new woodenwalls that are now covered with messages from fans and sake shops from all over Japan that visited the distillery. Seeing these messages, I got strong sense of the history of the place. The following month, I returned to Tokyo and drank the freshly brewed unfiltered "Toyobijin Namazake Genten".　The chestnut-like flavor of the malt reminded me of the sweet sake aroma that filled the distillery and I was filled with joy.　(Taeko Kikuchi, D&DEPARTMENT TOYAMA)

A café with an amazing view that's become a new Miyajima destination　I love Miyajima and visit it multiple times a year. On one visit, I found an alley that I'd never walked in off of "Machiya Dori", a street lined with souvenir shops. I climbed the stone stairs at the back of the alley and found "Tenshinkaku", a café housed in an old standalone home on a hill.　The home was once used as a summerhouse by an aristocratic family and renovated into a café by Keisuke Sasaki, owner of "Itsuki Coffee", also on Miyajima. On the café's property is a Japanese garden. The café also offers a view of a bright vermillion-lacquered five-storied pagoda, the formidable Senjokaku, and Itsukushima Shrine. I looked at the beautiful bay as I drank coffee made with home roasted beans and a rich chocolate terrine. I will return to this café and its view this year.　(Yuki Okamoto, female blacksmith)

🎵 みんなのおんがく
minon.info

037

香川
KAGAWA

くぼさんのとうふ
📍 香川県綾歌郡宇多津町浜三番丁 25-19
☎ 0877-49-5580
🏠 www.kubosannotofu.co.jp
Kubo-san no tofu
📍 Utazu-cho Hama Sanban-cho 25-19, Ayaka, Kagawa

滋味溢れ、雑味がない真っ当な味わい　宇多津町の「くぼさんのとうふ」ショップには、久保隆則さんが、契約栽培国産大豆と天日塩にがりで作った豆腐、豆腐の惣菜や菓子、「良い食品づくりの会」認定の食品などが沢山並ぶ。私は、工場で「櫂寄せ」の作業を見せてもらった。炊いた豆乳を大きな杓文字を使って一定のリズムで混ぜ、天然にがりを入れて一気に固める。濃い湯気の中で力強く混ぜる様子は、圧巻だった。「大切なのは、味と安全のために、素材や製法と向き合う事。そして、当たり前ですが、手をかける事です」と話す久保さんの豆腐は、丁寧に取った出汁だけに入れるなど、シンプルに食べるのが一番。ひと口目は、ぜひ、塩で。(こんどう みわこ／天然酵母パン「o-ba'sh crust」)

Proper-tasting tofu that's full of flavor and has no bitter-ness　"Kubo-san no tofu" in Utazu-cho sells tofu that Takanori Kubo makes with contract-farmed domestic soybeans and sun-dried salt bitterns; prepared foods and snacks made with the tofu; and other foods approved by "Yoi-shokuhin-zukuri-no-kai (Good Food Product Association)". At the factory, Kubo showed me the process of gathering the cooked soymilk with a big paddle in a steady rhythm. The natural bittern is mixed in and the soymilk solidifies into tofu at once. It was amazing to see him forcefully mixing the soymilk in the intensely humid room. He explained, "The important thing is to carefully consider your ingredients and production methods for the sake of flavor and safety. And this goes without saying, but you need to take great pains to make your product." His tofu is best eaten simply, for example in carefully made broth. (Miwako Kondo, o-ba'sh crust)

036

徳島
TOKUSHIMA

カフェ・ポールスター
📍 徳島県勝浦郡上勝町福原平間 32-1
☎ 0885-46-0338
🏠 cafepolestar.com
Cafe polestar
📍 Kamikatsu-cho Fukuhara Hirama 32-1, Katsuura, Tokushima

"ゴミをゼロに"を目指す、町と共にあるカフェ　勝浦川沿いの急坂を上がり、上勝町に入ると、美しい花や木々が目に入る。私は「カフェ・ポールスター」で、満開の枝垂桜を眺め、季節野菜の日替わりランチを頂いた。地元自慢の棚田米や、特産のユズや、ユコウ(ミカン科)を使ったドリンクが美味しい。上勝町は、2020年までに町から出るゴミをゼロにする「ゼロ・ウェイスト宣言」をした。「ポールスター」でも野菜の皮を剥かずに調理し、お客様の各々には紙ナプキンの代わりに、ハンドタオル等の持参を呼びかけている。また、ゲストを招いて、町の将来を考える「上勝百年会議」を毎月開催。町を愛する人を、確実に増やしている。(北室淳子／手延べ素麺「北室白扇」)

A café that coexists with a city that aims to eliminate trash　I saw beautiful flowers and trees as I climbed the steep hill along the Katsuura River and entered Kamikatsu-cho. At "Café polestar," I had the daily special lunch plate with seasonal vegetables as I looked at the weeping cherry trees that were in full bloom. Café polestar offers a great drink made with Tanadamai rice, a source of local pride, yuzu (a type of citron), a local specialty, and yuko (a type of tangerine). Kamikatsu-cho has declared that it will eliminate all trash and achieve "zero waste" by 2020. Café polestar cooks its vegetables without peeling them and, rather than providing paper napkins, asks customers to bring their own hand towels. The café also hosts the monthly "Kamikatsu Hundred Years Conference," to which guests are invited to consider the city's future. Café polestar is actively promoting love for its home city. (Junko Kitamuro, Kitamuro Hakusen)

半田手延めん
www.kitamuro.co.jp

039 高知 KOCHI

道の駅 キラメッセ室戸「食遊 鯨の郷」
📍 高知県室戸市吉良川町丙890-11
☎ 0887-25-3500（予約は電話で）
🏠 www.kiramesse-muroto.jp/syokuyu/goaisatsu/
Roadside Station Kira Messe Muroto "Shokuyu Isanogo"
📍 Kiragawa-cho hei 890-11, Muroto, Kouchi

038 愛媛 EHIME

IKEUCHI ORGANIC
📍 愛媛県今治市延喜762（今治ファクトリーストア）
☎ 0120-939-683
🏠 www.ikeuchi.org
IKEUCHI ORGANIC
📍 Engi 762, Imabari, Ehime（Imabari Factory Store）

美味しいクジラ料理を、いつでも味わえる店　捕鯨が盛んだった土佐湾には、現在も数種のクジラが回遊してくる。佐喜浜漁港からの漁船でホエールウォッチングに乗船し、斜め前方に上がる潮噴きを見たら、それはマッコウクジラだ。僕は、インドネシアで手投げ銛による捕鯨に同行した時、波打ち際で、即時解体したマッコウクジラの歯茎の生肉を、何も付けず、そのまま食べた美味さが忘れられない。ぜひ、窓から太平洋を一望できるレストラン「鯨の郷」で、クジラ料理を味わってほしい。歯茎の生肉はないが、さえずり（舌）の酢味噌和えや、竜田揚げ、赤身の刺身など、どれもこれも、全て美味い。クジラを詳しく学べる資料館「鯨館」も隣接。（前田次郎／d design travel 編集部）

良心溢れるタオルメーカー　1953年創業の「IKEUCHI ORGANIC（旧・池内タオル）」の池内計司さんは、コットン生産品に多量の農薬や枯葉剤が使われ、また、遺伝子組み換えによって作られている事を知り、製造する全てのタオルに、体に安全なオーガニックコットンの使用を決めたそうだ。2015年2月には、既存のオーガニックの幼児服に加え、縫い目がなく、より着心地のよい、ニットの帽子やストール、靴下なども発表。「池内タオル」から、その社名や、ロゴなどを一新したのは、オーガニック製品だけを提供したいという、池内さんの強い意志からだ。私の愛用するタオルは、「ORGANIC 120」。本当に気持ちのよい生地だ。（杉村希咲／D&DEPARTMENT TOKYO）

A restaurant serving delicious whale cuisine at all times　Whaling was once popular in Tosa Bay and several types of whales still make their way to it. Take a whale watching boat from Sakihama Fishing Port. If you see a whale spraying diagonally forwards, it's a sperm whale. I once accompanied a whaling trip in Indonesia where a sperm whale was harpooned by hand. I'll never forget the amazing taste of the whale's gums, which we ate raw and without any flavoring right on the beach. I recommend going to "Isanogo," a restaurant with an expansive view of the Pacific Ocean, to try whale cuisine. It doesn't offer raw whale gum, but it does serve whale tongue with miso and vinegar, fried whale meat, and whale sashimi. They are all delicious. The restaurant is also adjacent to "Kujirakan," an archive museum where you can learn all about whales. (Jiro Maeda, d design travel Editorial Team)

A conscientious towel manufacturer　Keiji Ikeuchi of "IKEUCHI ORGANIC (formerly Ikeuchi Towel)", established in 1953, found out that tons of defoliants and agricultural chemicals and genetically engineered cotton plants are used to produce cotton and decided that his company would only use organic cotton, which is safe to use on the body, to manufacture their towels. In February 2015, the company released its seamless knit hats and stoles that offer improved comfort in addition to its existent infants' wear line. The change in company name and logo was a result of Ikeuchi's strong desire to exclusively offer organic products. I use IKEUCHI OROGANIC's "ORGANIC 120". It really feels great to use. (Kisa Sugimura, D&DEPARTMENT TOKYO)

7days Hotel
www.7dayshotel.com

風で織るタオル I
IKEUCHI ORGANIC

041
佐賀
SAGA

塚本猪一郎
Iichiro Tsukamoto

微笑みの芸術家　佐賀市で、芸術家が多く集う「旬菜台所 あ・うん」の常連に、地元画家の塚本猪一郎さんがいる。周りには、いつも多くの人が集まり、笑い声が絶えない。大卒後、ラーメンの屋台で貯めたお金で、フランスやスペインへ留学。日本に戻って絵で食べていけるとは思っていなかったそうだが、毎年、自費で数百部作る手刷りのカレンダーが、多くの人に彼の絵のよさを知ってもらう切っ掛けになった。2007年には、パリの「idem（旧ムルロー工房）」で作品を制作。植物か、動物か、無為に描き、「人に見せるために意図的に絵は描かない。作為がなくなって描けて、初めて自分の作品が出来上がる」と塚本さん。彼は、いつも笑顔だ。（北島真由美／「パハプスギャラリー」）

Artist of Smiles　Iichiro Tsukamoto is a regular at Saga City's "A-Un", where many artists gather. He is always surrounded by people who are constantly laughing. After graduating from college, he studied abroad in France and Spain using money he had earned working a ramen stall. He did not think he'd able to make ends meet as an artist back in Japan, but his hand-printed and independently produced calendar, which he makes several hundred of annually, helped to spread his work to many. In 2007, he made work at "idem" (formerly Mourlot Studios) in Paris. He drew plants and animals without any grand design. "I don't draw to show people. It's only when the intention disappears that I can make my work," explained Tsukamoto, who always has a smile on his face. (Mayumi Kitajima, PERHAPS GALLERY)

040
福岡
FUKUOKA

「めんたいぴりり」（博多座）
piriri.tv
"Mentai piriri" (Hakataza Theater)

福岡県民が皆、虜の辛子明太子劇　「テレビ西日本」開局55周年記念で放送された「めんたいぴりり」は、日本初の辛子明太子を製造・販売した、「ふくや」をモデルに描いた、博多華丸・富田靖子さん主演のドラマ。2015年3月には、「博多座」で舞台化。劇中では本物の博多祇園山笠中洲流の昇き山が舞台上に登場し、その昇き手は実際に毎年山笠を担ぐ男達で、大

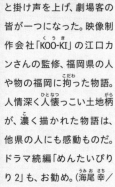

迫力で、一緒に「おいさ！」と掛け声を上げ、劇場客の皆が一つになった。映像制作会社「KOO-KI」の江口カンさんの監修、福岡県の人や物の福岡に拘った物語。人情深く人懐っこい土地柄が、濃く描かれた物語は、他県の人にも感動ものだ。ドラマ続編「めんたいぴりり2」も、お勧め。（海尾 幸／D&DEPARTMENT FUKUOKA）

A spicy cod roe drama that's captivated all Fukuoka citizens
Television Nishinippon aired "Mentai piriri", a drama based on the first spicy cod roe made and sold by "Fukuya" and starring Yasuko Tomoita and Hanamaru Hakata, to commemorate its 55th anniversary. In March 2015, the story was dramatized at the "Hakataza" theater. In the theater version, an actual *kakiyama* [portable shrine] used in the annual Hakata Gion Yamakasa Festival was carried on stage by the men who carry it every year at the same festival. With their syncopated "oisa!" cheers, they simultaneously created tremendous intensity and brought everyone in the theater together. The story, which deals with Fukuoka people and things, was supervised by Kanro Eguchi of the video production company "KOO-KI" and depicts the friendly and warmhearted locals in detail. It's a moving story for those who grew up outside Fukuoka as well. I also recommend the sequel "Mentai piriri 2". (Sachi Umio, D&DEPARTMENT FUKUOKA)

森正洋のミニカップブラウン
2003〜
http://www.design-mori.net

健康な体ときれいな水を守る。
シャボン玉石けん

043 熊本 KUMAMOTO

☕

PAVAO（パバオ）
📍 熊本県熊本市中央区南坪井町1-9
山村ビル（地獄温泉）2F
☎ 096-351-1158
PAVAO
📍 Jigoku Onsen 2F, Chuo-ku Minamitsuboi-
cho 1-9, Kumamoto, Kumamoto

センスよく、地元の器を伝える店　地元熊本で大学浪人していた時、友達の紹介で宝物のような店に出会った。熊本市の老舗銭湯「地獄温泉」2階の「孔雀」という名店「PAVAO」だ。店主が友人達と自ら改築した食堂とギャラリーに、孤高の画家・田上允克さんの絵や、民藝関連書物、熊本小代焼の器などが並び、それらが店独特のエキゾチックな雰囲気を盛り上げている。私は、今年3月に帰熊した時、幸運にも小代焼職人の井上尚之さんの個展に入場できた。県内外で引っ張りダコの井上さん、熊本県での個展は「PAVAO」だけだった。商品を選び切れずに困った私は、カフェでひと休みし、彼の器に盛られた料理に、私の美の想像力は逞しくされた。（宮崎琴子／d47 食堂）

A store with great taste and selection of local ceramics A friend introduced me to "PAVAO", a jewel of a store in Kumamoto, where I grew up, while I was preparing for my college entrance examination. Located above the old "Jigoku Onsen" hot spring in Kumamoto City, PAVAO, which means "peacock", comprises a Shokudo and gallery, which was renovated by the owner and his friends. It is filled with maverick painter Masakatsu Tagami's works, folk art-related books, and Kumamoto Shodaiyaki ceramics, which create an exotic ambiance. When I returned to Kumamoto in March, I was fortunate enough to catch the Shodaiyaki artist Naoyuki Inoue's solo exhibition. Inoue is very popular in and outside Kumamoto, but his only solo exhibition in Kumamoto was at PAVAO. Unable to choose a piece, I took a break in the café, where the food was served on Inoue's dishes, which strengthened my aesthetic imagination. (Kotoko Miyazaki, d47 SHOKUDO)

042 長崎 NAGASAKI

🛍

大山製茶園
📍 長崎県東彼杵郡東彼杵町中尾郷1556
☎ 0957-46-1349
🌐 ooyamacha.ocnk.net
Ooyama Seichaen
📍 Higashi-sonogi-cho Nakaogo 1556,
Higashi-sonogi, Nagasaki

大村湾を一望できる、約100年続く製茶園　大正7年創業「大山製茶園」の四代目の大山良貴さんは、20代まで渋谷のレコード店で働き、クラブでDJもしていた。現在は、お茶の楽しみ方を広めるため、DJやライブイベントなどでも、お茶を振る舞う活動をしている。東彼杵郡の、標高約330メートルの大自然に、家族4人で、土壌からこだわった滋味に満ちた茶畑を造った。「そのぎ茶」は、茶葉がクルクルと丸まった、蒸し製玉緑茶。ふくよかな香りで、渋みを抑えた、まろやか味わい。私は、びっくりする旨みを感じた。茶工場の傍の「茶飲み処 茶楽」では、お茶の淹れ方教室なども開催している。農林水産祭「内閣大臣賞」受賞歴あり。（澤田 央／d47 design travel store）

A nearly 100-years-old tea plantation with a view of Omura Bay Yoshitaka Ooyama, the fourth-generation owner of "Ooyama Seichaen", which was established in 1918, DJed clubs and worked at a record store in Shibuya until his 20s. He currently organizes tea service events at DJ and live events to spread knowledge about the enjoyment of tea. Located in Higashi-sonogi, 330 meters above sea level, the exquisite tea farm was created by the four-person family, who obsessed over every detail starting with the soil. "Sonogi Tea" is a steamed curled leaf tea. It has a robust aroma and mild, not very bitter, flavor. I was amazed by its tastiness. The teahouse "Chanomidokoro Charaku" hosts lessons on tea preparation, etc. Ooyama Seichaen is also a recipient of "Prime Minister Award at the Festival of Food, Agriculture, Forestry and Fisheries". (Hiro Sawada, d47 design travel store)

JIRO 長崎次郎書店　www.nagasaki-jiro.jp

The Porcelains
Made in Japan

黒木碁石店 蛤おはじき
📍 宮崎県日向市平岩8491
☎ 0982-54-2531
🌐 www.kurokigoishi.co.jp
Kurokigoishiten Clamshell Ohajiki Stone
📍 Hiraiwa 8491, Hyuga, Miyazaki

国本泰英
🌐 knmtyshd.com
Yasuhide Kunimoto

砂浜生まれの、おはじき お倉ヶ浜海岸は、明治時代から碁石が造られてきた。国内で唯一、碁石に適した厚さのスワブテ蛤貝が採れたが、現在は稀少、材料はメキシコ産に主に移行。碁石は、職人の手作業で造られるが、縞目や、色、きめなど、基準に満たない物は、赤や青、黄色などに染められ、「蛤おはじき」に造られる。最高峰の日向の蛤碁石が、値の張る商品としてではなく、おはじきとして、子供に親しまれている事が嬉しい。蛤碁石が地元特産である理由は、砂浜で遊んだ皆が記憶している。細かい海の砂が育んだ、日向産の蛤碁石の復活に、今後一層の期待をする。(前田次郎／d design travel 編集部)

別府の新名所を創った、若き画家 玖珠町に、ある画家がいる事を知った。アウトドアブランド「mont-bell」のTシャツデザインや、ギャラリーで作品を目にしてから、ずっと私の頭から離れなかった。そんな中、彼が別府温泉の「ホテルニューツルタ」で壁画を制作中と聞き、現場に向かい、ようやく会う事ができた。国本泰英さんという好青年で、故郷である玖珠町に住みながら制作している。彼は、人物を描く事で、その周りの風景も私達に想像させる。すぐに風景が見えてしまう、と言ったほうが正確だろう。彼の大きな作品を、いつでも見れる場所ができ、別府に足を運ぶ機会が増えそうだ。(原 茂樹／「日田シネマテーク・リベルテ」)

Beach-born *Ohajiki* marbles Okuragahama beach has produced *go* stones since the Meiji era. It was the only place in Japan where clamshells with the right thickness for *go* stones could be found. The clamshells are now scarce and primarily sourced from Mexico. *Go* stones are made by hand by craftsmen. Clamshells that do not meet the standards in terms of grain, color, and hatching are dyed in primary colors and turned into "clamshell *ohajiki* marbles". It's nice to know that the finest *go* stones made in Hyuga are transformed not into expensive products but rather toys for kids. Everyone who has played on the beach in Hyuga knows why it's known for its *go* stones. The uniquely hatched and polished Hyuga *go* stones are produced by the fine sand of its beaches. I strongly hope that Hyuga *go* stones will experience a revival. (Jiro Maeda, d design travel Editorial Team)

A young artist who created a new destination in Beppu I found out about a painter in Kusu-machi. I kept thinking about his work after I saw it in galleries and on t-shirts made by the outdoor brand "mont-bell". I then heard that he was painting a mural at "the Hotel New Tsuruta" in the Beppu hot spring region, went there, and finally met him. Yasuhide Kunimoto is a pleasant young man who lives and works in his hometown Kusu-machi. While his works are figurative, they also evoke surrounding landscapes. It's actually more accurate to say that one immediately sees a landscape in his work. With a readily viewable major work by Kunimoto, I'll likely visit Beppu hot springs even more frequently now. (Shigeki Hara, Hita Cinematheque Liberte)

白玄堂
www.hakugendo.com

鬼塚電気工事株式会社
ONIZUKA ELECTRIC WORKS

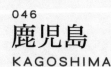

047
沖縄
OKINAWA

ハコニワ
📍沖縄県国頭郡本部町伊豆味2566
☎0980-47-6717
Cafe Hakoniwa
📍Motobu-cho Izumi 2566, Kunigami,
　Okinawa

046
鹿児島
KAGOSHIMA

JR大隅横川駅
📍鹿児島県霧島市横川町中ノ39-1
☎0995-72-0582(霧島市役所 横川総合支所)
Osumi-Yokogawa Station
📍Yokogawa-cho Nakano 39-1, Kirishima,
　Kagoshima

深緑の中の 琉球 古民家カフェ　沖縄本島北部の森の中に、ひっそりと佇む「ハコニワ」は、僕が、ドライブの際に必ず立ち寄る店だ。今は慣れたが、最初は緑深い山道を恐る恐る進んでいった。築50年以上の古民家を改築した店は、木々に囲まれ、木漏れ日が大変美しい。沖縄食材をふんだんに使った料理は、地元出身オーナーの谷口かおりさんが幼い頃から食べてきた料理をアレンジした物。使用する食器は、ご主人の室生さんが作陶する名護市「室生窯」の物。ダイナミックな絵付け皿に料理が映える。晴れた日が、お薦めだが、雨の日も、しとしとと瓦屋根に当たる雨音を聞きながら、ゆっくりとコーヒーを飲んでほしい。(山入端 俊／D&DEPARTMENT OKINAWA)

町の人々成長と共にある駅舎　明治36年に開業した「JR大隅横川駅」は、水戸岡鋭治氏デザインの「はやとの風」も停車する、登録有形文化財にも指定された、九州最古の木造駅舎。築110年を超えるホームの柱には、第二次世界大戦で受けた機統掃射の跡が今でも生々しく残る。夏祭りや平和コンサート、駅カフェといった様々なイベントが催され、世代を超えて町民の交流の場となっている。中でも、成人式がいい。長年利用してきた駅を背景に、新成人達は晴れ着姿で写真を撮る。彼らの表情は明るい。この駅は、町民の成長を見続け、立派な社会人へなるための始発駅なのだ。そして、私も、この駅で成人式を迎えた一人だ。(栗野良弥／D&DEPARTMENT KAGOSHIMA)

A café housed in an old Ryukyu-style folk home deep in the woods　I always stop by "Café Hakoniwa", hidden deep inside a forest in the northern part of the main island of Okinawa, when I go on a drive. I'm now used to it, but the first time I drove to the café, I hesitantly drove the deep woods mountain roads. Housed in renovated folk home that's over 50 years old, the café is surrounded by woods, and bathed in sunlight beautifully filtered through them. It serves food based on recipes its owner Kaori Taguchi grew up locally with and made with plenty of local ingredients. Beverages and food are served in wares made at "Murogama Pottery" by Taniguchi's husband Muroo Taniguchi. The dynamically painted ceramic wares perfectly match the food. I recommend slowly enjoying a coffee at Hakoniwa on a rainy day while listening to the rain hit the tiled roof. (Shun Yamanoha, D&DEPARTMENT OKINAWA)

A train station that stands by locals　Opened in 1903, "Osumi-Yokogawa Station" is Kyushu's oldest wooden train station. It is also a registered tangible cultural property and the Eiji Mitooka-designed "Hayato no Kaze" stops there. The pillars of the more than 110-years-old station remain pockmarked from the machine-gun fire it endured during World War II. The station hosts various events including summer festivals, peace concerts, and a "station café", and is used by local residents of all generations as a place to socialize. My favorite event there is the coming of age ceremony. The new adults have their picture taken in formal dress, with happy expressions, and in front of the station they've used for many years. The station watches the growth of local residents and sees them off as they start their journey into adulthood. I too had my coming of age ceremony here. (Fumiya Kurino, D&DEPARTMENT KAGOSHIMA)

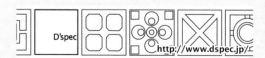

D'spec　http://www.dspec.jp/

D&DEPARTMENT
KYOTO

2014年、本山佛光寺の境内にオープンしたD&DEPARTMENT KYOTO。元はお坊さんたちの宿坊（僧侶のための宿泊施設）だった建物を使っています。畳敷きのスペースや小上がりなど、かつての気配が残るショップでは、京都府内の工芸品、食品などをご紹介。併設のギャラリーでは、京都の文化を伝える企画展を定期的に開催しています。佛光寺という地域に開かれたお寺の境内で、日本人の暮らしや、長く続く文化の背景を再編集し、地域コミュニティと連動した活動に取り組んでいます。

ショップに併設されたギャラリーでは、京都に長くつづく文化を学べる企画展を開催。ものづくりの現場で実際に使われている道具が並び、実演製作が行われていることも。

細い道も多い京都には自転車がぴったり。「BRUNO」のレンタルを実施しています。ご利用の方にはスタッフおすすめのスポットをご紹介した「ぐるぐるMAP」をプレゼント。

D&DEPARTMENT KYOTO
d SHOKUDO KYOTO

D&DEPARTMENT KYOTO / d食堂 京都

📍 京都府京都市下京区高倉通仏光寺下ル新開町397
本山佛光寺内

☎ 075-343-3217（ショップ）
　075-343-3215（食堂）

🏠 d-department.com/ext/shop/kyoto.html

🚇 地下鉄烏丸線「四条駅」5番出口より徒歩6分
　阪急京都線「烏丸駅」15番出口より徒歩6分

dd 食堂 SHOKUDO

佛光寺の「お茶所」の建物で、京都各地の食を提供しています。京都の郷土料理、調理法、食材や調味料、生産者など、さまざまな視点で、京都の「食」を編集した定食をはじめ、出汁を大切にした麺類、季節の果実を使ったドリンクやパフェなどの甘味もご用意。京都の知られているおいしさも、知られていない食文化も楽しんでいただけます。春はシダレザクラ、夏はサルスベリ、秋は真っ黄色になるイチョウの大木を縁側で眺めても。店内では天童木工の低座イスにゆったりと腰を下ろしてお寛ぎいただけます。

1.「京丹後定食」。100歳を超える人が国内平均の3倍という京丹後市。この地の祝い事に欠かせない郷土料理「鯖そぼろのばらちらし」をメインに、地域名産の海藻、アカモクのすまし汁など。

2.「苺と伊根満開甘酒のパフェ」。小島農園の苺を使い、日本酒「伊根満開」の酒粕を蒸しパンに、甘酒をクリームチーズの中に。湯葉のチョコクランチ、白味噌あんも。さっぱりとした後味。

3.「紫蘇シロップかき氷」。すっきりした味わいで、気持ちまでシャキッとする紫蘇シロップは、京の漬物処「志ば久」の大原の畑から届く生赤紫蘇で作っています。

4. 夏が過ぎ、涼しくなり始めた中秋（9〜10月の十五夜）に、和ろうそくの灯りで、空に浮かぶ月と、おつまみと飲み物を楽しむ夕べ。毎年趣向が変わります。

D&DEPARTMENTの活動を通じて「ながくつづく」を研究、紹介、活用しながら、いい店や場所、生活道具がいつまでも存在し続くように、そこに大切な意識を広める場として発足した「ロングライフデザインの会」。地域や仲間と繋がり、持続性を生み出す活動を、年間を通して応援いただく会員制度です。

会員みんなでつくる

ロングライフ
デザインの会
会員紹介

今村製陶［JICON］

version zero dot nine

漆工芸大下香仙株式会社
［Classic Ko］

亀崎染工有限会社

カリモク家具

株式会社キャップライター

ダイアテック［BRUNO］

大地の芸術祭

デザインモリコネクション

株式会社東京チェンソーズ

ドライブディレクション

日本デザイン振興会

株式会社藤栄 ニーチェアエックス

FUTAGAMI

株式会社プラス

※2024年3月末までに入会された個人・法人会員の内、お名前掲載に同意いただいた方々をご紹介しています。

AHH!! ／アールズスタジオ 村上理枝／四十沢木材工芸／浅井勇樹／あさのゆか（朝から晩まで）／浅見要介／安積とも絵／飯島俊幸／礒 健介／inutaku3／入多由紀恵／石見神楽東京社中 小加本行広／株式会社 INSTOCK／江原明香／mldkdesigns LLC ／ MT ／ August Kekulé／大崎真弓 株式会社大崎材木店／大治将典／有限会社 大鷹／大山 曜／オクムサ・マルシェ／カーサプロジェクト株式会社／風の杜／弁護士法人 片岡総合法律事務所／金子さつき／河野秀樹／菅野悦子／機山洋酒工業 株式会社／Cuet Inc. ／中野結衣／国井純（ひたちなか市役所）／黒野 剛／桑原宏充／桑原宏充／藝ノ日 藤崎眞弓／ Code for FUKUI ／コクウ珈琲／九十百千 KOTOMOCHI ／小湊美輝／コルポ建築設計事務所／ COMFORT STYLE Co.,Ltd. ／今 由美／齊藤鷹之／酒井貴子／株式会社サカエマーク／坂口慶樹／坂本正文／佐賀義之／サトウッヨシ／佐藤丈公／讃岐かがり手まり保存会／ saredo されど／志ば久 久保統／ JunMomo ／白崎龍弥・酒井晴菜／白藤協子／村主暢子／ STAN STORE TOKYO ／ sail 中村圭吾／曽山 茂／タイタイスタジオ／竹原あき子／ちいさな庭 智里／土原翔吾／株式会社 津乃吉／妻形 円／紡ぎ詩／水流一水／つるまきばね／ Daiton ／ DESIGN CLIPS ／ tetora ／ DO-EYE-DO ／とくら建築設計／友員里枝子／鳥居大資／ DRAWING AND MANUAL ／永田 智／中村亮太／ Nabe ／南條百恵実／西山 薫／梅月堂／821&350 ／原田將裕（茅ヶ崎市役所）／ハルバル材木座／パンのGORGE ／ HUMBLE CRAFT ／東尾厚志／東島未来／日の出屋製菓 千種啓資／ひろ／ Hiroshi Tatebe ／fhans-satoshi ／POOL INC. 小西利行／深石英樹／藤枝 碧／藤原慎也／ FURIKAKE 得丸成人／古屋万恵／古屋ゆりか／株式会社ぶんぶく／ホテルニューニシノ／ Marc Mailhot ／松田菜央／matsumoto tomoco ／マルヒの干しいも 黒澤 欽／みうらけいこ／道場文香／峯山 大／宮崎会計事務所／メノワカ食堂／モノ・モノ／森内理子／森 光男／八重田和志／谷澤咲良／宿たゆたう／山口愛由子／ヤマコヤ やまさき薫／山崎建設株式会社／山崎義樹／山田敬志／山次製紙所／ヤマモト ケンジ／山本文子／山本八重子／山本 凌／梁 有鎮／yurie ／横山純子／横山正芳／吉永ゆかり／若松哲也

他 匿名48名（五十音順・敬称略）

D&DEPARTMENT STORE LOCATION

D&DEPARTMENT HOKKAIDO
by 3KG
📍北海道札幌市中央区大通西17-1-7
☎011-303-3333
📍O-dori Nishi 17-1-7, Chuo-ku,
Sapporo, Hokkaido

D&DEPARTMENT SAITAMA
by PUBLIC DINER
📍埼玉県熊谷市肥塚4-29 PUBLIC DINER
屋上テラス
☎048-580-7316
📍PUBLIC DINER Rooftop Terrace
4-29 Koizuka, Kumagaya, Saitama

D&DEPARTMENT TOYAMA
📍富山県富山市新総曲輪4-18
富山県民会館 1F
☎076-471-7791
📍Toyama-kenminkaikan 1F, Shinsogawa
4-18, Toyama, Toyama

D&DEPARTMENT MIE
by VISON
📍三重県多気郡多気町ヴィソン 672-1
サンセバスチャン通り6
☎0598-67-8570
📍6 Sansebastian-dori, 672-1Vison,Taki-cho,
Taki-gun Mie

D&DEPARTMENT KAGOSHIMA
by MARUYA
📍鹿児島県鹿児島市呉服町6-5
マルヤガーデンズ 4F
☎099-248-7804
📍Maruya gardens 4F, Gofuku-machi 6-5,
Kagoshima, Kagoshima

D&DEPARTMENT SEOUL
by MILLIMETER MILLIGRAM
📍ソウル市龍山区梨泰 院 路240
☎+82 2 795 1520
📍Itaewon-ro 240, Yongsan-gu,
Seoul, Korea

D&DEPARTMENT HUANGSHAN
by Bishan Crafts Cooperatives
📍安徽省黄山市黟县碧阳镇碧山村
☎+86 13339094163
📍Bishan Village, Yi County, Huangshan City,
Anhui Province, China

D&DEPARTMENT FUKUSHIMA
by KORIYAMA CITY
📍福島県郡山市燧田 195 JR郡山駅 2F
こおりやま観光案内所内
☎024-983-9700
📍JR Koriyama Station 2F
（Koriyama tourist information center），
195 Hiuchida, Koriyama, Fukushima

D&DEPARTMENT TOKYO
📍東京都世田谷区奥沢8-3-2-2F
☎03-5752-0120
📍Okusawa 8-3-2-2F, Setagaya-ku, Tokyo

d news aichi agui
📍愛知県知多郡阿久比町矢高五反田37-2
☎0569-84-9933
📍Yatakagotanda 37-2, Agui-cho,
Chita-gun Aichi

D&DEPARTMENT KYOTO
📍京都府京都市下京区高倉通仏光寺
下ル新開町397 本山佛光寺内
☎ショップ 075-343-3217
食堂 075-343-3215
📍Bukkoji Temple, Takakura-dori Bukkoji
Sagaru Shinkai-cho 397, Shimogyo-ku,
Kyoto, Kyoto

D&DEPARTMENT OKINAWA
by PLAZA 3
📍沖縄県沖縄市久保田3-1-12 プラザハウス
ショッピングセンター 2F
☎098-894-2112
📍PLAZA HOUSE SHOPPING CENTER 2F,
3-1-12 Kubota, Okinawa, Okinawa

D&DEPARTMENT JEJU
by ARARIO
📍済州島 済州市 塔洞路 2ギル 3
☎+82 64-753-9904/9905
📍3, Topdong-ro 2-gil, Jeju-si,
Jeju-do, Korea

d47 MUSEUM / d47 design travel store /
d47食堂
📍東京都渋谷区渋谷 2-21-1 渋谷ヒカリエ 8F
☎d47 MUSEUM/d47 design travel store
03-6427-2301　d47食堂 03-6427-2303
📍Shibuya Hikarie 8F, Shibuya 2-21-1,
Shibuya, Tokyo

高木 崇雄　Takao Takaki
工藝風向 店主
福岡民藝協会事務局になりました。
ぜひご参加下さい。

田代 淳　Jun Tashiro
うるしぬりたしろ
d金継ぎ部員の成長が目覚ましく、
顧問の私は嬉しい。

田中 信宏　Nobuhiro Tanaka
COCOROSTORE ココロストア
山陰近県で自然と共に生きる人や技、
繋がりをご紹介しています

谷口 亮太郎　Ryotaro Taniguchi
diatech products プロモーション担当
trip tour travel journey tools BRUNO

谷 周子　Shuko Tani
ハーブ料理研究家
日本の誇り京都を感じ考える機会を、
有難うございます。

辻井 希文　Kifumi Tsujii
イラストレーター
イラストをかいております。
楽しみにしていた京都号です。

土屋 裕一　Yuichi Tsuchiya
suiran
群馬を拠点に、本のある生活を
提案しています。

土屋 有加　Yuka Tsuchiya
D&DEPARTMENT KYOTO
by 京都造形芸術大学
佛光寺で、心地よい食堂やってます。

寺崎 美緒　Mio Terasaki
アーバンリサーチドアーズ ブランド販促
今回の「In-Town Beauty」は、新鮮だけど
京都らしい。京都に行ったら鴨川へ！

鳥原 嘉博　Yoshihiro Torihara
指物職人・二級建築士
日本一？優雅な自転車通勤で
仕事をしています。

中川家　Nakagawa-ke
清(父) 彰子(母) 久子(長女)
元喜(長男) 清香(次女)
みんな小さい頃からよく遊んだ御所。
今日も散歩へ！

中村 新　Shin Nakamura
昇苑くみひも　営業・企画
「京くみひも」の奥深さに、
どっぷりはまってます。

中村 千晶　Chiaki Nakamura
d47 design travel store
出会いが楽しいd47♪ハロー 你好어서 오세
요。和菓子づくりも継続してます。

中山 小百合　Sayuri Nakayama
d47食堂
人々や暮らし、風景が浮かぶ。
郷土料理って面白い。

成田 舞　Mai Narita
フォトグラファー
ただいま丸太町に写真館を製作中です。

沼田 健一　Kenichi Numata
trattoria blackbird シェフ
クッキングスクール開催中。
詳細は■ blackbird-mito.com

野口 忠典　Tadanori Noguchi
d47 design travel store 店長
京都には、誇り高い「ほんまもん」が
あります。

原 茂樹　Shigeki Hara
日田リベルテ支配人・映画技師など
大分県日田市で映画館を営んでおります。
■ www.hita-liberte.com

針谷 茜　Akane Hariya
D&DEPARTMENT PROJECT
ご褒美は、木屋町「モリタ屋」の
すき焼きがいいです。

廣瀬 智也　Tomoya Hirose
D&DEPARTMENT YAMANASHI
by Sannichi-YBS
新たな気持ちで、今年2周年を迎える
山梨店です。

万城目 絢子　Ayako Makime
d47食堂
ビール担当になりました。
日々ビールを飲み比べているので、
ビールっ腹が心配です。

ますだ けんたろう　Kentaro Masuda
8175 inc. 代表
かなりのおせっかい焼き。京都の中華、
ご案内します(＾＾)

益田 晴子　Haruko Masuda
IKEUCHI ORGANIC
店舗統括マネージャー兼京都 Store 店長
京都にお越しの際は、
IKEUCHI ORGANIC にお立ち寄り下さい。

松本 伸哉　Shinya Matsumoto
ホホホ座 顧問
下條家文化事業企画室長兼任。

ミツモリ ヨシヒロ　Yoshihiro Mitsumori
トマト　TOMATO
美容師「LINE hair salon & OTAKU)
世界を挑発する ■ www.otaku-project.com

宮越 葉子　Yoko Miyakoshi
D&DEPARTMENT HOKKAIDO by 3KG
北海道らしいもの、こと、を考え
探していきます。

宮崎 琴子　Kotoko Miyazaki
d47食堂
d47で日本を学び、
将来は地元熊本にdを！

村井 一気　Kazuki Murai
Life is Beautiful 実行委員
立山の麓で、緩やかに音楽フェス
やっています。

村木 諭　Satoshi Muraki
Producer
美味しい珈琲とタマゴサンドが好きです。

売豆紀 拓　Taku Mezuki
シマネプロモーション
YUTTE プロデューサー
島根のいいもの集めてギフト作ってます。
■ http://yutte.com/

森 有子　Yuko Mori
株式会社太陽薬品 薬剤師
初詣は毎年千本鳥居の伏見稲荷へ。
好きな場所はインクライン。

八木 浄顕　Kiyoaki Yagi
佛光寺総務
コーラスをしています。

安永 ケンタウロス　Kentauros Yasunaga
カメラマン
dが見つける「京都」楽しみです。

山下 賢二　Kenji Yamashita
ホホホ座 座長
京都は伝統だけでは成り立たず、
前衛との共犯関係があるのです。

山田 藤雄　Fujio Yamada
DEAN & DELUCA
「ぐっと」来る場所を探して、
街をさまよっております。

山入端 俊　Shun Yamanoha
ファーマー
(元 D&DEPARTMENT OKINAWA)
格好いい農業を日々、模索しています！

山本 哲　Satoshi Yamamoto
鴨川オタク
奥深く魅力尽きない鴨川を、
あなたも体感しませんか。

吉田 茜衣　Akane Yoshida
D&DEPARTMENT KYOTO
by 京都造形芸術大学
朝茶が習慣。京都店からワクワクを
お届けします！

ワタナベシンヤ(B)　Shinya B Watanabe
テンプル大学 アート学科 准教授
佐々木信さん、空閑さんと「DIAMONDS
ARE FOREVER」に行きました。

CONTRIBUTORS

相馬 夕輝　Yuki Aima
D&DEPARTMENT PROJECT
常連になってみたい京都が
たくさんあった。通います！！

浅野 浦乃　Urano Asano
D&DEPARTMENT KYOTO
by 京都造形芸術大学
スタッフの平均年齢を上げています。

石井 唯　Yui Ishii
D&DEPARTMENT TOYAMA ショップ店長
大阪店から富山店へ。北陸新幹線で
富山へお越しください！

伊藤 愛　Ai Ito
マフラー制作
宮城県大崎市にて、寒い冬に
もってこいなマフラーをつくっています。

岩井 巽　Tatsumi Iwai
東北芸術工科大学 学生
京都造形大と、東北芸工大は姉妹校。
卒業制作展は見応えアリです。

宇治田 沙季　Saki Ujita
善称寺 坊守
和歌山市のちいさなお寺で、
日々精進のオテライフ。
🏠 zensho-ji.com

内田 幸映　Yukie Uchida
d47食堂 店長
素敵な仲間のおかげで、
食堂のおばちゃん4年目突入です！

海尾 幸　Sachi Umio
D&DEPARTMENT FUKUOKA
福岡のよかとこば見にこんね？

うめの たかし　Takashi Umeno
ホホホ座／homehome
北九州市の情報誌『雲のうえ』の
応援団もやってます！
🏠 kumonoue-fanclub.net/

岡竹 義弘　Yoshihiro Okatake
d47食堂
京都の中華、おいしく頂きました。
毎日マンプクでした。

岡本 友紀　Yuki Okamoto
鍛冶屋
照明やオブジェなど制作。
資生堂や金麦のCMにも出演。
🏠 forgerone.com

小鹿 由加里　Yukari Ojika
農学部芸術学科
企画と野良仕事。
🏠 www.nougei.tumblr.com

小野 文子　Fumiko Ono
株式会社 庵プロデュース
「暮らすような旅」ができる、まちづくりの
お手伝いをしています。

小原 龍樹　Ryuki Obara
D&DEPARTMENT KYOTO
by 京都造形芸術大学
京都を楽しんでいます。

ガイセ キキ　Cristina Lucia Geisse Bottles
丸久小山園 営業部／陶々舎
一服如何ですか。
🏠 www.totousha.com

菊地 妙子　Taeko Kikuchi
D&DEPARTMENT TOYAMA ダイニング店長
「富山は豊か！食も人も！そして酒も！」

喜多 和夫　Kazuo Kita
「工場跡」オーナー
ナガメル春の会@京都に参加。
いやぁ、楽しかったです。

北島 真由美　Mayumi Kitajima
パンプスギャラリー
佐賀県佐賀市で、楽しいギャラリーを
運営しています。

北室 淳子　Junko Kitamuro
有限会社北室白扇
四国徳島でおいしい お素麺を
作っています。

久保 常次　Tsuneji Kubo
理想の森プロジェクト世話役
川下の人達に美しい水を流す事を、
誇りにしています。

栗野 良弥　Fumiya Kurino
D&DEPARTMENT KAGOSHIMA by MARUYA
僕も焼酎は年中お湯割りを飲みます。

黒江 美穂　Miho Kuroe
d47 MUSEUM 事務局
京都の中華料理に興味があります。

近藤 太一　Taichi Kondo
京桶職人(桶屋近藤 代表)
桶が無ければ本当の京料理も和菓子も
漬物も出来ません。
🏠 oke-kondo.jimdo.com

こんどう みわこ　Miwako Kondo
オーバッシュクラスト STAFF
bakery & cafe で働きながら徳島の
旬×パンを楽しむ毎日。
🏠 o-bashcrust.com

齊藤 望　Nozomu Saito
NPO 弘前こども
コミュニティ・ぴーぷる 理事
今日も明日も「こどもを真ん中に＾＾」

三枝 里真　Rika Saegusa
ライター
京都に行くと、必ず訪れるのは
南禅寺です。

坂田 佐武郎　Saburo Sakata
デザイナー
御苑と鴨川が大好きです。

坂本 大三郎　Daizaburo Sakamoto
山伏／絵描き
これまで行く機会が少なかった京都。
この本をにぎりしめて観光したい！

迫 一成　Kazunari Sako
hickory03travelers
2015年の夏は「にいがた水と土の芸術祭」
へ。旧二葉中でお店を展開します。

佐藤 晶　Akira Sato
d47 design travel store
デザイントラベルを楽しんでいます。
d47에도 오세요！

澤田 央　Hiro Sawada
d47 design travel store
京都がこんなに東京から近いとは！
日帰りでも充実！！

下元 利之　Toshiyuki Shimomoto
合同会社shimogen代表
京都で人と人をつなげる会社を運営！
京都の人と街が好きです。

城 敬之　Takayuki Shiro
D&DEPARTMENT KYOTO
by 京都造形芸術大学 ショップチーフ
京都の魅力を発信するきっかけに
なりたい。

新海 康介　Kosuke Shinkai
アネックスホテル福井／二ノ丸グリル
福井で小さなホテルと小さな洋食屋を
やっています。

進藤 仁美　Hitomi Shindo
d47 design travel store
旅の計画中。

すが かつみ　Katsumi Suga
昆虫・両生類研究、校閲
先日、ケンカ血まみれで、嵐の「Sakura」を
熱唱、他の客を呆然とさせました。

杉村 希咲　Kisa Sugimura
D&DEPARTMENT TOKYO
ようやく自転車を買いました。
今年の目標は100km走ること。

鈴木 苑子　Sonoko Suzuki
京都造形芸術大学 広報室
平安の歌人が詠んだ風景に
折々遭遇する京都生活は楽しい。

園部 暁子　Akiko Sonobe
d47 design travel store
京都、哲学の道を散歩したい、
夏には鴨川のそばでビールものみたい。

「D&DEPARTMENT KYOTO
by 京都造形芸術大学」の話

Osamu Kuga
空閑 理

「京都府号」の取材中、毎日のように通った「イノダコーヒ本店」の住所は、故・高田渡の歌の「三条堺町の……」のフレーズでお馴染みだが、実際に京都で見聞きしたのは、最も一般的なのが「堺町通り三条下ル（縦の通りを先に述べ、縦の通りにだけ「通り」を付ける）」。次いで「堺町三条下ル（通り）を省略。普通、「通り」を省略すると、三条下ル（縦の通りを先に述べ、縦の通りにだけ「通り」を付ける）」。や、または「堺町通り三条通り下ル（縦横の通りに「通り」を付ける）」と呼ぶ者は、ほとんどいない。では、「堺町通り三条下ル」だけが正しくて、他は誤りか？と京都の人々に訊くと、「いや、誤りとは言えない」という答え。「その人が言うのが、いいのだ」「無理に統一する必要はない」と、"これが正しい"という答え。は、ないのだ。

今回、「京都府号」取材の編集室代わりとなったのは、高倉通り仏光寺下ル（正しいのだろうか……と考えてはいけない）の本山佛光寺の境内にある「D&DEPARTMENT KYOTO by 京都造形芸術大学」だった。立派な銀杏が一本と、しだれ桜の並木がある境内の、毎朝、ご近所の方々がラジオ体操を行う、市民に開かれた、とても清々しい寺だ。ショップチーフの城 敬之さんをはじめ、スタッフの皆さんには、食堂で美味しいうどんを食べさせてもらったり、自転車を預かってもらったり、洗濯させてもらったり、定休日にはゲストハウスに皆で泊まったり、納涼床でビールを飲んだりして、「一つにまとめきれない、まとめてはいけない京都"を共に考え、悩み、そして楽しみながら、この「京都府号」を完成させる事ができました。いつも助けられました。本当に、ありがとうございました。

その「D&DEPARTMENT KYOTO」のオーナーである「京都造

Design at this university; his students do not stay in classroom but also go into D&DEPARTMENT KYOTO where they work as interns at the shop as salespeople and curators. For these students, everyone is their teacher: not just people who visit Kyoto, but the city itself teaches them about what makes designed products "super-long life design". And I also think that these students contribute to the essence of what makes Kyoto unique.

Often times, Kyoto is defined and categorized by people who do not really know, or live, in Kyoto. However, people here do not really care about that. They go through each season, enjoying what they want to enjoy whether it's the river or the clouds in the sky or the colors of the sky. They live without limits. They live according to their own rhythms and aesthetics. That is what Kyoto taught me: to be yourself.

形芸術大学」のキャンパスは、左京区の瓜生山にあり、山頂付近からは如意ヶ岳の大文字が間近に見え、京都市街を一望できる能舞台もある。急な斜面に数多くの棟が建っていて、それらが坂道や階段で複雑に繋がり合い、その全容はハッキリとは掴めない。建物の奥深く（と感じられる）にはアーティストのヤノベケンジ氏の「ウルトラファクトリー」があったり、山の頂上には日本人初の宇宙飛行士で農家の秋山豊寛氏が指導する農園があったりして、創造的な仕事の現場が、教育の現場でもあるのだ。そして、「ロングライフデザイン」を教える、本誌発行人でもあるナガオカケンメイの講義も行われ、学生達は、店頭に立って商品をお客様に説明したり、併設のギャラリーで展覧会を企画したりする。京都に訪れる人みんなが教授で、京都の街そのものが、"超ロングライフなキャンパス"であり、講義室なのだ。そして、京都から学ぼうとする、彼ら学生達自身も、また「大切な京都らしさ」の大きな一部でもある。

京都には、他所者が勝手に、何か一つの考え方で簡単に対象をまとめて、「京都とはこうだ」と決めつけられてしまう事が、とても多い。だが、そんな「決めつけの京都」など構わずに、勝手に時の流れに流してしまって、自分達は、鴨川を流れる水や、その四季折々の風景や、その上を吹き抜ける風、その上に広がる空の色や雲の形、それらが、いつも違う事を楽しむ――その瞬間、瞬間を、それを眺める人が、美しく感じるのか、寂しく感じるのか、と同じように――個々が、素直に物事を感じ、自由に生きている。その素直さと自由さが、僕達が京都から教えられた"素敵な答え"でした。

Instead of the Afterwards by the Editor-in-Chief, a word about "D&DEPARTMENT KYOTO by Kyoto University of Art and Design"

Our temporary editorial team for this Kyoto issue was at "D&DEPARTMENT KYOTO by Kyoto University of Art and Design" inside the Bukko-ji temple property, a wonderful place where there's an ancient gingko tree and where neighbors come to sit and chat. Takayuki Shiro, the head manager and the rest of the shop staff took care of us by feeding us in their cafeteria and hosting us by letting us stay at the guesthouse overnight, and drank beer together on the wooden platforms by the river.

The campus of Kyoto University of Art and Design, D&DEPARTMENT KYOTO's owner, is in the Uryuyama neighborhood of Sakyo-ku with a Noh stage where we can observe the entire city of Kyoto. This creative educational campus also has Ultra Factory, the atelier of Kenji Yanobe; a farm atop the mountain supervised by Toyohiro Akiyama, the first Japanese astronaut to go to space. And our very own Kenmei Nagaoka, the publisher of this magazine, teaches courses in Long-Life

d MARK REVIEW KYOTO INFORMATION

1 鴨川 (→p. 024)
Kamo River (→p. 025)

2 河井寛次郎記念館 (→p. 026)
♀ 京都府京都市東山区五条坂鐘鋳町 569
☎ 075-561-3585
KAWAI KANJIRO'S HOUSE (→p. 027)
♀ Gojozaka Kanei-cho 569, Higashiyama-ku, Kyoto, Kyoto

3 磔磔 (→p. 028)
♀ 京都府京都市下京区富小路通仏光寺下ル筋屋町 136-9
☎ 075-351-1321
Taku Taku (→p. 029)
♀ Sujiya-cho 136-9, Tominokoji-dori Bukkoji Sagaru, Shimogyo-ku, Kyoto, Kyoto

4 ちいさな藍美術館 (→p. 030)
♀ 京都府南丹市美山町北上牧 41
☎ 0771-77-0746
The Little Indigo Museum (→p. 031)
♀ Kita-kamimaki 41, Miyama-cho, Nantan, Kyoto

5 セイボリー (→p. 032)
♀ 京都府京都市中京区東洞院通三条下ル三文字町 220 八百一本館 3F
☎ 075-223-2320
Savory (→p. 033)
♀ Yaoichi Honkan 3F, Higashino-toin-dori Sanjo Sagaru Sanmonji-cho, Nakagyo-ku, Kyoto, Kyoto

6 十二段家 本店 (→p. 034)
♀ 京都府京都市東山区祇園町南側 570-128
☎ 075-561-0213
JUNIDANYA (→p. 035)
♀ Gion-machi Minamigawa 570-128, Higashiyama-ku, Kyoto, Kyoto

7 田歌舎 (→p. 036, 132)
♀ 京都府南丹市美山町田歌上五波 1-1
☎ 0771-77-0509
Tautasha (→p. 037, 130)
♀ Tota Kamigonami 1-1, Miyama-cho, Nantan, Kyoto

8 辻森自転車商会 (→p. 038)
♀ 京都府京都市中京区東洞院通六角上ル三文字町
☎ 075-221-5732
Tsujimori Cycle (→p. 039)
♀ Higashino-toin-dori Rokkaku Agaru Sanmonji-cho, Nakagyo-ku, Kyoto, Kyoto

9 有次 (→p. 040)
♀ 京都府京都市中京区錦小路通御幸町西入ル
☎ 075-221-1091
Aritsugu (→p. 041)
♀ Nishikikoji-dori Gokomachi Nishi-iru, Nakagyo-ku, Kyoto, Kyoto

10 志ばφ (→p. 042, 122, 137)
♀ 京都府京都市左京区大原勝林院町 58
☎ 075-744-4893
Shibakyu (→p. 043, 120, 137)
♀ Ohara Shorinin-cho 58, Sakyo-ku, Kyoto, Kyoto

11 内藤商店 (→p. 044)
♀ 京都府京都市中京区三条大橋西詰北側
☎ 075-221-3018
Naito Shoten (→p. 045)
♀ Sanjo-Ohashi Nishizume Kitagawa, Nakagyo-ku, Kyoto, Kyoto

12 イノダコーヒ 本店 (→p. 046, 082, 137)
♀ 京都府京都市中京区堺町通三条下ル道祐町 140
☎ 075-221-0507
Inoda Coffee Honten (→p. 047, 083, 137)
♀ Sakaimachi-dori Sanjo Sagaru Doyu-cho 140, Nakagyo-ku, Kyoto, Kyoto

13 一保堂茶舗 喫茶室 嘉木 (→p. 048, 078)
♀ 京都府京都市中京区寺町通二条上ル
☎ 075-211-3421
Ippodo Tea Main Store in Kyoto Kaboku Tearoom (→p. 049, 079)
♀ Teramachi-dori Nijo Agaru, Nakagyo-ku, Kyoto, Kyoto

14 美山粋仙庵 SAI (→p. 050, 136)　※休業
♀ 京都府南丹市美山町内久保下カルノ 54-1
☎ 0771-75-1555
Miyamasuisen-an SAI (→p. 051, 136)
♀ Uchikubo Shimo-karuno 54-1, Miyama-cho, Nantan, Kyoto

15 FACTORY KAFE 工船 (→p. 052, 137)
♀ 京都府京都市上京区河原町通今出川下ル梶井町 448 清和テナントハウス 2F G 号室
☎ 075-211-5398
FACTORY KAFE KOSEN (→p. 053, 137)
♀ Kawaramachi-dori Imadegawa Sagaru Kajii-cho 448 2F Room G, Kamigyo-ku, Kyoto, Kyoto

16 京の宿 石原 (→p. 054)　※休業・再開予定あり
♀ 京都府京都市中京区柳馬場通姉小路上ル柳八幡町 76
☎ 075-221-5612
Ishihara (→p. 055)
♀ Yanagino-banba-dori Aneyakoji Agaru Yanagi-hachiman-cho 76, Nakagyo-ku, Kyoto

17 小宿 布屋 (→p. 056)
♀ 京都府京都市上京区油小路通丸太町上ル米屋町 281
☎ 075-211-8109
Oyado Nunoya (→p. 057)
♀ Aburanokoji-dori Marutamachi Agaru Komeya-cho 281, Kamigyo-ku, Kyoto, Kyoto

18 KYOTO ART HOSTEL kumagusuku (→p. 058)
♀ 京都府京都市中京区壬生馬場町 37-3
☎ 075-432-8168
KYOTO ART HOSTEL kumagusuku (→p. 059)
♀ Mibu-banba-cho 37-3, Nakagyo-ku, Kyoto, Kyoto

19 西陣伊佐町 町家 (→p. 060)　※休業
♀ 京都府京都市上京区大宮通上立売上ル西入ル
Nishijin Isa-cho Machiya (→p. 061)
♀ Omiya-dori Kamitachiuri Agaru Nishi-iru, Kamigyo-ku, Kyoto, Kyoto

d 20 堀部篤史(恵文社一乗寺店) (→p. 062)

♀ 京都府京都市左京区一乗寺払殿町 10
☎ 075-711-5919
Atsushi Horibe (Keibunsha Ichijoji) (→p. 063)
♀ Ichijoji Haraitono-cho 10, Sakyo-ku, Kyoto, Kyoto

d 21 湊 三次郎(サウナの梅湯) (→p. 064)
♀ 京都府京都市下京区木屋町通上ノ口上ル岩滝町 175
☎ 080-2523-0626
Sanjiro Minato (Sauna Umeyu) (→p. 065)
♀ Kiyamachi-dori Kaminokuchi Agaru Iwataki-cho 175, Shimogyo-ku, Kyoto, Kyoto

d 22 藤原 誉(→7. 田歌舎) (→p. 066)

Homaru Fujiwara (→ 7. Tautasha) (→p. 067)

d 23 黒木裕行(株式会社ルーフスケイプ) (→p. 068)

♀ 京都府八幡市美濃山ヒル塚 100-9
☎ 075-925-8240
Hiroyuki Kuroki (Roofscape Architect) (→p. 069)
♀ Hiruzuka100-9, Minoyama, Yawata, Kyoto

飯尾醸造 (→p. 121, 137)
♀ 京都府宮津市小田宿野 373
☎ 0772-25-0015
Iio Jozo (→p. 120, 137)
♀ Odashukuno 373, Miyazu, Kyoto

 西冨家コロッケ店 河原町店 (→p. 140)
♀ 京都府京都市下京区河原町通松原下ル
植松町 735
☎ 075-202-9837
Nishitomi-ya Croquette Shop (Kawara-machi branch) (→p. 140)
♀ Kawaramachi-dori Matsubara Sagaru Uematsu-cho 735, Shimogyo-ku, Kyoto, Kyoto

 ますだ茶舗 (→p. 141)
♀ 京都府宇治市宇治蓮華 21-3
☎ 0774-21-4034
MASUDA TEA STORE (→p. 141)
♀ Ujirenge 21-3, Uji, Kyoto

 COFFEE HOUSE maki 出町店 (→p. 141)
♀ 京都府京都市上京区河原町今出川上ル
青龍町 211
☎ 075-222-2460
COFFEE HOUSE maki (Demachi-ten) (→p. 141)
♀ Kawaramachi-dori Imadegawa Agaru Seiryu-cho 211, Kamigyo-ku, Kyoto, Kyoto

 京のすし処 末廣 (→p. 141)
♀ 京都府京都市中京区寺町通二条上ル
要法寺前町 711
☎ 075-231-1363
SUEHIRO (→p. 141)
♀ Teramachi-dori Nijo Agaru Yohojimae-cho 711, Nakagyo-ku, Kyoto, Kyoto

 京極 かねよ (→p. 142)
♀ 京都府京都市中京区六角通新京極東入ル
松ヶ枝町 456
☎ 075-221-0669
Kyogoku Kaneyo (→p. 142)
♀ Rokkaku-dori Shinkyogoku Higashi-iru Matsugae-cho 456, Nakagyo-ku, Kyoto, Kyoto

 喫茶 マドラグ (→p. 143)
♀ 京都府京都市中京区上松屋町 706-5
☎ 075-744-0067
La Madrague (→p. 143)
♀ Kamimatsuya-cho 706-5, Nakagyo-ku, Kyoto, Kyoto

 えびす屋 京都嵐山總本店 (→p. 167)
♀ 京都府京都市右京区嵯峨天龍寺
芒ノ馬場町 3-24
☎ 075-864-4444
Ebisuya (→p. 167)
♀ Saga Tenryuji Susukinobaba-cho 3-24, Ukyo-ku, Kyoto, Kyoto

26 ホホホ座（→p. 102, 109, 111, 112）
📍 京都府京都市左京区浄土寺馬場町 71
ハイネストビル 1 階・2 階
☎ 075-741-6501
HOHOHOZA（→p. 100, 109, 111, 113）
📍 Hainesuto Bldg 1F・2F, Banba-cho 71, Jodoji,
Sakyo-ku, Kyoto, Kyoto

27 古書 善行堂（→p. 102）
📍 京都府京都市左京区浄土寺西田町 82-2
☎ 075-771-0061
Kosho Zenkodo（→p. 103）
📍 Nishida-cho 82-2, Jodoji, Sakyo-ku, Kyoto, Kyoto

28 カフェ進々堂 京大北門前（→p. 105）
📍 京都府京都市左京区北白川追分町 88
☎ 075-701-4121
Café Shinshindo Kyodai Kitamon-mae（→p. 102）
📍 Oiwake-cho 88, Kita-shirakawa, Sakyo-ku, Kyoto,
Kyoto

29 出町ふたば（→p. 105）
📍 京都府京都市上京区出町通今出川上ル
青龍町 236
☎ 075-231-1658
Demachi Futaba（→p. 102）
📍 Seiryu-cho 236, Demachi-dori Imadegawa Agaru,
Kamigyo-ku, Kyoto, Kyoto

30 北野天満宮（→p. 106）
📍 京都府京都市上京区馬喰町
北野天満宮社務所
☎ 075-461-0005
Kitano Tenman-gu Shrine（→p. 105）
📍 Kitano Tenman-gu Shamusho, Bakuro-cho,
Kamigyo-ku, Kyoto, Kyoto

31 長文屋（→p. 106, 137）
📍 京都府京都市北区北野下白梅町 54-8
☎ 075-467-0217
Chobunya（→p. 107, 137）
📍 Kitano Shimo-hakubai-cho 54-8, Kita-ku, Kyoto,
Kyoto

32 興石・中村外二工務店（→p. 106）
📍 京都府京都市北区紫野西御所田町 15
☎ 075-451-8012
KOHSEKI（→p. 107）
📍 Nishi-goshoden-cho 15, Murasakino, Kita-ku,
Kyoto, Kyoto

33 源光庵（→p. 107）
📍 京都府京都市北区鷹峯北鷹峯町 47
☎ 075-492-1858
Genko-an Temple（→p. 107）
📍 Kita-takagamine-cho 47, Takagamine, Kita-ku,
Kyoto, Kyoto

34 光悦寺（→p. 107）
📍 京都府京都市北区鷹峯光悦町 29
☎ 075-491-1399
Koetsu-ji Temple（→p. 106）
📍 Koetsu-cho 29, Takagamine, Kita-ku, Kyoto, Kyoto

35 プラッツ（→p. 114）
📍 京都府京都市右京区嵯峨天龍寺造路町 5
☎ 075-861-1721
Platz（→p. 115）
📍 Ukyo-ku Saga Tenryuji Tsukurimichi-cho 5, Kyoto,
Kyoto

36 かみ添（→p. 114）
📍 京都府京都市北区紫野東藤ノ森町 11-1
☎ 075-432-8555
Kamisoe（→p. 114）
📍 Higashi-fujinomori-cho 11-1, Murasakino, Kita-ku,
Kyoto, Kyoto

37 東哉（→p. 115）
📍 京都府京都市東山区五条橋東 6-539-26
☎ 075-561-4130
Tosai（→p. 114）
📍 Gojobashi Higashi 6-539-26, Higashiyama-ku,
Kyoto, Kyoto

38 アサヒビール大山崎山荘美術館（→p. 127）
📍 京都府乙訓郡大山崎町銭原 5-3
☎ 075-957-3123（総合案内）
Asahi Beer Oyamazaki Villa Museum of Art（→p. 127）
📍 Zenihara 5-3, Oyamazaki-cho, Otokuni, Kyoto

39 月桂冠大倉記念館（→p. 127）
📍 京都府京都市伏見区南浜町 247
☎ 075-623-2056
Gekkeikan Okura Sake Museum（→p. 127）
📍 Minami-hama-cho 247, Fushimi-ku, Kyoto, Kyoto

40 黄桜カッパカントリー（→p. 127）
📍 京都府京都市伏見区塩屋町 228
☎ 075-611-9919
Kizakura Kappa Country（→p. 127）
📍 Shioya-cho 228, Fushimi-ku, Kyoto, Kyoto

41 ダイヤテックプロダクツ（→p. 127）
📍 京都府京都市伏見区柿木浜町 431
☎ 075-644-7776
Diatech Products（→p. 127）
📍 Kakinokihama-cho 431, Fushimi-ku, Kyoto, Kyoto

42 酒蔵 Bar えん（→p. 128）
📍 京都府京都市伏見区今町 672-1
☎ 075-611-4666
Sakagura Bar En（→p. 129）
📍 Ima-machi 672-1, Fushimi-ku, Kyoto, Kyoto

43 朝日焼 作陶館（→p. 128）
📍 京都府宇治市宇治山田 11
☎ 0774-23-2517
Asahiyaki Sakutokan（→p. 129）
📍 Uji-yamada 11, Uji, Kyoto

44 グンゼ博物苑（→p. 130）
📍 京都府綾部市青野町亀無 6
☎ 0773-43-1050
GUNZE Museum（→p. 128）
📍 Kamenashi 6, Aono-cho, Ayabe, Kyoto

45 竹松うどん店（→p. 130）
📍 京都府綾部市志賀郷町儀市前 13
☎ 0773-21-1665
Takematsu Udon-ten（→p. ）
📍 Shigasato-chogiichi-mae 13, Ayabe, Kyoto

46 かやぶきの里（→p. 130）
📍 京都府南丹市美山町安掛下 23
☎ 0771-75-1906（美山町観光協会）
Kayabuki no Sato（→p. 128）
📍 Agake Shimo 23, Miyama-cho, Nantan, Kyoto

47 カネマスの七輪焼き（→p. 132）
📍 京都府宮津市漁師 1714
☎ 0772-25-0058
Kanemasu Shichirin-yaki（→p. 133）
📍 Ryoshi 1714, Miyazu, Kyoto

48 向井酒造（→p. 133, 136）
📍 京都府与謝郡伊根町平田 67
☎ 0772-32-0003
Mukai Shuzo（→p. 132, 136）
📍 Hirata 67, Ine-cho, Yosa, Kyoto

49 舟屋の里 伊根（→p. 135）
📍 京都府与謝郡伊根町亀島 459
☎ 0772-32-0680
Funaya no Sato Ine（→p. 132）
📍 Kameshima 459, Ine-cho, Yosa, Kyoto

50 舟屋の宿 鍵屋（→p. 135）
📍 京都府与謝郡伊根町亀島 864
☎ 0772-32-0356
Kagiya（→p. 132）
📍 Kameshima 864, Ine-cho, Yosa, Kyoto

51 村上開新堂（→p. 078, 136）
📍 京都府京都市中京区常盤木町 62
☎ 075-231-1058
Murakami Kaishindo（→p. 079, 136）
📍 Tokiwagi-cho 62, Nakagyo-ku, Kyoto, Kyoto

52 丸久 小山園（→p. 136）
📍 京都府宇治市小倉町寺内 86
☎ 0774-20-0909
Marukyu Koyamaen（→p. 136）
📍 Ogura-cho Terauchi 86, Uji, Kyoto

53 阿闍梨餅本舗 満月（→p. 136）
📍 京都府京都市左京区鞠小路通今出川上ル
☎ 075-791-4121
Ajari Mochi Honpo Mangetsu（→p. 136）
📍 Marikoji-dori Imadegawa Agaru, Sakyo-ku, Kyoto,
Kyoto

54 麩嘉（→p. 137）
📍 京都府京都市上京区西洞院通椹木町上ル
東裏辻町 413
☎ 075-231-1584
Fuka（→p. 137）
📍 Nishino-toin-dori Sawaragi-cho Agaru
Higashi-uratsuji-cho 413, Kamigyo-ku, Kyoto,
Kyoto

d design Travel KYOTO INFORMATION

1 庶民 (→p. 077)
京都府京都市下京区大宮通四条下ル
四条大宮町 18-6
Shomin (→p. 076)
Omiya-dori Shijo Sagaru Shijo Omiya-cho 18-6,
Shimogyo-ku, Kyoto, Kyoto

2 モリカゲシャツ キョウト (→p. 077)
京都府京都市上京区河原町通丸太町上ル
枡屋町 362-1
075-241-7746
MORIKAGE SHIRT KYOTO (→p. 076)
Kawaramachi-dori Marutamachi Agaru
Masuya-cho 362-1, Kamigyo-ku, Kyoto, Kyoto

3 井川建具店 (→p. 078)
京都府京都市中京区東九軒町 328
075-231-2646
Ikawa Tateguten (→p. 076)
Higashi-kyuken-cho 328, Nakagyo-ku, Kyoto,
Kyoto

4 キンシ正宗 堀野記念館 (→p. 078)
京都府京都市中京区堺町通二条上ル
亀屋町 172
075-223-2072
Kinshi Masamune Horino Memorial Museum
(→p. 079)
Sakaimachi-dori Nijo Agaru Kameya-cho 172,
Nakagyo-ku, Kyoto, Kyoto

5 三月書房 (→p. 078)
京都府京都市中京区寺町通二条上ル西側
075-231-1924
Sangatsu Shobo (→p. 079)
Teramachi-dori Nijo Agaru, Nakagyo-ku, Kyoto,
Kyoto

6 芸艸堂 (→p. 078)
京都府京都市中京区寺町通二条南入
妙満寺前町 459
075-231-3613
Unsodo (→p. 079)
Teramachi-dori Nijo Minami-iru Myomanji-mae-
cho 459, Nakagyo-ku, Kyoto, Kyoto

7 鳩居堂 (→p. 079)
京都府京都市中京区寺町通姉小路上ル
下本能寺前町 520
075-231-0510
Kyukyodo (→p. 078)
Teramachi-dori Aneyakoji Agaru, Nakagyo-ku
Shimo-Honnoji-mae-cho 520, Kyoto, Kyoto

8 スマート珈琲店 (→p. 080, 140)
京都府京都市中京区寺町通三条上ル
天性寺前町 537
075-231-6547
Smart Coffee (→p. 078, 140)
Teramachi-dori Sanjo Agaru Tenshoji-mae-cho
537, Nakagyo-ku, Kyoto, Kyoto

9 スターバックスコーヒー 京都三条大橋店
(→p. 081)
京都府京都市中京区三条通河原町東入ル
中島町 113 近江屋ビル 1F
075-213-2326
Starbucks Coffee Kyoto Sanjo Ohashi (→p. 081)
Sanjo-dori Kawaramachi Higashi-iru Nakajima-
cho 113, Nakagyo-ku, Kyoto, Kyoto

10 元・立誠小学校 (→p. 082)
京都府京都市中京区備前島町 310-2
Rissei Elementary School (→p. 080)
Bizenjima-cho 310-2, Nakagyo-ku, Kyoto, Kyoto

11 モリタ屋 木屋町店 (→p. 082)
京都府京都市中京区木屋町通三条上ル
上大阪町 531
075-231-5118
Moritaya Kiyamachi (→p. 080)
Kami-osaka-cho 531, Kiyamachi-dori Sanjo Agaru,
Nakagyo-ku, Kyoto, Kyoto

12 島津製作所 創業記念資料館 (→p. 082)
京都府京都市中京区木屋町二条南
075-255-0980
Shimadzu Foundation Memorial Hall (→p. 080)
Kiyamachi, Nijo Minami, Nakagyo-ku, Kyoto,
Kyoto

13 イノダコーヒ 三条支店 (→p. 083)
京都府京都市中京区三条通堺町東入ル
枡屋町 69
075-223-0171
Inoda Coffee Sanjo (→p. 083)
Masuya-cho 69, Sanjo-dori Sakaimachi
Higashi-iru, Nakagyo-ku, Kyoto, Kyoto

14 京極スタンド (→p. 084)
京都府京都市中京区新京極通四条上ル
中之町 546
075-221-4156
Kyogoku Stand (→p. 082)
Nakanomachi 546, Shin-kyogoku-dori Shijo
Agaru, Nakagyo-ku, Kyoto, Kyoto

15 homehome (→p. 085)
京都府京都市下京区早尾町 313-3
五条モール 201
homehome (→p. 085)
Gojo-mall 201, Hayao-cho 313-3, Shimogyo-ku,
Kyoto, Kyoto

16 倉日用商店 (→p. 085)
京都府京都市上京区堀川下立売上ル
4-55 堀川商店街内
075-841-7304
Kura Daily Store (→p. 084)
Horikawa-shotengai-nai, Horikawa Shimodachiuri
Agaru, Kamigyo-ku, Kyoto, Kyoto

17 神馬 (→p. 086, 140)
京都府京都市上京区千本通中立売上ル
西側玉屋町 38
075-461-3635
Shinme (→p. 084, 140)
Tamaya-cho 38, Senbon-dori Nakatachiuri Agaru
Nishigawa, Kamigyo-ku, Kyoto, Kyoto

18 OGAWA COFFEE 京都駅店 (→p. 099)
京都府京都市下京区東塩小路町 地下鉄京都
駅 中央 1 改札口北側コトチカ京都内
075-352-0808
OGAWA COFFEE Kyoto Station (→p. 099)
Higashi-shiokoji-cho, Shimogyo-ku, Kyoto, Kyoto

19 京都 たかばし 本家 第一旭 (→p. 099, 140)
京都府京都市下京区東塩小路向畑町 845
075-351-6321
Dai-ichi Asahi (→p. 099, 140)
Mukaihata-cho 845, Higashi-shiokoji,
Shimogyo-ku, Kyoto, Kyoto

20 新福菜館本店 (→p. 099)
京都府京都市下京区東塩小路向畑町 569
075-371-7648
Shinpukusaikan Honten (→p. 099)
Mukaihata-cho 569, Higashi-shiokoji,
Shimogyo-ku, Kyoto, Kyoto

21 教王護国寺 (→p. 099)
京都府京都市南区九条町 1
075-691-3325
Kyoogokoku-ji (→p. 099)
Kujo-cho 1, minami-ku, Kyoto, Kyoto

22 細見美術館 (→p. 100)
京都府京都市左京区岡崎最勝寺町 6-3
075-752-5555
Hosomi Museum (→p. 101)
Saishoji-cho 6-3, Okazaki, Sakyo-ku, Kyoto, Kyoto

23 ロク (→p. 100)
京都府京都市左京区聖護院山王町 18
メタボ岡崎 101
075-756-4436
Roku (→p. 101)
Metabo Okazaki 101, Shogoin San-no-cho 18,
Sakyo-ku, Kyoto, Kyoto

24 グリル 小宝 (→p. 101, 141, 142)
京都府京都市左京区岡崎北御所町 46
075-771-5893
Grill Kodakara (→p. 101, 141, 142)
Okazaki Kitagosho-cho 46, Sakyo-ku, Kyoto, Kyoto

25 金地院 (→p. 101)
京都府京都市左京区南禅寺福地町 86-12
075-771-3511
Konchi-in (→p. 100)
Fukuchi-cho 86-12, Nanzenji, Sakyo-ku, Kyoto,
Kyoto

OTHER ISSUES IN PRINT

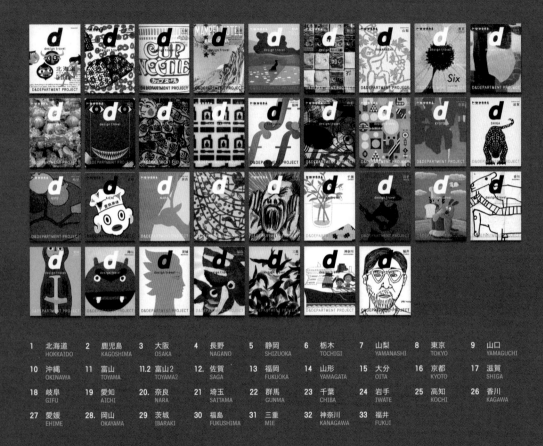

1	北海道 HOKKAIDO	2	鹿児島 KAGOSHIMA	3	大阪 OSAKA	4	長野 NAGANO	5	静岡 SHIZUOKA	6	栃木 TOCHIGI	7	山梨 YAMANASHI	8	東京 TOKYO	9	山口 YAMAGUCHI
10	沖縄 OKINAWA	11	富山 TOYAMA	11.2	富山2 TOYAMA2	12.	佐賀 SAGA	13	福岡 FUKUOKA	14	山形 YAMAGATA	15	大分 OITA	16	京都 KYOTO	17	滋賀 SHIGA
18	岐阜 GIFU	19	愛知 AICHI	20.	奈良 NARA	21	埼玉 SAITAMA	22	群馬 GUNMA	23	千葉 CHIBA	24	岩手 IWATE	25	高知 KOCHI	26	香川 KAGAWA
27	愛媛 EHIME	28.	岡山 OKAYAMA	29	茨城 IBARAKI	30	福島 FUKUSHIMA	31	三重 MIE	32	神奈川 KANAGAWA	33	福井 FUKUI				

HOW TO BUY

「d design travel」シリーズのご購入には、下記の方法があります。

店頭で購入
Physical Stores
- D&DEPARTMENT 各店（店舗情報 P.181）
- お近くの書店（全国の主要書店にて取り扱い中。在庫がない場合は、書店に取り寄せをご依頼いただけます）

ネットショップで購入
Online Stores
- D&DEPARTMENT ネットショップ 🛒 www.d-department.com
- D&DEPARTMENT global site 🛒 www.ddepartment.com
- Amazon 🛒 amazon.co.jp
- 富士山マガジンサービス（定期購読、1冊購入ともに可能）🛒 www.fujisan.co.jp

＊書店以外に、全国のインテリアショップ、ライフスタイルショップ、ミュージアムショップでもお取り扱いがあります。
＊お近くの販売店のご案内、在庫などのお問い合わせは、D&DEPARTMENT PROJECT 本部・書籍流通チームまでご連絡ください。（☎03-5752-0520 🕘平日9:00～18:00)

編集後記

神藤秀人 Hideto Shindo

京都は取材するまで、何度も何度も通った店が多かった。行く度に少しずつ、その店の事、店主の事、商品の事、段々と分かっていった、充実の制作期間。そして、それが当たり前なのだと、気付かせてくれた旅でもあった。だから、本誌掲載を快諾していただいた日には、嬉しくてしょうがなくて、二日酔いを恐れず、立ち呑み「庶民」で祝杯を上げた。また来ます、京都。何度も、必ず。

前田次郎　Jiro Maeda

京都の行事を調べ、京都の手土産をいただき、本誌コーナーでご紹介いただいた、本を読み、CDを聴き、映画を観ながら、「タカラ can チューハイ」を毎晩のように飲みました。「d design travel KYOTO」の制作を通して、独創的な活動をたくさん知りました。そして、新しい京都を知りました。一歩一歩、あっという間の3ヶ月。ご協力いただいた皆さん、ありがとうございました。

佐々木晃子　Akiko Sasaki

京都取材が始まったばかりの4月初旬に、本誌「静岡号」の立役者で、「ケンブリッジの森」を主宰する藤原慎一郎さんの"京都建築探訪"に、お供した日がありました。「今年は京都に、たくさん来る事になりそうだから、いい本作ってね！」と、笑顔で激励して下さった藤原さんが、2015年6月17日、永遠の眠りにつかれました。心から、ご冥福をお祈りいたします。

発行人 / Founder
ナガオカケンメイ　Kenmei Nagaoka（D&DEPARTMENT PROJECT）

編集長 / Editor-in-Chief
空閑 理　Osamu Kuga（D&DEPARTMENT PROJECT）

副編集長 / Deputy Editor
神藤秀人　Hideto Shindo（D&DEPARTMENT PROJECT）

編集 / Editors
前田次郎　Jiro Maeda（D&DEPARTMENT PROJECT）
佐々木晃子　Akiko Sasaki（D&DEPARTMENT PROJECT）
松崎紀子　Noriko Matsuzaki（design clips）

執筆 / Writers
相馬夕輝　Yuki Aima（D&DEPARTMENT PROJECT）
うめの たかし　Takashi Umeno（HOHOHOZA）
坂本大三郎　Daizaburo Sakamoto
高木崇雄　Takao Takaki（Foucault）
野口忠典　Tadanori Noguchi（d47 design travel store）
松本伸哉　Shinya Matsumoto（HOHOHOZA）
山下賢二　Kenji Yamashita（HOHOHOZA）
深澤直人　Naoto Fukasawa

デザイン / Designers
遠藤直人　Naoto Endou（D&DEPARTMENT PROJECT）
高橋恵子　Keiko Takahashi（D&DEPARTMENT PROJECT）
中川清香　Sayaka Nakagawa（D&DEPARTMENT PROJECT）
加瀬千寛　Chihiro Kase（D&DEPARTMENT PROJECT）

イラスト / Illustrator
辻井希文　Kifumi Tsujii

翻訳・校正 / Translation & Copyediting
グレイ俣野ゆき子　Yukiko Matano Gray（GT Partners / Spice Rack）
永井真理子　Mariko Nagai（Temple University Japan）
ネトルトン・タロウ　Taro Nettleton
ワタナベシンヤ(B)　Shinya B Watanabe（Temple University Japan）

制作サポート / Production Support
京都造形芸術大学　Kyoto University of Art and Design
岡竹義弘　Yoshihiro Okatake（d47 SHOKUDO）
針谷 茜　Akane Hariya（D&DEPARTMENT PROJECT）
瀧口陽子　Yoko Takiguchi（D&DEPARTMENT PROJECT）
高野知子　Tomoko Takano（3KG）
D&DEPARTMENT FUKUOKA
D&DEPARTMENT HOKKAIDO by 3KG
D&DEPARTMENT KAGOSHIMA by MARUYA
D&DEPARTMENT KYOTO
D&DEPARTMENT OKINAWA by OKINAWA STANDARD
D&DEPARTMENT OSAKA
D&DEPARTMENT SEOUL by MILLIMETER MILLIGRAM
D&DEPARTMENT SHIZUOKA by TAITA
D&DEPARTMENT TOKYO
D&DEPARTMENT TOYAMA
D&DEPARTMENT YAMANASHI by Sannishi YBS
GOOD DESIGN SHOP COMME des GARÇONS D&DEPARTMENT PROJECT
d47 design travel store
d47 MUSEUM
d47 食堂　d47 SHOKUDO
Drawing and Manual

広報 / Public Relations
松添みつこ　Mitsuko Matsuzoe（D&DEPARTMENT PROJECT）
清水 睦　Mutsumi Shimizu（D&DEPARTMENT PROJECT）

表紙に、ひとこと

「八つ橋」 神坂雪佳（1866年－1942年）

京都市にある、手摺木版の出版社「芸艸堂」で、明治から昭和にかけて活躍した、京都の画家・図案家の神坂雪佳を知った。琳派の伝統的な技法やモチーフを、斬新かつモダンな感性で継承し、尾形光琳や酒井抱一も描いた、「八橋図」「燕子花図」の、定番的とも言える風景を、大胆な構図で、鮮やかな青と緑でフラットに描いた本件をクローズアップして、「京都府号」の表紙とさせていただいた。現在でも、類い稀な美しさを、僕は感じる。（空閑 理）

A Word on the Cover

"Yatsuhashi" by Sekka Kamisaka（1866–1942）

I learned of Sekka Kamisaka, an artist from Meiji and Showa eras, at Unsodo, a publisher of woodblock printing in Kyoto. Sekka took the traditional process and motifs and rendered them from an avande-garde sensibility. Traditional motifs of *Yatsuhashi* and *Kakitsubata* landscapes which have been drawn by artists such as Korin Ogata and Hoitsu Sakai were made startlingly modern by Sekka with bold strokes and vivid use of blue and green. We used the close-up of this painting for the cover of Kyoto issue. Even after 80 years, this painting is quite modern.（Osamu Kuga）

---

d design travel KYOTO

2015年 7月25日　第1版 / First printing: July 25, 2015
2015年10月25日　第1版 第2刷 / Second printing: October 25, 2015
2018年 7月25日　第1版 第3刷 / Third printing: July 25, 2018
2024年 6月10日　改訂版 第1刷 / Revised Edition First printing: June 10, 2024

発行元 / Distributor
D&DEPARTMENT PROJECT
📍 158-0083 東京都世田谷区奥沢8-3-2
　Okusawa 8-3-2, Setagaya, Tokyo 158-0083
☎ 03-5752-0097
🏠 http://www.d-department.com/

印刷 / Printing
株式会社サンエムカラー SunM Color Co., Ltd.

ISBN978-4-903097-85-5 C0026

Printed in Japan

本誌掲載の写真・記事の無断転用を禁じます。
Copyright©2024 D&DEPARTMENT PROJECT. All rights reserved.

掲載情報は、2022年1月時点のものとなります。
一部、2018年7月時点のものがあります。
定休日・営業時間・詳細・価格など、変更となる場合があります。
ご利用の際は、事前にご確認ください。
掲載の価格は、特に記載のない限り、すべて税込み価格です。
定休日は、年末年始・GW・お盆休みなどを省略している場合があります。
本文中の「D&DEPARTMENT KYOTO by 京都造形芸術大学」は、
2018年3月よりD&DEPARTMENTの直営店になりました。
The information provided herein is accurate as of January 2022. Some information provided is accurate as of July 2018. Readers are advised to check in advance for any changes in closing days, business ho urs, prices, and other details. All prices shown, unless otherwise stated, include tax. Closing days listed do not include national holidays such as new year's, obon, and the Golden Week. "D&DEPARTMENT KYOTO by Kyoto University of Art and Design" in the main text has become a directly managed shop of D&DEPARTMENT since March 2018.

全国の、お薦めのデザイントラベル情報、本誌の広告や、
「47都道府県応援バナー広告」（P.154〜177のページ下に掲載）
についてのお問い合わせは、下記、編集部まで、お願いします。

宛て先
〒158-0083 東京都世田谷区奥沢8-3-2 2F
D&DEPARTMENT PROJECT
「d design travel」編集部宛て
d-travel@d-department.jp

公式サイト（日本語）
🏠 http://www.d-department.com

グローバルサイト（多言語）
🏠 http://www.ddepartment.com